VALUES, SELF, AND SOCIETY

VALUES, SELF, AND SOCIETY

Toward a Humanist Social Psychology

M. Brewster Smith

Transaction Publishers
New Brunswick (U.S.A.) and London (U.K.)

Library of Congress Catalog Number: 90-40000
ISBN: 0-88738-373-4
Printed in the United States of America

Library of Congress Cataloging-in-Publication Data

Smith, M. Brewster (Mahlon Brewster), 1919–
    Values, self, and society : toward a humanist social psychology /
M. Brewster Smith.
        p.   cm.
    Includes bibliographical references and index.
    ISBN 0-88738-373-4
    1. Social psychology. 2. Humanistic psychology. 3. Personality
and culture. 4. Social values. I. Title.
HM251.S662   1990
302—dc20   90-40000
                                                                              CIP

To my grandchildren
—Garrett, Melanie, Bryan, Jesse, and Masumi—
and to the future of everyone's children
and grandchildren in the twenty-first century

Contents

Acknowledgments

The chapters originally appeared in the following books or journals. In each case, permission to reprint my copyrighted material is gratefully acknowledged.

Chapter 1: "Psychology and values," *Journal of Social Issues* 34 (4) (1978): 181–99. Copyright © 1978 by the Society for the Psychological Study of Social Issues.

Chapter 2: "Perspectives on selfhood," *American Psychologist* 33 (1978): 1053–63. Copyright © 1978 by the American Psychological Association. Reprinted by permission.

Chapter 3: "Attitudes, values and selfhood," in H. E. Howe and M. M. Page, eds., *Nebraska Symposium on Motivation 1979*. Lincoln: University of Nebraska Press, 1980. Copyright © 1980 by the University of Nebraska Press.

Chapter 4: "The metaphorical basis of selfhood," in A. J. Marsella, G. De Vos, and F. L. K. Hsu, eds., *Culture and self: Asian and Western perspectives*. New York and London: Tavistock Publications, 1985. Copyright © 1985 by Anthony J. Marsella, G. De Vos, and Francis L. K. Hsu. A passage is drawn with permission from "The cognitive model of anger inherent in American English," by G. Lakoff and Z. Kövecses, in D. Holland and N. Quinn, eds., *Cultural models in language and thought*. New York: Cambridge University Press, 1987. Copyright © 1987 by Cambridge University Press.

Chapter 5: "Toward a secular humanistic psychology," *Journal of Humanistic Psychology* 26 (1) (1986): 7–26. Copyright © 1986 by Association for Humanistic Psychology. Represented by permission of Sage Publications.

Chapter 6: Metapsychology, politics, and human needs," in R. Fitzger-

Introduction

I still think of myself as a social psychologist (psychological rather than sociological variety), but the conception of social psychology with which I feel at home no longer fits the way the present field defines itself. Today's journals, textbooks, and conferences represent a vigorous but rather narrow scientific specialty in psychology, the practitioners of which are more exclusively in communication with each other, more closely focused on agendas that are primarily and often only intelligible within the subdiscipline, than was the case when I formed my identity as a psychologist. When I was an undergraduate in the 1930s, my kind of social psychology was being launched by creative generalists like Gordon Allport (1937), Gardner and Lois Murphy (1931), Theodore Newcomb (1943), Otto Klineberg (1940), Kurt Lewin (1936), and Muzafer Sherif (1936), who mostly had strong interdisciplinary ties and who mostly also contributed to the emergence of personality as a differentiated academic field. (The phrase *personality and social psychology* was typically used to label a single entity.) These founders were characteristically involved in the human problems of the social and political world, on which they sought to bring the emerging concepts and methods of social psychology to bear.

Over more than four decades, my own efforts have involved me in the mainstream of psychology, in which I have paddled up the current more often than not. As I wrote at midpassage in an autobiographical item,

> With increasing clarity, I have struggled to make sense of an emerging three-way commitment: to a psychology that seeks to come to grips with human experience (and in that sense is "humanistic"), to a psychology that broadly abides by the rules of the game of science as a public, self-critical, and therefore cumulative social enterprise aimed at the comprehensive understanding of the phenomena in its territory, and to one that bears helpfully on the urgent social problems that hinge on an ingredient of human cussedness. That has made me a

generalist—at a time when ever more intensive specialization has been the predominant trend. The things I have done that have pleased me most, in writing and teaching and consultation, have been efforts at conceptual mapping and clarification, of establishing relevance and cutting across established boundaries, more than the direct products of my research. To an extent greater than I sometimes like to admit, I have been an "armchair psychologist." If there is an "Establishment" in psychology and the social sciences, I am nevertheless surely a member of it but—I hope—I am something of a maverick. (1972, p. 214)

During the nearly two decades since I thus described my endeavors in psychology, I have maintained the same three commitments, in the context of a changing world and a considerably modified psychological scene. I have continued to be involved with the psychology of social problems, in recent years particularly with problems of human survival in the nuclear age, which are taking a hopeful new turn just now. I have continued to be committed to a scientific approach in human psychology, but I have had to rethink my conception of human science to take responsible account of the demise of logical positivism, which was the regnant view when I was being socialized as a "behavioral scientist," and also to come to terms with the "postmodern" critics of positivism in psychology, whose alternatives of constructivism, hermeneutics, critical theory, and the like have sometimes seemed to me to discard the goal of cumulative knowledge and the discipline of respect for evidence. Neither the Old Testament of logical positivism as I had once received it, nor the New postmodern Testament being heralded but hardly delivered by recent John the Baptists seemed satisfactory to me in the forms in which they were being offered. Much of my recent writing has been an attempt to salvage for myself and others the aspects of scientific empiricism that seemed to me essential to save, and to pick and choose among aspects of the postmodern perspective.

As for my commitment to a humanistic psychology that seeks to come to grips with human experience, that has led me into a closer involvement with the humanistic psychology movement than I could have anticipated. As a relatively friendly critic of the movement, I found myself coopted in 1985 as president of the American Psychological Association's Division of Humanistic Psychology. Sharing enough common goals and enough common criticisms of mainstream psychology with the leaders of humanistic psychology to bond me to my role, I found it necessary not only to work out the relations between scientific and humanistic conceptions of the psychological enterprise beyond my previous thought on the subject but also to articulate my own secular humanist perspective in distinction from the tide of "transpersonal" mysticism that was attracting so many participants in the humanistic psychology movement. Not surprisingly, my version of humanistic psychology looks both to the evocative and interpretative traditions of the arts and humanities and to the causal-explanatory traditions of science, viewing them as not merely complementary but as intersecting in our most promising attempts to understand selfhood.

Because I have often addressed audiences other than my colleagues in social psychology, my writings have been scattered in publications that are not easily accessible to any particular set of readers. So I have published two previous collections (Smith, 1969a, 1974) in the hope of reaching a broader audience for the perspectives that I have advanced. The present volume is similarly motivated. While the chapters and essays that I gather here are occasional pieces written in response to particular requests, I have selected the occasions to which I have responded and the pieces to be reprinted so as to allow me to develop the themes with which I have been concerned in a coherent way. In other words, to anticipate an editorial criticism with which I empathize readily as a former editor and frequent editorial consultant, I put forward the confident claim that this is a *book,* not just a collection. Its ingredients date from 1977 to 1990, with the more recent dates predominating.

There are three interrelated sections. The first, Values and Selfhood, includes the chapters that are in strongest continuity with my earlier work on opinions, attitudes, and values (Smith, Bruner, & White, 1956; Smith, 1963), and that are my major contribution to the mainstream of personality and social psychology. My treatment of selfhood, developed in cultural context, amounts to an empirically oriented variant of an existentialist perspective on the human condition. The second section, Humanistic Psychology and Human Science, contains essays in which I work out the relations between humanistic and scientific approaches in the present postpositivist setting, which is very different from that in which humanistic psychology was launched as a "Third Force" beside behaviorism and psychoanalysis. I propose and elaborate upon my own conception of human science. In Humanism and Social Issues, the final section, I deal with several contemporary problems, applying the metatheoretical perspectives that I develop earlier in the book, and analyze the distinctive contribution that psychology has made and can make toward their amelioration.

Chapter 1, "Psychology and Values," was my offering in a lecture I gave at Harvard in memory of my doctoral mentor, Gordon Allport. In it, I discuss the various ways in which psychologists have tried to deal with values (conceptions of the preferable), including the serious but unsuccessful attempts by Gestalt psychology and radical behaviorism, and the misleading claims of bridging the gap between facts and values in terms of mental health and Piagetian developmentalism. I try to clarify how psychology can participate legitimately in the dialectic of value controversy, using Allport's (1954) *Nature of Prejudice* as a model for the psychologist's contribution. A more recent example of my own attempt to come to grips with insistent value conflicts in the contemporary United States may be found in chapter 14.

Of almost the same vintage (1978) is chapter 2, "Perspectives on Selfhood," which was my presidential address to the American Psychological Association. It presaged the surge of interest in self theory and research in social psychology, psychoanalysis, and cultural anthropology during the next decade: for once in my career, I have the retrospective thrill of being a surfer, riding on the front of a wave I did not cause— though of course at the time I was unaware of the wave that was to follow me. In that chapter, I take selfhood—not "the" self—as a label for criterial features of the human condition that are linked to reflexive self-awareness, and examine selfhood from three perspectives: evolutionary or phylogenetic, cross-cultural and transhistorical, and developmental or ontogenetic. The reflexiveness of selfhood makes our theories about it important in partly constituting the persons that we are. I argue that if psychology is to begin to grasp the phenomena of selfhood, it needs to work in both the causal and the interpretative traditions, taken as complementary—a theme that is one of the distinctive messages that I am eager to communicate. It recurs throughout the rest of the book. And I conclude with a look at the perils of selfhood in our own time, suggesting that an avowedly historical approach to understanding how to formulate these perils and how to cope with them provides personality and social psychology with a thoroughly challenging agenda.

Chapter 3, "Attitudes, Values, and Selfhood," my contribution to the long series of the Nebraska Symposium on Motivation, was also presented in 1978 and seeks to integrate the perspectives developed in chapters 1 and 2 with my earlier work on the psychology of opinions and attitudes. There is some repetitious overlap as I recapitulate the main points of these chapters—the reader's forgiveness is requested. The chapter contains my criticism of mainstream social psychology, which would not be very different today. It also presents my functional map of political attitudes and behavior in their personal and social context and discusses it as an example of the sort of conceptualized interpretation that seems to me a realistic goal in many sectors of behavioral and social science. An outgrowth of my earlier work on opinions and personality (Smith, Bruner, & White, 1956), my map has played a larger role in the emerging interdisciplinary field of political psychology (Stone & Schaffner, 1988; Greenstein, 1975) than in psychologists' social psychology.

"The Metaphorical Basis of Selfhood," chapter 4, carries my analysis of selfhood further by examining how culturally provided symbol systems participate in our self-constitution as persons. Here I draw gratefully on Lakoff and Johnson (1980) and Kövecses (1986), linguists who have greatly advanced our understanding of how networks of metaphoric thought, which we imbibe with our native tongue, provide warp and web for our thinking about self and world.

My approach to values and selfhood is humanistic in its preoccupation with the interpretative realm of meanings, its emphasis on the existential implications of reflexive self-awareness, and its focus on human agency, but it certainly also aspires to contribute to the cumulative process of science. It reflects, I hope, the humanistic influence of two of my most significant mentors, Gordon Allport and Henry Murray, to whom my two earlier collections were respectively dedicated. They and the other two principal founders of the psychology of personality as a recognized subdis-cipline—Gardner Murphy and George Kelly—were also among the organ-izers of humanistic psychology when it emerged in the 1960s as an alternative to the mechanistic behaviorism and the substantially reduction-istic psychoanalysis that dominated American psychology then. They hoped to redirect psychological science; they did not intend to oppose science. Soon, the humanistic psychology movement was captured by the irrationalist counterculture of the hippies and their psychedelic drugs, Esalen, body-oriented therapies, and Eastern religion—and its links with the academic psychology of personality atrophied (see Smith, 1984). The movement had peaked and was in substantial decline when I found myself elected president of the American Psychological Association's Division of Humanistic Psychology. It was an honor that I accepted with much ambivalence.

My treatment of humanistic psychology and human science begins with chapter 5, "Toward a Secular Humanistic Psychology," which was my presidential address. In it, I suggest a taxonomy of divergent humanistic approaches, distance myself from the increasingly influential "transper-sonal" psychology with its transcendental or spiritual commitments, and identify myself with a secular humanist position in the tradition of Mon-taigne, Nietzsche, the early Marx, Henry Murray, and Erich Fromm, which it seemed to me had received insufficient emphasis in the movement. I also offer a secular "origin myth" drawing on anthropology and prehis-tory to elaborate on "what it means to be human" as a way of interpreting the unprecedented modern predicament in which we find ourselves. Giving up the faith in progress that buoyed our hopes after traditional religious views were initially undermined in the modern world, I nevertheless find grounds for hope in a secular appraisal of the challenges that humankind now faces.

Chapter 6, "Metapsychology, Politics, and Human Needs," addresses some consequences for political theory that follow from my view of human nature as a transactional, dialectical emergent in history and culture. I sort out the confusing references to needs in theories of motivation and personality, giving particular attention to the hierarchy of needs proposed by Abraham Maslow, the humanistic psychologist who has been most influential in political psychology. I am critical of Maslow's formulations, as paradoxically pseudobiological and insufficiently humanistic, whereas I give more favorable notice to conceptions of personal control and efficacy, which fared well in the ensuing decade.

Chapter 7, "Encounter Groups and Humanistic Psychology," examines what became in the 1960s and 1970s the central phenomenon of the humanistic psychology movement, scrutinizing its characteristics critically, and accounting speculatively for its wide appeal, especially to young middle-class adults, in terms of its responsiveness to three interrelated lacks felt in contemporary society: deficits in meaning, in hope, and in community. After I had published that analysis, it struck me when I was discussing the topic with a ministerial group that I might as well have phrased the lacks in terms of the traditional Pauline virtues of faith, hope, and charity!

"Can There Be a Human Science?" chapter 8, was my contribution to a symposium organized shortly after Carl Rogers's death around the rhetorical question, "After Maslow and Rogers—a new humanistic psychology?" I used the occasion to examine how Maslow, Rogers, and May—the primary leaders in the humanistic movement—had conceived of their relations with science (very differently!), and to disentangle the meanings that have accrued to the term *human science*. Probably the most frequently recurrent sense in which this positively valued but ambiguous term gets used is as a translation of the German *Geisteswissenschaften*, otherwise rendered as cultural or mental sciences. I find this usage unfortunate because it obscures basic differences between the sciences, on the one hand, and the arts and humanities, on the other, in objectives and approach. Yet as I note in my treatment of selfhood (chapters 2–4), psychology actually does bring the causal-explanatory approach of science and the interpretative-meaningful approach of the humanities into joint focus effectively when it treats the causes and consequences of people's self-understanding as helpless or efficacious. I would reserve the term *human science* for such efforts, which in their intrinsic reference to meaning are inherently humanistic, but in their concern for lawful causal explanation are scientific in the useful traditional sense, which, I assert, has survived the demise of logical positivism as the commonly accepted philosophy of science.

Chapter 9, "Psychology and the Decline of Positivism: The Case for a

Human Science," continues my exploration of human science, here in relation to the positivist tradition in the social and behavioral sciences rather than to the special meanings of human science in the humanistic psychology movement. I review the enthusiasm for behavioral science when the term was introduced shortly after World War II, and how the positivistic worldview with which it was linked began to be shaken in the 1960s. The decline of positivism was liberating, but it was also confusing. In my attempt to clarify the opportunities of our present position for human science, I stress our new alertness to the importance of historical and cultural context, the very different routes that theorists can take in revolt against linear, mechanical conceptions of social and psychological causation, and the promise of an ethnopsychology of selfhood, harking back to issues treated in chapter 4.

Chapter 10, "Beyond Aristotle and Galileo: Toward a Contextualized Psychology of Persons," continues my attempt to salvage a postpositivist human science, this time rescuing it from a third set of dangers in addition to those examined in chapters 8 and 9: dangers presented by the extreme versions of "postmodern" alternatives to positivism being offered by contemporary polemicists. My title alludes to an influential essay by Kurt Lewin (1931) in which he criticized the essentialist aspects of the psychology of his day as Aristotelian and laid the basis for his "Galilean" field theoretical approach. I agree with the contextualist and constructivist critical position that calls into question Lewin's aspirations for a timeless, value-free science, but I challenge the version of contextualism that eminent social and developmental psychologists have derived from the philosopher Stephen Pepper (1942). My reading of Pepper indicates that he was addressing a classification of metaphysical systems that has only limited applicability to the options that are now available to us in psychology and social science. I strongly insist that we need to attend more closely to historical and cultural context than has been our usual practice, but I reject contextualism as it is currently being advocated. The essay ends with a statement of my agenda of central theoretical problems for the psychology of personality conceived as human science.

There is no developmental progression in the five essays constituting the final section, Humanism and Social Issues. These essays variously apply perspectives and intellectual strategies developed earlier in the volume. Chapter 11, "Psychology and the Public Interest," examines the role that the American Psychological Association has played over the years in regard to "public interest" issues. The task requires me to consider what we can mean by the public interest, and I conclude that defining the public interest is inherently a political process—in terms of a humanistic conception of politics that I honor in the writings of Isaiah Berlin (1978) and

Hannah Arendt (1958), which I found missing in the pseudobiological doctrine of Abraham Maslow (chapter 6). I therefore support continued debate in the association about the appropriateness of advocacy on social issues, also noting (in disagreement with many in the academic scientist faction) that the contribution of psychology is not limited to reporting conclusive research data (data are seldom if ever conclusive); it is also and maybe more importantly the redefining of policy questions by raising awareness of unconsidered possibilities or by reconceptualizing familiar dilemmas.

Chapter 12, "McCarthyism: A Personal Account," is just that. As a delayed result of my involvement with Stalinist radicalism during my undergraduate years before the war, I was called up before the Senate Internal Security Subcommittee during the heyday of McCarthyism, and also was blacklisted for a decade by the National Institute of Mental Health. Through the provisions of the Freedom of Information Act, I was able a few years ago to gain access to the main documents bearing on my encounter with McCarthyism. I do not emerge as a hero. In my Senate subcommittee hearing, I protected myself by "naming names" of some of my fellow student radicals, feeling worthless and wretched after having done so, even though, in retrospect, I believe I did no one actual harm. I include this somewhat confessional piece because contemporaries who underwent similar experiences have told me that my honesty about my encounter is helpful, and because my account throws light on one of the dehumanizing episodes of my times, which it remains humanly important for new generations to remember so as to forestall any future recurrence. As a personal document, it also provides context for my views on the variety of other matters treated in this book: the postmodernists are right that science and scholarship cannot safely be depersonalized when matters of human experience and value are at issue.

Chapter 13, "War, Peace, and Psychology," reviews the modest contributions of psychology to matters of war and peace since the emergence of social psychology before World War II through the period when the threat of nuclear Armageddon was the horror that most psychologists (along with everybody else) were unable to bring themselves to face. I became active in a minority group of psychologists, Psychologists for Social Responsibility, which had as its principal *raison d'être* the aim of getting more psychologists involved in the attempt to avoid nuclear war. The chapter contains details to back up the point I make in chapter 11, that psychologists can make and have made significant contributions by helping to redefine policy problems. A focus on the predictable features of the conflict process, including similar and reciprocal enemy images, leads to very different consequences from a focus on the evil essence of one's national antagonist as such. The chapter also uses my analysis of the empowering effects of hope and the demoralizing effects of hopelessness, drawing on my earlier treatment of the self-confirming prophecy as inherent in selfhood (chapter 2 and recurrently throughout this book). The wave of new hope spreading through the world as this volume goes to press creates a setting in which people should be less motivated to avoid the issues involved in the continued presence of the nuclear arsenal—*if* they can remain aware of the problem.

Chapter 14, "Value Dilemmas and Public Health," is based on a memorial lecture honoring Andie Knutson, a former Berkeley colleague whose research on cultural and religious factors affecting people's definitions of when a human life begins anticipated the present bitter debates about abortion. In the course of reviewing a variety of developments that make medical ethics a topic of lively current interest, I carry forward the consideration begun in chapter 1 of the social scientist's role at a time of value dissensus ("assumptive worlds in collision"). I share in what I detect as the growing nostalgia for the value consensus that could be taken for granted in traditional communities, but I see community in that traditional sense as beyond our reach, and in terms of my own value perspective, not even desirable. Rather to my surprise, I come out an articulate defender of liberalism.

Chapter 15, "Hope and Despair: Keys to the Sociopsychodynamics of Youth," is my fullest development of the theme that more than any other binds the book together. Theorists writing from quite different research traditions have assembled convergent evidence that hope and despair are central to the maintenance of vicious or benign circles, to self-fulfilling prophecies. People who hope engage in active coping that makes it possible for some of their hopes to be realized; people who despair are likely to withdraw from the fray, assuring more negative outcomes. I apply this dynamic to interpreting problems of youth that have been the topic of much recent political concern—especially drugs, crime, and violence, which have put the lives of young black and Hispanic males in the central-city ghettos of our metropolises so seriously at risk. The data I review on fears of nuclear catastrophe on the part of youth in general are no longer current, of course. But the rise of the counterculture of the 1960s (see chapter 7), the prevalence of the drug problem across lines of class and race, and the disturbing rise in suicide rates among the young (still low in absolute terms) suggest that my analysis is just as germane to young people in general—to their elders, too.

This way of framing the problem is a good example of how psychology is relevant to social policy in ways beyond providing conclusive data from policy research. To the extent we take this analysis seriously, current popular remedies to the drug problem on both the supply side and the demand side have little promise: attempts to block the production and distribution of drugs, or to induce would-be users to "just say No." In the central-city ghetto, what realistic basis for hope do young people have to induce them to delay gratification, and to invest effort in schooling? In a society in which its national leaders have set wretched examples of the pursuit of rampant self-interest, and duplicity to boot, why should young people not get what kicks they can from life? If our political "leaders" avoid leadership on the transparently obvious problems that are eroding the quality of our lives, problems that bid fair to let the world end "not with a bang but a whimper" (now that we are less worried about the Bang), how can we expect better of the young, especially those whose grounds for hope are shakiest?

I

Values and Selfhood

1

Psychology and Values

Among my various mentors at Harvard and elsewhere, Gordon Allport now seems to me to have been most nearly a father to me, in all of the complexity of connotation that the image evokes. Events at the close of his humane and productive life sealed this image permanently for me. My biological father, whom Gordon had known, had just recently died of cancer at a ripe age when I learned, close to the end, of Gordon's similar fatal illness. I was still full of gratitude to my father for the grace and dignity of his death in which I had just participated—for me a lifting of unacknowledged terrors and a final establishment of loving and respectful closeness. That gave me heart to risk writing Gordon very openly, talking about my father's death and saying what I could about what Gordon had meant to me. I got back a warm vicarious note from his perennial secretary and protectoress, Eleanor Sprague, saying that Gordon was then too weak to write his own reply. But inscribed on the note, in Gordon's hand, was the symbol of a happy face with which he often signed letters of good cheer. Gordon is therefore established permanently as a father figure in my personal pantheon.

Relations with father figures are complex and change and ripen over the life course. I remember how as a graduate student I was particularly eager to differentiate my bumptious young conceptions and approaches from his, to the point of mocking his evident discomfort with psychoanalytic ideas and complaining about what then seemed to me his inadequate grasp of the interdisciplinary syntheses that we of the new generation thought we were about to reach in the just created Department of Social Relations. In retrospect, I become increasingly aware of deep and major ways—also funny minor ones—in which I see Gordon's example and influence recurrently emerging in the kind of psychologist that I have become. I have come to realize that I am far more indebted to Gordon than I can formulate explicitly.

3

This chapter was originally presented in Allport's memory. Its title labels an arena of concern that prevaded Gordon Allport's work. From his postdoctoral *Wanderjahr,* Allport brought back news of the value-laden humanistic tradition in German psychology. In his own work and thought thereafter, an inner dialectic between the conceptions of that tradition and the norms of American empirical psychology gave form to the major theme in his life work, the development of a psychology of personality. His *Study of Values* (Allport, Vernon, & Lindzey, 1951) with Philip Vernon and, later, Gardner Lindzey, was a substantial by-product on the empirical side. His structural and developmental formulation of personality came to a focus in an explicitly evaluative view of psychological maturity: how people ought to become (Allport, 1937). As a social psychologist, Allport was ever the responsible citizen upholding humane and democratic values, as he did in his classic book, *The Nature of Prejudice* (1954), an exemplary marshaling of empirical research and psychological analysis in the service of these values. We will return to it later.

Yet even though Allport's writings were infused with values, there is a sense in which he tended to take them for granted. In William James's phrasing (1985), he was on good healthy-minded terms with them, without the scruples of a sick soul. The rising tide of relativism did not seem to trouble him; he was able to maintain his own firm commitments in a context of tolerance and tentativeness. Our later generations have been too much buffeted by rapid and disorienting cultural change to move in the realm of values with as much mature assurance. A major recent turning point dates at about the year of Allport's death, 1967 (Chilman, 1978). Almost perforce, psychologists who are concerned with values now have to become more self-conscious and critical about their concern.

Fifteen years ago I tried to sort out my own thinking in an essay, "Personal Values in the Study of Lives" (Smith, 1963), that I contributed to a Festschrift for Allport's eminent friend, colleague, and sparring partner, Harry Murray, another of my revered Harvard mentors. This seems an appropriate occasion for me to return to the task. Very selectively, I want to examine some major ways in which psychology has dealt with values, especially some recent attempts by psychologists to span the gap between fact and value that rarely seemed to trouble Allport but has been an enduring obstacle to the development of a psychology that is both humanistic and scientific, Allport's lifelong objective, which I now realize is also mine. I want finally to take a few steps toward a way of thinking about the place of values in psychology that might help us, as psychologists and social scientists, to play a legitimate and needed part in reestablishing our human sense of direction in a perilous, novel world, a world that increasingly is one of our own making but one in which we feel less and less at home.

An Approach to Personal Values

Precise definition is not essential to what I want us to think about. All the same, since psychologists, other social scientists, and philosophers have used the word *values* to refer both to features of the world toward which people are oriented and to features of people that govern their orientation toward the world, I have to make clear at the outset that I will be talking about the latter—about personal values. So was Allport, so is Milton Rokeach (1973), who has done some of the most interesting recent research. Clyde Kluckhohn's familiar definition (which I will not belabor in detail) provides a good starting point:

> A value is a conception, explicit or implicit, distinctive of an individual or characteristic of a group, of the *desirable* which influences the selection from available modes, means, and ends of action. (1951, p. 395; italics mine)

Kluckhohn goes on to say that such conceptions of the desirable are usually fused with beliefs about the nature of reality: *value orientations* is his term for the fusions that constituted the concrete subject matter in which he was most interested.

The key word in Kluckhohn's definition is *desirable,* and the key distinction that it carries implicitly is between the desirable and the merely desired; between values in a strict sense and mere wants or preferences. We all make the distinction in the language with which we comment on our own and one another's activity in everyday life. We find ourselves wanting and other people doing things that we don't find desirable; we regret that we don't want or do what we are somehow convinced that we ought to. We criticize and sometimes alter our actions in terms of such considerations. In my essay for the Murray Festschrift, I drew on Fritz Heider (1958) to emphasize that the realm of *ought,* of the desirable and preferable, has the phenomenal quality of objectivity and intersubjective validity. From the perspectives of each of us, what we regard as desirable or preferable, what we feel we ought to want or do, seems to be objectively given, not a matter of our personal whim. Even if we are tolerant of other people's different values, we are convinced of the rightness of our own. Values as the explicit or implicit standards involved in these occasions of valuing have the quality of objective requiredness emphasized by Gestalt psychology (Köhler, 1938). This quality of experienced objectivity seems important in the role that values play in giving sense and direction to our lives.

I went on to suggest that we can usefully distinguish types of phenomenally objective requiredness in the realm of values, and to give a provisional account of their basis in psychological development and their functional meaning for personality. First there is *social requiredness*. In infancy, the distinction between want and ought first arises from baby's reactions to the parents' expressions of approval or disapproval of baby's impulsive actions, later from their demands and admonitions. The parents are the most salient constituent of absolute reality as the infant first comes to know it. No wonder that their requirements are felt as objective requiredness by the infant at the beginning of personhood.

In a traditional society in which there is strong consensus on the proper ways of acting in each of the finite array of situations that life has to offer, the prototypical social requiredness of family values merges seamlessly with the right and proper as it is taken for granted and supported by everyone in one's social world—the ghosts of one's ancestors and the gods, too, in the mythic order that people in such societies elaborated to make their mortal lives with one another significant and livable (Smith, 1978c). Social requiredness would seem to be at the basis of the objective requiredness of values.

Under conditions of rapid social change, secularization, worldwide cultural contact, and shaken social consensus, such as have increasingly prevailed in modern Western history, a more gyroscopic source of orientation and guidance is needed, to borrow David Riesman's (1950) metaphor—some form of what I called *personal requiredness* of values, arrived at through processes of "internalization" as studied and debated by developmental psychologists. I suggested two subtypes of personal requiredness: superego requiredness and self requiredness.

Following Freud (1961/1923), I saw *superego requiredness* as resulting from the internalization of socially required values at a developmental phase prior to the firm establishment of reflective selfhood, and therefore characterized by inflexibility, irrationality of application, implicitness, and the burden of amorphous guilt that attends transgression. Superego values can persist into adulthood, as we well know, sealed off from inner discourse, immature, and unintegrated in the self. In contrast are personal values characterized by what I called *self requiredness*. These standards

> are actively embraced by the person and thus become constituents of the self, part of what the person feels himself to be and to stand for. Characteristically their application involves more finely differentiated . . . discrimination that is the case with superego values, and they can therefore be applied with more

flexibility, appropriateness, and rationality. As one measures oneself and one's behavior against these standards, his self esteem rises or falls; at low ebb there is a sense of shame or worthlessness to correspond to the superego affect of guilt. . . . Since they are integrated in the self rather than sealed off in an infantile form, they are open to progressive modification and elaboration. They retain the phenomenal character of objective requiredness emphasized by Heider but are sustained by the individual's active commitment to them as the values that he chooses to live by. (Smith, 1963, p. 339)

(Please excuse my sexist phrasing of the early 1960s—I have tried to learn to do better since!)

But this mode of valuing, the most mature one according to my scale of values—which was also Allport's and, as we will see, Lawrence Kohlberg's and Jane Loevinger's too—is vulnerable to collapse into mere preferences. It rests on personal commitment, the worth and substance of which depends on the integrity of the self. In the absence of social support from significant others or from general consensus, value commitments may be hard to sustain, especially in the prevailing corrosive atmosphere of hedonistic individualism. And as Robert Penn Warren (1975) has suggested, integral selfhood itself is seriously at risk in a culture in which historical continuities and communally shared meanings are depleted. There seems to be a strong pull, at present, away from the objective requiredness of self values, leaving people exposed with their unguided wants. "If it feels good, do it!" one increasingly hears, maybe more often in California than elsewhere.

So the status of personal values is crucially in question. Must the phenomenal objectivity of values fade in the light of modern sophistication? Can psychology contribute to the clarification, the criticism, the elaboration and legitimation of values, or is it limited to mere description, to documenting aspects of what it is easy to see as our common plight?

Values in Gestalt and Skinnerian Psychology

Two of the more ambitious and coherent postures that psychologists have taken toward the realm of values seem to me to give us remarkably little help in pursuing these questions—those of Köhler's Gestalt psychology and of Skinner's behaviorism. Köhler's rich and closely reasoned book, *The Place of Value in a World of Facts* (1938), came from his William James Lectures at Harvard in the fall of 1934. My account of the phenomenal requiredness of experiences of value, which I took as a starting point, derives by way of Heider from Köhler's analysis. But Köhler was mainly concerned with the philosophical standing of the structural correspondences or isomorphisms that his Gestalt psychology proposed as existing between experience, brain processes, and the physical world. He was not concerned with the critique of values, with grounds beyond mere preference for choice among them. In regard to values, he was satisfied to find that they do indeed have a place in the world of facts, but he did not interest himself in the warrant for the place that particular values have in the lives of particular persons or peoples.

An important Gestalt psychologist of the following generation who is still among us, Solomon Asch, went further toward addressing our present problems. In his *Social Psychology* (1952), he subjected the prevalent doctrines of cultural relativism to radical attack, arguing that while diverse cultures indeed provide people with differing definitions, different views of reality, within these separate cultural worlds people everywhere experience much the same value requiredness, make the same reasonable choices according to their several lights. This is a useful line of argument, I think, since it calls attention to the possibility that people may resemble one another more closely in their standards of the preferable than in the contexts of existential beliefs with which these standards are fused in the value orientations that govern what people do. For example, California ranchers of the 1880s who regarded the Indians of the Sierra foothills as subhuman "varmints" could engage in genocide for sport while holding more or less to what they and their contemporary descendants regarded as Christian values in their dealings with those whom they saw as people (see Kroeber, 1961). All the same, Asch surely maintained an exaggerated view of human reasonableness, and the experience of requiredness, descriptively important as it is, falls short of explaining or legitimizing values even when it is bolstered by the mysteries of isomorphism.

As for Skinner's (1971) radical behaviorism, when he applies it to the problem of values it can seem helpful only to those who welcome his attempt to cut the Gordian knots of human freedom and dignity. Value, for Skinner, is external and it reduces to what is positively reinforcing. We say we "ought" to do things for which we have received the reinforcement of social approval—and so on. To translate this view of external programming into the perspective of the behaving person (not a translation that Skinner himself would ever make), Skinner has in effect reduced values to preferences; he denies the merit of the distinction with which the present analysis begins. True, he introduces the criterion of survival as a kind of superordinate value: individual survival in the course of evolution, as it partly determines what from a species perspective has become reinforcing, and the survival of cultures, as the governing criterion for engineers of cultural redesign. But to be consistent with his premises, he can have nothing helpful to say about what sorts of cultures ought to survive. And this is something that thoughtful people need to be able to talk about.

Values Applied to Personality

Rather than looking further at how systematic psychologies have dealt with human values in general terms, we may make more headway by narrowing the scope of our inquiry to examine how psychologists of personality have dealt with the value implications of their subject matter— Gordon Allport's home ground. Because the study of personality emerged in close relation to the practical endeavors of psychotherapy and education, personality psychology, like its older cousins, abnormal psychology and mental hygiene, has always included evaluative concepts of good functioning, of "mental health." The preoccupation of the 1920s and 1930s was with "adjustment," which at the time looked to many like a technical, scientific, value-free concept. It was only after social critics of conformity had belabored the point that it became commonly recognized that "adjustment" as a criterion carries with it a culture-bound commitment to prevailing values and practices, whatever they may be. The criterion is not value-free at all, and its use has the danger that its frieght of values is implicit: When mental health professionals purvey adjustment, they may be accepted as technical experts when they are actually covert gurus of value advocacy.

In times since, the roles of guru and of mental health professional have become more explicitly mixed, especially in California, and this is hardly an improvement! Take, for example, the famous Gestalt Prayer offered by Fritz Perls, since his death the patron saint of Gestalt therapy (not to be confused with Köhler's Gestalt psychology, as I try ineffectually to convince my students):

> I do my thing and you do your thing.
> I am not in this world to live up to your expectations,
> And you are not in this world to live up to mine.
> You are you and I am I;
> If by chance we find each other, it's beautiful.
> If not, it can't be helped.

Its deeper meaning may be clarified by a recent parody attributed to Jon Carroll, whose words, as Thomas Greening (1977) says in providing us with both these versions and others, "convey the authenticity of deep I-thou encountering, beautifully expressive of our capacity for caring and Being":

> I do my laundry, and you do yours.
> I am not in this world to listen to your ceaseless yammering,
> And you are not in this world for any discernible reason at all.

You are you, and I am I, and I got the better deal.
And if by chance we find each other, it will be unspeakably tedious.
Fuck off.

Even without the benefit of this translation, we see that Perls is asking us to accept a version of rampant individualism, a value orientation decried by Marin (1975) and Lasch (1976) as the "new narcissism" and, in another variant, challenged by Edward Sampson (1977) as the prevailing implicit value assumption of much contemporary American social psychology.

Psychologists have proposed various lists of criteria of positive mental health (Jahoda, 1958) or of the mature personality (Allport, 1961), containing such hallmarks as extension of the sense of self; warm relating of self to others; emotional security (self-acceptance); realistic perception, skills, and assignments; self-objectification; insight and humor; and a unifying philosophy of life (here I draw on Allport, 1961). At about the time that these lists were being offered to the psychologically alert public, I wrote a paper that has often been reprinted (Smith, 1961), calling attention to the fact that each of these proposed criteria of maturity or mental health represents a value claim about the nature of the good life, about the kind of personality that is desirable or preferable. It seemed to me that there was little point in psychologists arguing with one another about just which criteria belonged on these largely overlapping lists ("mental health" in this context is more a chapter heading for "personality evaluated" than a specifiable scientific concept), but that there was considerable point in their organizing research to discover the developmental or therapeutic conditions under which each proposed evaluative criterion can be realized at an optimal level, and the individual and social consequences and side effects of realizing the criterion. This was to say that psychologists have no special privileged position as value advocates; their scientific-technical expertise should lie rather in the working out of means-end relationships that bear on the realization of values.

In the years since, I have remained confident about my criticism of surreptitious value advocacy in the name of supposedly value-free technical concepts like adjustment or mental health. But I soon came to feel less secure about the limits that I tried to draw about the role of psychology in the elaboration and criticism of values. It may move our inquiry forward to look at several attempts by psychologists to use empirical methods to establish evaluative criteria of mental health or maturity.

Self-Actualization and Other Bridges between Facts and Values

The first of these attempts to be considered, Maslow's (1954) description of self-actualizing people, which was already available to our list makers of the 1960s, is surely the best known. Though its empirical grounding is remarkably weak in view of the burden of argument that Maslow and others subsequently rested on it, the study is especially instructive about the traps that beset the psychologist who seeks a simple bridge across the gap between facts and values.

You will remember that Maslow set out to discover what self-actualizing people have in common. He writes that "for the purposes of this discussion, [the self-actualization syndrome] may be loosely described as the full use and exploitation of talents, capacities, potentialities, etc. Such people seem to be fulfilling themselves and to be doing the best that they are capable of doing, reminding us of Nietzsche's exhortation, 'Become what thou art!' '' (1954, pp. 200–201). To get a relatively pure criterion group of people who had realized their potentialities to the fullest, he spread his net to include historical figures as well as acquaintances and notable contemporaries. The specimens that he caught, among historical figures, were Lincoln, Jefferson, Einstein, Eleanor Roosevelt, Jane Addams, William James, and Spinoza as clear cases, together with some whom he regarded as more doubtful. What seemed to distinguish this remarkable group from ordinary people? Maslow's list of hallmarks of self-actualization includes (to take a partial sampling) acceptance of self, others, and nature; spontaneity; problem-centeredness rather than ego-centeredness; detachment and a need for privacy; autonomy; capacity for deep intimacy; openness to mystical experiences; identification with humankind. Maslow's self-actualizers were indeed fine people! I admire them as much as he did.

But consider what Maslow has really done. Starting with the idea of full actualization of potentialities, the Nietzschian exhortation, he has assembled a collection of his own heroes and heroines, who inevitably exemplify Maslow's own humane values. Where is Napoleon on this list? Where is Alexander the Great? Where the young Casanova, Thomas Edison, Benvenuto Cellini, John D. Rockeffeller, Sr.—other people's heroes who seem to fit the self-actualization criterion just as well as Maslow's heroes but who exemplify different potentialities realized, different values in the spectrum of human potential? Where, indeed, are actualizers of evil? Maslow has built no bridge between facts and values after all, not even a shaky one. He has stayed in the closed circle of his own values. He has, I should add, engaged in what could be a legitimate form of value advocacy—holding forth examples of values that one hopes other people will become sensitized to appreciate and cherish—but he has done so under the false colors of his claim to have provided empirical evidence substantiating a particular set of values for appraising personality.

It is only a step from Maslow's informal study to more formal and systematic research that uses criterion groups selected by appropriate panels of judges to identify empirically the characteristics that distinguish "personal soundness" (as in Frank Barron's [1954] study of Berkeley graduate students) or "maturity" (as in Douglas Heath's [1965] research on Haverford undergraduates). The broadly based sets of judges who made the ratings in terms of which criterion groups were selected in these studies give their findings a firmer status than is possible in Maslow's very personal exploration. But is their status so different, as putative bridges between facts and values in the appraisal of personality?

What the studies provide, on closer consideration, is the empirical and analytic description of "current concepts of positive mental health" (to borrow the title of Marie Jahoda's (1958) book on which I have previously drawn)—current, that is, among the population that the judges sample, at the time of each study. They are empirical explications of mental health values, not empirical justifications of them. One could expect the features that distinguish criterion groups to differ across subcultures and over time—so it is of real interest that Heath (1977) now finds the criteria of "maturity" to be much the same for Turkish and Italian youth and their raters as at Haverford. Of course, these studies too provide no magic bridge. They contribute, however, to making our thought and discourse about values more explicit. They are not trivial.

Piagetian Developmentalism: A New Bridge?

This line of criticism has been available for a long time (Smith, 1959), though I doubt that it has really permeated the thinking of the mental health community. Meanwhile, there dawned a new source of hope for a differently constructed bridge, stimulated by Jean Piaget's fertile ideas and investigations concerning psychological development—which together with computer science have surely been the most important source of new perspectives in psychology during the third quarter of this century, though his contributions began a full quarter century before. Piaget's lifetime project of working out a developmental approach to human knowing led him to distinguish sequential stages of thought from infancy to adult competence in one cognitive domain after another. His claim—still of course the subject of debate and qualification—was that the sequence of stages is intrinsically determined: subsequent stages build on the thought processes attained in earlier ones, restructured at a more complex, flexible, and adaptively powerful level of organization. Development, according to Piaget, is not a matter of passive response to external programming but occurs in predictable steps as the child, interacting with the world, both assimilates the world to his or her existing mental structures and accommodates these structures better to fit the exigencies of new encounters.

The outcome of this interactive process is a progressively better fit between the world as the child constructs it and the world that the child encounters. Piaget properly regards his enterprise as developmental epistemology: an account of the validity of human knowledge by means of structures emerging in developmental process.

Among Piaget's earlier books, written before his formal program had taken its mature shape, was *The Moral Judgment of the Child* (1932), in which, for example, he used careful questioning to trace the development of children's thinking about the status of the rules of the games that they play. Much later, Lawrence Kohlberg (1969) refined and built upon Piaget's analysis of moral judgment to produce evidence for six stages in the development of children's reasoning about standard moral dilemmas presented in a story form. The stages fall into three broad levels: a premoral level, in which the reasons given have to do with the attainment of gratification and the avoidance of punishment; a level of conventional morality, in which the reasons concern what is lawful, right, and proper; and a postconventional level characterized by reasoning in terms of social contract theory or self-accepted principles. The evidence for and against Kohlberg's theory is by no means all in, but over the past fifteen years it has been the target of much fruitful research and controversy.

Let's pause a moment to note the possible claims of the Piaget-Kohlberg approach as a new bridge between facts and values. At first blush they are impressive. If a firmly invariant sequence of stages in the development of moral judgment were to be established empirically, we are likely to be ready to agree that the developmentally later attainments are superior to developmentally earlier ones. It is hard not to believe in progress in the case of the cognitive development of the growing child! I'll postpone raising doubts until we have looked at an extension and generalization of the approach to a point of full juncture with the analysis of psychological maturity as we have seen it treated by Allport, Heath, and others.

In *Ego Development*, written within a broadly psychoanalytic framework, Jane Loevinger (1976) elaborates a stage theory of personality development à la Piaget, which is based substantially on Kohlberg but integrates congruent ideas derived from several other theorists. Rather than limiting her concern to the narrow sphere of moral judgment, the whole span of ego processes is encompassed in principle by her formulation. Development extends from stages characteristic of infancy and early childhood, which she labels presocial, symbiotic, and impulsive, through intermediate stages that she calls conformist, conscientious, and individualistic, to rarely attained heights of maturity in autonomous and integrated stages (the last she identifies with Maslow's concept of self-actualization). For each stage she suggests milestones in regard to impulse control and character, interpersonal style, conscious preoccupations, and cognitive style. As is the case with Kohlberg's narrower theory, the stages are not merely an account of a supposed invariant sequence in the course of individual development; they also generate a typology of people in terms of how far up the ladder they have managed to progress. Her own research using a sentence-completion test with a carefully prepared scoring manual has participated in the refinement and elaboration of her scheme, but she can hardly claim to have tested it.

I confess to considerable enthusiasm about Loevinger's proposal, and I think it is worth substantial effort to see whether, in spite of the difficult measurement problems, something like her scheme of stages and milestones can be approximately established. Within our own contemporary culture, it seems to organize the facts about personality development and individual differences in personality in a way that is very relevant to our existing tradition of liberal values, helping us to formulate goals and checkpoints for parenting, education, and psychotherapy and to adapt our educational or therapeutic strategies to the stages along the way. Has she slipped those values in surreptitiously? I don't think so; nor do we have to interpret her as seeking to legitimize values by developmental facts, the magic bridge. Rather, she is attempting to sort out the developmental facts in a way that immediately engages some of our central values for the appraisal of personality.

There are serious problems with Loevinger's scheme, as with Kohlberg's scheme, when we view it in transhistorical and cross-cultural perspective. I am less worried about the cross-cultural applicability of both schemes than I am about their cross-cultural relevance. In a few test cases, Kohlberg has shown that the sequence of his stages seems to be properly invariant across cultures—but some cultures fail to show the highest stages at all. Is that because these cultures are inimical to the development of moral judgment? Or is it rather that the higher stages of a scoring scheme developed in our culture will inevitably (and I think quite properly) reflect the direction of intrinsic developmental possibility that accords with the challenges and opportunities provided by our culture, with its distinctive value emphases?

A Kohlberg or a Loevinger working within Far Eastern traditions might develop scales of intrinsically ordered developmental stages that would probably share with ours a common base in childhood universals but, toward their summits, might scale quite different peaks of human potential for the realization of diverse values. Given the individualistic emphasis on autonomous choice of both Kohlberg's and Loevinger's schemes at their higher reaches, I think it is premature—indeed wrong—to conclude that either of them has vanquished the problem of cultural relativism. Long ago, St. John Climacus offered to Eastern orthodoxy his "ladder of divine ascent" (see Braun, 1978), a Kohlberg-Loevinger scale for monks and mystics. Kohlberg and Loevinger now construct promising human ladders with quite different rungs. Why, after all, should we want a single universal ladder?

Indeed, if we take Gordon Allport's commitment to human individuality—to uniqueness—seriously, we ought to retain some skepticism about general-purpose ladders even for single cultures. Human potentiality is various and open in essential respects, within limits set by biology, culture, and history, and within new limits set by the strained ecology of our finite planet. The routes to the realization of human values are also many. Case studies presented by McDowell (1978) of self-transformation in adult lives suggest that even for us modern Americans, the Kohlberg-Loevinger ladder can at best be a rough approximation.

Psychology and the Dialectic of Values

It is time to draw some conclusions from our long though selective review of how psychologists have dealt with the problem of evaluating personality. There is indeed no magic bridge between facts and values. No more than anyone else can psychologists prove the preferability of particular values by considerations of fact. If our values are more than what our social world expects of us or what has been instilled in us before we knew any better, they are products of a social and personal process of reflective and creative choice and commitment, to be informed by fact but never dictated by it. All the same, psychologists from Allport on who have treated the evaluation of personality in light of empirical facts have not engaged in an empty, futile enterprise. In a way that uses the special assets of psychology, they have contributed to the ongoing dialogue or dialectic through which values are differentiated, transmitted, and sometimes transformed.

I agree with the ethical philosopher Harry Girvetz[1] (1973) that when we are functioning at our most fully human level, valuing is a reflective and creative process, developed in inner and outer dialogue, in which real choices made by our reflective selves are sometimes capable of transcending our existing entrenched patterns of interests, even going beyond the implicitly or explicitly codified sets of standards and principles that embody the wisdom of personal and social experience. Values have their standing in social experience or in internalized versions of it, and it is social and inner dialogue that sustains or transforms them. But this dialogue is not a matter of empty words; it engages and evokes people's different native sensitivities and their wants and interests and their new sensitivities that emerge in the interplay of experience. It engages the world of events as these unfold and the world of facts, themselves transformed in interaction, which Piaget's view of development helps us to formulate. The dialogue is the living substance of the human enterprise, in which, since the dawn of human speech maybe some fifty-thousand years ago, people have been shaping their own human nature as they create culture and give meaning to self and world (see Smith, 1978c).

Psychologists do have a distinctive role in this ongoing dialectic—not as gurus, I hope (we don't have the right credentials!), but as scientists of a difficult terrain and as professionals whose human service roles give some of us a privileged window on human experience (Smith, 1977). To illustrate the special role of psychology and its place in a dialectic process that does not stay still, I can do no better than to call our attention to the historical significance of Gordon Allport's (1954) classic, *The Nature of Prejudice,* which I was recently asked to reappraise after a quarter century, having reviewed it for what had been Gordon's *Journal of Abnormal and Social Psychology* when it first appeared (Smith, 1955, 1978b).

In the book, Allport did not offer a theory of prejudice but sought to put existing theories and the evidence for them in perspective and, taking theory and evidence into account, to provide guidelines for social action in the service of democratic values in intergroup relations. The facts that Allport had to work with are out of date, of course, but the principles that he drew from them have proved remarkably durable—for example, that contact between members of majority and minority groups is likely to reduce ethnic or religious prejudice when the members of the respective groups are equal in status and are interdependent, in pursuit of common goals, especially when their cooperative relationship is sanctioned by institutional supports.

Nearly a generation of readers has been influenced by this careful, wise, and humane work of applied social science, and I am sure that democratic values have been advanced. It is not just that Allport used the resources of psychology and social science very effectively to *clarify causal and means-end relationships*—how best to proceed to attain valued goals. His close examination of the nature and manifestations of bigotry surely made many of his readers more thoughtful and self-critical about ways in which they too had played the bigot unthinkingly: a role of *sensitization* that can lead to the emergence of new values, and a role of *encouraging Socratic self-confrontation* that can lead to the reordering of the reader's values and behavior toward more inclusive, self-chosen patterns of consistency. Milton Rokeach's (1973) research focuses on the latter process. And Allport's own example of scrupulous fairmindedness—seeing problems in their complexity, weighing evidence carefully and objectively, never settling for shoddy "simple and sovereign" theories or remedies—was surely a cogent contribution to the dialectic of values: *modeling* has a role in the dialectic, too.

Allport's principles of prejudice and intergroup relations have been durable over a quarter century, as I have said. But there is a way in which the book is certainly dated, even something of a period piece. For our present purpose, it is especially instructive to grasp what it is in the book that clashes with our present perspective. It has to do with the book's implicit aim, its assumed audience, and the point of view assumed by the writer. As a liberal white gentile, Allport was appropriately concerned in the early 1950s with spreading the gospel of liberalism and tolerance among gentiles and whites. From the standpoint of white experience, prejudice seemed more central than the discrimination and injustice encountered by Jews and blacks, which was of course also very much in view in his book. We need to remember also that Allport was writing at a time when Gunnar Myrdal (1944) could call the "Negro problem" really a white problem (a truth then that now appears as a half-truth); a time when Robin Williams (1947) could take for granted the consensual objective of "the reduction of intergroup tensions" (the title of his important monograph)—certainly not what either Malcolm X or Martin Luther King could be said to have been up to in the meantime.

Our evaluative frame for judging these matters has shifted radically over a period that witnessed the *Brown v. Board of Education* decision, the nonviolent protest of Martin Luther King, the proud and truculent separatism of Malcolm X, the emergence of articulate and insistent Third World voices abroad and at home. Suddenly, respect (for one's own group, as well as between groups) seemed much more important and consequential than liking or disliking (which is what prejudice is mainly about). And *racism,* a rhetorical term identified with minority protests—which for all its ambiguities implies consequential effects more than subjective feelings and intentions—began to replace *prejudice* as the main target of concern. It was soon joined by *sexism,* as the call for respect and justice spread to new quarters.

So Tom Pettigrew and Bernard Kramer cannot revise *The Nature of Prejudice* to bring it up to date, as Tom tells me that they first intended. They will have to rewrite it if they are to be true to Allport's legacy. That they have to do so seems to me a sign of the vitality of the book, not of its weakness. It follows from the fact that Allport was engaged in the book with the significant contexts of his time. Not only the factual context of current history has changed since then but also the context of human values that call for priority in personal action in research, and in public policy. A splendid example of the complex interrelation of psychology and values, the book participated consequentially in the dialogue by which our democratic values have been transformed in significant respects.

This is an appropriate note on which to bring to an end this offering in honor of Gordon Allport's memory. Some of my colleagues in social psychology have been shocked, lately, at Kenneth Gergen's (1971) announcement that their field should be properly construed as an historical discipline, not a timeless science on the model of Newton or Einstein. My reply, and I think it would have been Allport's, is: if our field is to have human significance, if it is to make a difference to the central human concerns that touch our values, of course it is historical; of course it is a part of history. I think that is the nature of our field. I regard it not as a limitation but a strength and a challenge. If more of us were able to follow Gordon Allport's memorable example, we might even hope to have an effect on history through our part as psychologists in the continuing dialectic process of collective human self-understanding.

Notes

1. I find the treatment of moral discourse by Girvetz (1973) especially helpful and relevant to a psychologist's concerns. Though he makes no reference to Kohlberg, his classification of the views that moral philosophers have taken of the good fits the Kohlberg levels, though with a slightly different cut. First there are what he calls aesthetic and prudential uses of *good, right,* and *ought*: what is good is merely the object of an interest, or it is what is consistent with our prevailing pattern of preferences or interests. Second are moral or jurisprudential uses of *good* and *right* according to which conduct is good not because it serves a desire or fits a pattern of desires but because it accords with law or with accepted standards of morality. Conduct is good not because of its consequences but because it is right. Finally, Girvetz distinguishes a realm of the truly ethical, which emerges only in dilemmas for which the person's existing standards give no adequate guidance. Girvetz sees the ethical as *reflective* morality in which the self wills courses of action according to what the self undertakes to become, transcending the totality of one's prevailing interests.

2

Perspectives on Selfhood

In this chapter, my presidential address to the American Psychological Association, I took the opportunity to develop and promulgate a point of view that seemed to me to make a difference for how we shape a major part of our science, how we pursue our profession, and how we contribute to human welfare.

At a previous Canadian meeting of the Association, Donald Hebb's (1974) address to us was entitled "Psychology: A Biological Science." Psychology *is* that—but more. More recently, Bill McKeachie (1976) told us, in his presidential address, that we are converging on a consensual all-American psychology of "cognitive behaviorism." So we may seem to be, and the underlying metaphor of information processing bequeathed us by the computer has certainly liberated us, as new metaphors do, from the constrictions of the more crudely mechanistic metaphors that had previously bemused us. But I am not sure that such easy convergence is what psychology needs just now or in the long run. Even liberalized cognitive behaviorism falls short of doing justice to the vast domain that psychology has staked out for itself, a domain that may be susceptible to treatment more in terms of dialectical oppositions than of eclectic synthesis.

Selfhood as Being Human

"Selfhood," in my title, is a label for the criterial features of the human condition, and over the millennia since people became *self*-consciously aware of their special place in the world it has been the prime puzzle (along with the cosmological puzzle) to which myth, religion, and philosophy have been addressed. I see it as the central concern of psychology as a humanistic science.

I am not talking at this point about *the* Self as a successor to the Soul, or even about the *self-concept*. Nothing that *thing*-like, substantive, or concrete can ground our consideration appropriately. I am talking, rather, about universal features of being a person, distinctive features that we find fascinating and, when we take them seriously, as mysterious as the frontiers of cosmology. So: Selfhood involves being *self-aware* or *reflective; being* or *having* a body (a large debate here);[1] somehow taking into account the *boundaries of selfhood* at birth and death and feeling a *continuity of identity* in between; placing oneself in a *generational sequence and network of other connected selves* as forebears and descendants and relatives; being in partial *communication and communion with other contemporary selves* while experiencing an irreducible *separateness of experience and identity;* engaging in joint and individual *enterprises* in the world with some degree of *forethought and afterthought* (not just "behaving"); *guiding* what one does and *appraising* what one has done at least partly through *reflection* on one's performance; feeling *responsible,* at least sometimes, for one's actions and holding others responsible for theirs. I could go on, but this already covers a lot of ground. These are features that a *human* psychology, let alone a humanistic one, has to take into account. All of these terms involve presuppositions, of course. I run through them lightly simply to identify the domain with which I am concerned.

The puzzle of selfhood—of what it means to be human—does not lend itself to *definitive* solution by psychology or other human disciplines, since human beings are prolific creators of novel meaning. Yet three major contemporary perspectives with roots in modern scientific and humanistic inquiry carry our thinking about selfhood beyond the rich symbolic presentations of myth and common sense, religion and philosophy and literature, and seem to me, taken together, to provide a foundation for more specific psychological formulations. These are an *evolutionary* or *phylogenetic* perspective, how we got to be human in the first place; a *cross-cultural* and *transhistorical* perspective, looking at empirical variants of selfhood; and a *developmental* or *ontogenetic* perspective, how we attain personhood in our individual lives. The first two of these perspectives require us to look outside the customary confines of psychological inquiry.

The Evolutionary Perspective

First, the evolutionary perspective.[2] The new vision that we have recently gained of human evolution serves both to make the boundary between the prehuman animal and the truly human being more ambiguous for us and to make the distinctive features of humanness more remarkable. We have pushed our divergence from our closest primate cousins back many million years. We have learned that our Pliocene ancestors could already walk bipedally and were first using, then making, crude tools long before they developed the big brains that underlie our present complexity of experience and behavior. This greatly expanded time frame for human evolution is a matter of fact. On it we have built the speculative construction (Washburn, 1959, 1978) that manipulation, tool use, and toolmaking— phenomena of incipient "material culture"—gave important selective advantage to the genes that govern brain size and neural complexity. According to this now-plausible view, material culture and distinctive human biology evolved interactively.

Such speculations about the causal processes underlying one distinctively human feature, our technology, rest on the factual basis of dated sequences of bones and hearths and artifacts that we have unearthed. The development of symbolic culture and language unfortunately leaves no such traces until very late in the course of human emergence, in Neanderthal burial sites dating from about the time that our own subspecies of *Homo sapiens* appeared. Burial in graves lined with flowers (Marshak, 1976) surely attests to well-elaborated cultural beliefs in an afterlife. But fifty thousand years ago for the flower-lined graves and seventy thousand for other evidence of deliberate burial (Butzer, 1977) is only yesterday in the evolutionary time span that has recently opened out behind us.

Prelinguistic communication must have been just as selectively advantageous as manipulative tool use to those bands of protohuman hunters and gatherers on the East African savannahs who excelled in it, and selection for communicative capacity was probably also involved in the rapid increase in brain size in later Pleistocene times. What is certain is that the capacity to learn the elaborate structures of human speech is built into the human brain in intricate, fundamental ways, and that the immensely flexible two-stage coding system of phonemes and lexical units elaborated in syntactical structures that is universal in human speech is a uniquely human emergent (Washburn, 1978). Contemporary conjecture suggests a remarkably late date for this crucial attainment, maybe about fifty thousand years ago among members of our own subspecies equipped genetically as we are today (Harnad, Steklis, & Lancaster, 1976)—a date that leaves extremely difficult puzzles about the previous evolution of the neural and articulatory bases of human language. So recent a date does fit the sudden efflorescence and diversification of Late Paleolithic culture beginning about then.

Let's consider, briefly, the emergent situation of people newly possessed of true language. The Acheulian bands of hunter-gatherers had been poised for more than a million years at the juncture of Nature and Culture (Butzer, 1977). They had been part of Nature. Their slowly evolving culture of crudely flaked stones and fire (surely sticks, too, but they don't last) and, at the boundaries of the last glaciation, of clothing and constructed shelter—also of social organization and protolinguistic communication— fed back to give a selective biological advantage to those whose bigger and more complex brains made them adept first at using, then at inventing, culture. But this insecure, partly cultural adaptation within Nature was ever so stable. Protopeople depended more than other animals on learning, but hardly on innovation. For countless millennia, their toolmaking culture had a universal sameness that approached the stereotyped behavior traits of other species of mammals.

The attainment of language gave its speakers immense practical advantages: in the coordination of joint activities through social organization, in the socialization of the young, in the potentiation of thinking. Forethought and afterthought became possible. People could now make plans, undertake commitments, recognize and correct errors—all essential adaptive ingredients of human social life as we know it.

In our present context, it is fair to say that selfhood as we experience it emerged with language. Although Gallup (1977) has recently shown that chimpanzees at the mirror are capable of responding appropriately to themselves as social objects in ways not demonstrated for other mammals, G. H. Mead (1934) was surely right in emphasizing the *reflexiveness* of language as centrally involved in the human capacity and propensity to take the self as object, figuratively to look at the self as if through the eyes of others. When we speak, we understand ourselves as if from the perspective of our hearers. We are part of our audience, sharing meanings in terms of a shared symbol system.[3]

Mead argued persuasively that the development of reflexive selfhood, the *self*-conscious sense of *me*-ness, is crucially "functional" in that the implicated ability to "take the role of the other" is essential for our participation in the coordinated activities of organized social life and gives us the tools for individual thought as well. So it surely is. Yet as surely there were heavy costs in the side effects of attaining articulate selfhood. Human self-consciousness breaks the unity of people with Nature. Self-consciousness with forethought and afterthought gives rise to the human existential predicament. At least for the past fifty thousand years, we and our forebears have faced the puzzle (which we have had the words to pose to ourselves) of whence we came into the world, why we are here, and what happens when we die. But as we know, this is no matter of mere curiosity. Since reflective language made us persons, we have cared about ourselves and each other *as* persons. So the inevitability of the eventual death of self and loved ones and the arbitrary unpredictability of death from famine, disease, accident, predation, or human assault become the occasion not only for momentary animal terror but also for potentially unremitting human anguish. And the quest for meaning, for meanings compatible with a human life of self-conscious mortality, becomes a matter of life-and-death urgency. I don't think that Ernest Becker (1973) exaggerated the importance of this theme in the history of human culture, though he tried hard to do so.

Yet, contrary to the old myth, our forebears cannot have been cast out of Nature's Garden of Eden in a sudden, tragic "birth trauma." Even if the final, full attainment of language competence worked itself out very rapidly once the basic structural-generative principles of human language had been hit upon, self-conscious selfhood, with its imperative challenge to find supportive meaning in the face of creature mortality, must have emerged over a period of time.

If so, the symbolic resources of language-bearing human communities could meet the need for meaning as it arose. Thus emerged the many worlds of myth, ritual, and religion that provided the traditional answers to the question of what it means to be human. They were good answers, proclaiming the value of each communicating tribal group as *The* People, legitimizing its way of life as ordained to their ancestors in the nature of things, giving intelligible meaning to the exigencies of life and death, providing appropriate ways in which individual and community could participate in the encouragement of auspicious outcomes and in the avoidance of ominous ones (Berger & Luckmann, 1966). The traditional mythic answers could not fully eliminate occasions for anguish and terror, but they could give intelligible shape to formless terror, and they could make the blows of fate more bearable to the victim and certainly more endurable to the victim's kindred and community. They allowed life to go on quite satisfactorily between emergencies.

We are in trouble now with the collapse of these mythic meanings under the corrosive impact of impersonal science and of a technological, segmentalized world that seems for the time being quite unfriendly to coherent human meaning in any frame of reference. The evolutionary perspective on selfhood, nevertheless, leaves us with the knowledge that our status as persons is a natural but surprising emergent from evolutionary process and with the speculation that our existential predicament as persons is an inherent side effect of our gift of symbolization and language.[4]

The Cross-cultural, Transhistorical Perspective

The second perspective on selfhood, cross-cultural and transhistorical, grows naturally out of the evolutionary point of view. Selfhood as it has emerged through the millennia of biocultural evolution is always phrased in the terms of a *particular* temporally dated culture (Geertz, 1973), and these historical-cultural versions of selfhood, as of the world, may be radically different. We psychologists, with our preoccupation with universal processes, have a strong bias against historical-cultural modes of thought and therefore risk being culture- and history-bound. I begin with a cross-cultural example because I think it produces the more plausible shock to our accustomed ways of thinking. But conceptually and methodologically, I see no essential difference between the cross-cultural and the transhistorical points of view as correctives to our temptation to phrase our ethnocentric, *un*historical observations in the language of *a*historical, Newtonian science.

The anthropological literature that bears explicitly on the conceptualization and nature of selfhood in persisting nonliterate cultures is surprisingly sparse, given the current emergence of a psychological anthropology that inherits the older culture-and-personality tradition of Ruth Benedict, Margaret Mead, and Abram Kardiner. I am talking here of explicit contributions to "ethnopsychology," construed to parallel other branches of "ethnoscience." The raw materials are surely available to be mined, but there have been few miners. The best explicit cross-cultural analysis of selfhood that I've encountered is provided by Clifford Geertz (1973, 1975).[5]

Geertz (1973) writes in interesting detail about selfhood in Bali, the Indonesian culture whose shadow plays and ceremonial life of dance and trance have become somewhat familiar to social scientists as well as to tourists. In a fine instance of the "thick description" that he sees as the anthropologist's task, Geertz communicates a believable picture of a world that minimizes individualized selfhood. People's names, the hooks upon which they hang their identity, show this. The Balinese have elaborate systems of birth-order names, status names, and names that they acquire as parents or grandparents of particular offspring. The complex naming system fits into a kind of stop-time social drama without climax, in which the members of the society link past and future in skillfully enacted simultaneity. Let me quote:

> The most striking thing about the culture patterns in which Balinese notions of personal identity are embodied is the degree to which they depict virtually everyone—friends, relatives, neighbors, and strangers; elders and youth; superiors and inferiors; chiefs, kings, priests, and gods; even the dead and unborn—as stereotyped contemporaries, abstract and anonymous fellowmen. Each of the symbolic orders of person-definition, from concealed names to flaunted titles, acts to strengthen the standardization, idealization, and generalization implicit in the relation between individuals whose main connection consists in the accident of their being alive at the same time and to mute or gloss over those implicit relations between . . . persons intimately involved in one another's

biographies, or between predecessors and successors. . . . The illuminating paradox of Balinese formulations of personhood is that they are—in our terms anyway—depersonalizing. (Geertz, 1973, pp. 389–90)

I commend to you the details of Geertz's full account, which really are required to make this schematic summary plausible, and his briefer comparison (Geertz, 1975) with selfhood in Java and Morocco, in both of which cultures he has worked.

As I have said, historical comparisons have the same conceptual status as cross-cultural ones, with the addition of opportunities to examine continuity and change in a single sequence. But on the transhistorical front, the trouble is that we cannot gain access to the kinds of representative data that field anthropologists provide. We are tied to what has survived, and the richest sources are the sophisticated documents of high literary culture. So long as we remember that we are dealing with conceptions of selfhood among elites, this is not a crucial handicap—especially because elites are more articulate than others about contemporary meanings, and may also contribute disproportionately to formulating the meanings definitive of selfhood that shape the self-conceptions and therefore the empirical selves of many more of us.

Our own Western literary tradition is particularly rich from this perspective because of its strong cultural bias, since the Renaissance, toward an emphasis on individuality. Cross-culturally, we have hovered near an opposite pole from Geertz's Balinese—something that we need to remember as we erect general theories of selfhood and personality from our special perspective. Yet within our tradition, there has also been substantial historical change in the meaning of selfhood. A number of recent literary critics who have dealt with this theme provide us with suggestive guidance. (See, for example, Quentin Anderson [1971], Leo Bersani [1976], Robert Langbaum [1977], Lionel Trilling [1972], and Robert Penn Warren [1975].)

With his broad sweep of humanistic scholarship and special involvement in psychoanalytic strands of thought, the late Lionel Trilling is an especially provocative guide. His final book, *Sincerity and Authenticity* (1972), written at the culmination of a distinguished career, is a brilliant account of vicissitudes of selfhood in the European literary tradition.

He begins with the classic statement of the ideal of *sincerity*, as Shakespeare's Polonius put it in his sententious advice to the young Laertes:

> This above all: to thine own self be true
> And it must follow, as the night the day,
> Thou canst not then be false to any man.

Trilling notes that the ideal of sincerity as a state or quality of the self is a kind of moral mutation in Western culture; it doesn't make sense to talk of sincerity in connection with the patriarch Abraham, or the hero Achilles—or Geertz's Balinese. Sincerity as an ideal emerges with Western individualism as celebrated in Shakespearian drama and in the self-explorations of the extravert Cellini and the introvert Montaigne and the new portraiture of Titian, Holbein, Dürer, and Rembrandt. Trilling traces the concept of sincerity—the sincerity of an intact selfhood in which actions and words correspond to inner feelings and convictions—through its literary transformations to our present dilemmas, when we are so acutely aware of the erosions of selfhood under the felt assault of society. Well before Freud, the ideal of sincerity as the virtue of integral selfhood-in-society had become suspect, and Freud raised serious questions about its very possibility. In the example of his own life (the stoic austerity that Trilling admired), as well as in his writings, Freud held forth the related but different ideal of *authenticity*, the responsible *owning* of what most people exclude from experienced selfhood—indeed a difficult ideal. But Trilling reminds us that authenticity to unconscious impulse and fragmented identity is a peril to integral selfhood. He is no friend to the ideas of R. D. Laing (1967).[6]

As a man of letters, Trilling focuses upon the shifting moral dimensions within which self-aware people in the Western tradition have encountered life as meaningful tragedy or comedy; it was not his project to write a general history of the consciousness of self. Yet it follows from the reflexiveness of human symbolic thought that such historically evolving moral ideas are partly *constitutive* of selfhood, of what it means to be human. Our own academic and would-be scientific accounts of selfhood risk being parochial—and unhelpful as a basis for critical perspectives on our human options—if they lack historical depth such as Trilling adumbrates for us.

The transhistorical perspective merges with the cross-cultural one, then, in reminding us that the very nature of selfhood, not just its context, is historically and culturally conditioned, because selfhood is a historical emergent in a changing world of cultural diversity. True, there are common points of reference that arise from common features of the human condition in all times and cultures since we first became humans. These are crucial to our attempts to gain a degree of interpretative understanding of selfhood in other times and places; otherwise we would be isolated in our own time and place by an absolute barrier. All the same, I can conclude only that however well other aspects of psychology may fit the ahistorical ideal of Newtonian and post-Newtonian science, psychological accounts of selfhood have to be framed in historical context if they are to be scientifically adequate; they cannot be timeless like the laws of physics.

Taken as a formulation applying to selfhood in his own times, Freud's own version of psychoanalytic theory stands up better than its present critics, including the feminists, generally allow. By the same token, currently fashionable accounts such as Goffman's (1959, 1974) that dissolve selfhood into fragmented transactions and roles can be seen as reasonably defensible versions of salient aspects of selfhood among us *now*—testimony, if you will, to pathological aspects of our present culture—though they may do little justice to human potentiality in the longer run and provide inadequate guidance for its development.

The Developmental or Ontogenetic Perspective

The third general perspective on selfhood, ontogenetic or developmental, is the one that contains most of the specific contributions and speculations of psychologists, psychiatrists, and social scientists. For this very reason, it is neither feasible nor appropriate for me to touch on here, let alone to summarize or criticize, the lines of thought on the development of selfhood linked with James (1890) and Cooley (1902), with Freud (1961/1923) and Jung (1966), with Fairbairn (1954) and Guntrip (1971), Jacobson (1964) and Kohut (1971, 1977), Sullivan (1953) and Erikson (1959).[7] In keeping with what I have tried to do with the evolutionary and the cross-cultural/transhistorical perspectives, I want rather to focus on core guiding ideas that have emerged as promising in the developmentalist perspective, ideas that seem to me to point directions in which a scientific humanism of selfhood can be elaborated. That is, I am still working on prolegomena. For me as for many others, a starting point can be found in the life contributions of Jean Piaget and of George Herbert Mead.

Babies are not born as persons or selves; they achieve selfhood. But by now it is a commonplace that they are not born as blank slates either. From the very beginning, babies learn about their worlds by interacting with them. Piaget (1952) opened our eyes to the active basis of the development of mind, in interaction with an environment that is assimilated selectively to the infant's emerging schemas—organized and active frames for making a coherent selection from the available plenitude and coming to terms with it. His developmental interactionism cut radically through the long-term opposition in psychology between the unacceptable empiricism of Locke and Hume—still substantially entrenched in American psychology—and the equally unacceptable a priorism of the Kantian tradition, which has deeper roots in continental Europe. Quite apart from the details of his formalized stage theories, it provided an interpretation of

Mind, hence of major aspects of selfhood, in the context of a view of adaptation rooted firmly in the evolutionary perspective.

I have already made use of George Herbert Mead's (1934) central idea that selfhood and symbolic communication emerge together, in the individual life as in the history of humankind. According to the tradition of "symbolic interactionism" that he launched, one comes to respond to oneself as an object—to be self-aware—by taking the role of the other in symbolic communication. Selfhood arises in the course of communicative interaction, which, from inept beginnings, gets progressively more precisely attuned to the general code as exemplified in communications originating from already socialized adults. But contrary to the perception of some psychologists—Gordon Allport (1968) for one—Mead did *not* regard selfhood, which encompassed both the *I* and the *me* for him, as a passive social product. In Mead's view, the *me* in reflective thought does indeed have social origins in role taking, but the acting and experiencing *I* is one step ahead: acting in the light of conversation with others and with the *me*, and transforming the *me* in the process.

Of course, important empirical issues lurk here that remain to be clarified in research. Language as such may not be so indispensable to the beginnings of selfhood as Mead believed, and Piagetian research indicates that the emergence of mind is a much more complex process than Mead envisioned; he never studied it empirically. How to merge the Piagetian account—increasingly nonsocial in its mature version—with the Meadian social account poses other interesting questions. But I am concerned here not with the controversial details of Meadian and Piagetian theory but with their preempirical working premises, which help to define a developmental framework for a psychology of selfhood. Actually, such a framework was sketched well before their time by the early, partly Hegelian Karl Marx (Bottomore, 1964).

In his conception of "dialectical" development, Marx held that people work upon the world, and in shaping their world, by the same token, people are shaped by it. The process is interactive, but it is also cumulative. As Marx said, people *create* their human nature, in major respects, as they create their world—both in the individual life span, where the materials they have to work with are genetic and cultural, and in history, where the result can transcend what any single individual brings to the process.[8]

The view of developing selfhood that follows from such a congenial synthesis of the metapsychologies of Marx, Piaget, and Mead sees selfhood as emergent: socioculturally and genetically conditioned, yes, but partly self-created. At the beginning of the life course, we are dealing with biological psychology's familiar formula: organism interacting with environment. But the formula becomes inadequate once the person becomes a virtuoso in symbolization, as we all do very early in life, once the regnant processes of the organism get organized into selfhood. The development of reflective selfhood is a spiraling process, in which, when things go well, people have progressively greater say in selecting or shaping the environments they "interact" with. People can emerge as "Origins" in De Charms's (1968) sense—people who *lead* rather than follow their lives—or they can be stuck as "Pawns" of externally driven vicissitudes or of their own unassimilated impulses.

A radically and cumulatively interactive—that is to say dialectical— approach to the development of selfhood, as we find in Piaget and Mead, seems appropriate to human phenomena. But as we know, Piaget and Mead in their concrete theorizing were so preoccupied with the cognitive side of selfhood that they gave little attention to the life of impulse and affectivity. We must turn elsewhere, especially to the psychoanalytic traditions, for initial ideas to guide a developmental approach to these essential components of selfhood. The British analysts of the so-called object-relations school (Fairbairn, 1954; Guntrip, 1971) seem to me to frame their suggestions along lines that are quite compatible with the interactive or dialectical account of selfhood.

The ontogenetic perspective on selfhood complements the phylogenetic, evolutionary perspective. How does it interlace with the historical and cross-cultural perspective? In fact, most theorizing and research on the development of selfhood has been done in modern Western contexts, with only those contexts in mind. For the earliest phases in becoming a person, this may not make much difference: At the beginning of the life course, development is probably determined mainly by biological maturation in interaction with fairly universal variants of the human and impersonal environment of babyhood. (But one can readily think of drastic exceptions!) The further we move through the life course along the developmental trajectory, the more we should expect cultural and historical differentiation in the agenda and in the very structure of selfhood.[9]

So I draw from the developmental perspective further grounds for an open, multipotential conception of selfhood as a creative enterprise. Such a view does not require of us scientific metaphors that regard people as less than people. Selfhood is an achievement—evolutionary, historical, and personal—not a given, and within limits and with odds that often seem to be stacked unfairly, people can take charge of their lives to different degrees, individually and collectively. Their lives can become infused with coherent meaning, or they can be bungled or meaningless.

The three broad perspectives that I have been pursuing establish a framework for thinking psychologically about selfhood. To bring this thinking more directly to bear on our activity as psychologists, I need to take a few steps further toward "personality theory," the subdiscipline that my concerns most obviously bear on and the details of which I have to rule out of bounds for my discussion here. I will therefore comment briefly on three matters that may help in building the bridges that are needed: the interplay between attributional and archetypal aspects of selfhood, some considerations of conceptual strategy for advancing the psychology of selfhood, and some final comments on the special problems of selfhood in our time.

Attributional and Archetypal Aspects of Selfhood

The feature of selfhood that has particularly captured the imagination of social psychologists is its reflexiveness: our capacity to turn back on ourselves in self-awareness, to take ourselves as objects—and to guide our actions accordingly with evaluative forethought and afterthought. This, of course, is a central concern of Meadian symbolic interactionist theory; it follows from this view that our perceptions, concepts, and theories (Epstein, 1973) about ourselves as persons become at least partly constitutive of who we are as persons. How we construe ourselves, as George Kelly (1955) put it, is an essential component of who we are. It is because I take seriously the idea that selfhood is a prime realm for the self-fulfilling prophecy that I have been so much concerned about American psychology's predilection for reductionist or demeaning conceptions of what it means to be human.

The insight, rather venerable by now, that how we construe ourselves makes an important difference,[10] has been picked up and elaborated upon by social psychologists working in the broad context of attribution theory (Jones, Kanouse, Kelley, Nisbett, Valins, & Weiner, 1972). I think considerable good has come of this endeavor. For example, attributed locus of control—external or internal—which Julian Rotter (1966) had introduced in an utterly different theoretical context, has been elaborated upon as a dimension of selfhood with causes and consequences that have been pretty well explored by now. This seems to me a substantial advance from the rather sterile current of research on the "self-concept" (Wylie, 1961, 1974).

But there is something one-sided and wrong about a purely cognitive psychology of selfhood, attributional or otherwise. For a corrective, I have to draw on a perspective on selfhood that I have previously scanted, that of Jung (e.g., Jung, 1966). Here we are no longer dealing with the neat cognitive constructions of the Socratic "well-examined life"—the self as it appears in the looking glass of Meadian I-me dialogue—but are con-

fronted with eruptive and affect-laden templates of thought from unconscious sources. We are told of recurrent images in dream and myth that
enter into the shaping of people's lives, and we are offered a strange
vocabulary of animus/anima, persona, shadow, and the like to describe
selfhood, in which the Self as a meaningful integration is also an emergent
and dynamic archetype that may eventually become central if the challenges of individuation are met. The new time depth of human evolution
that we lightly explored earlier makes me more open-minded about the
scientific acceptability of such archetypal templates than I was when I
began studying psychology. And the time depth accumulated in my own
life has also contributed to my taking them seriously. Of course, Jung is a
particularly exasperating guide for scientific psychology because his way
of interpreting selfhood draws on mythology to elaborate a whole set of
new myths of his own. All the same, it seems to me that we have somehow
to take into account—and, if we are scientists, to domesticate conceptually—the very different vision of selfhood that emerges from his writings.
Somehow, attributions, archetypes, and masks (Goffman [1959, 1974] and
the dramaturgical theorists also have their contribution) are all needed in a
psychology of selfhood.

Some Considerations of Conceptual Strategy

This apposition of social psychological attribution theory to Jungian
archetypes illustrates a state of affairs in the theory of selfhood—by now I
should say personality theory—that warrants comment. Systematic textbooks on personality written from a single theoretical position or from an
eclectic one have found it hard to compete with the successive revisions
of Hall and Lindzey's (1957) textbook, perhaps because the complexity,
the plenitude, of selfhood is better evoked by a succession of disparate
perspectives than by any forced synthesis. How far, we should ask, will it
be productive to push toward integration and synthesis? Are there polari-
ties or complementarities that defy synthesis and require a radically
different treatment? Just posing these questions seriously may represent a
step ahead in personality theory, which has languished in doldrums since
its halcyon days as represented by Henry Murray (1938), Gordon Allport
(1937), Gardner Murphy (1947), and George Kelly (1955).
    Surely there are areas of theorizing about selfhood, currently existing in
relative mutual isolation, that call for being brought together and shaken
down in synthesis, guided by empirical research. I have suggested as much
in regard to the cognitively based theorizing stemming from Piaget or
Mead and theories—not as yet well elaborated—concerning the impulsive
and affective aspects of selfhood. Here, in terms of the fable of the blind

men, it is a matter of trying to piece together a clear and coherent view of the elephant of selfhood. Even such clashing, competitive developmental theories as Piagetian structuralism and incremental social learning theory face eventual mutual accommodation or replacement by more general synthetic accounts of how people function, people who are still capable of producing data that sustain the hopes of theorists from both camps.

I think the case is different with phenomenological and existential (May, 1977) theories, which take a perspective on the person that is incommensurate with the theories cast in causal/functional terms. Here we may be trying, ineptly so far, to deal with a true complementarity, like the relation between wave and quantum formulations in physics. I believe that the phenomena of selfhood—its subjectivity and intentionality on the one hand, and its embeddedness in causal process on the other—require complementary formulations to begin to do it justice.

There is a familiar ideal-typical contrast with a long history in modern social thought, beginning with Dilthey's turn-of-the-century distinction between the natural and the cultural or mental sciences (*Naturwissenschaften* versus *Geisteswissenschaften*): the contrast between causes and reasons, between efficient causes and telic ones, between empirical lawfulness and normative regulation. For my present purposes, I would phrase the distinction as that between the perspective of *causal* understanding, traditionally but not essentially from a standpoint *external* to the behaving person and that of *interpretative* understanding, traditionally from one *internal* to the person's own perspective, a realm of feeling, meaning, and values.[11]

The causal perspective, as applied to human beings, finds continuity with the natural sciences. The interpretative perspective emphasizes the uniqueness of humankind as symbolizing, culture-bearing, historical creatures who act in a frame of past and future, who can make sense or nonsense to themselves, and who are capable of deceiving themselves and others and of seeing through one another's deceptions. One perspective *assumes* the principle of determinism, though it need not be dogmatic about it; the other assumes the reality of human choice and therefore of contingent human freedom. Both obviously apply to human beings!

Both perspectives are required, it seems to me, to make sense of such phenomena of selfhood as intentionality and responsibility; both are required for the guidance of the interpersonal strategies of applied psychology, which have to be as much concerned with effects in the causal world as they are with meanings in the personal one. We have not been able to synthesize the two perspectives coherently, although the phenomena of selfhood tempt us on occasion to risk trying to do so.[12] We should realize, I think, that we are dealing with a true complementarity.

Toward a Psychology of Selfhood in Our Own Time

Selfhood is self-transforming and historical, I have been arguing. So, as I have said, the kind of science that is appropriate for dealing with the phenomena of selfhood cannot be timeless on the Newtonian model. That does not prevent psychologists from pursuing a special interest in the relatively more enduring or recurrent aspects of selfhood (Triandis, 1977). From an evolutionary perspective, even those aspects that are substantially rooted in human biology are historical! But I agree with Geertz (1973) that we stand the best chance of discovering constants of process and relationship if we look closely at the variants of selfhood across cultures and through human history.

An avowedly historical approach frees us to try to contribute to understanding the special problems of selfhood in our own time, an agenda for social/personality psychology that is quite sufficiently challenging.[13] Here I think of the chronic attrition of meaning, hope, and community—the basic supports of selfhood labeled by the Christian tradition as faith, hope, and charity—that has generally accompanied technological modernity and the decline of mythic world views (see chapter 7). And especially I think of the challenge to humankind posed by the many awesome novelties in the human situation as we push the limits of growth in a finite planet under the tacit threat of our new powers of absolute destruction. Even to begin to deal with these matters, which should concern us all, would require another, even longer essay!

In the present context, I would make only two further points. The individualistic version of selfhood that has characterized our Western tradition since the Renaissance, which we Americans have managed even to exaggerate, seems an increasingly poor fit to our requirements for survival in unavoidable interdependency. I agree with Ed Sampson's (1977) strictures on the prevalence of individualistic value assumptions in American personality and social psychology. There are similar biases in the humanistic psychology of the human potential movement (see chapter 7). The historical and cross-cultural perspective that I have been advocating might help psychology to move beyond the role of merely resonating to cultural trends that have dubious human consequences. Psychology has its own legitimate contribution to make to social criticism!

My second point also hinges on how our often tacit interpretations of selfhood can make a difference. As I recently noted (Wertheimer et al., 1978), what differentiates Robert Heilbroner's (1974) grimly pessimistic reflections on the human prospect from John Platt's (1966) persistently optimistic ones is Heilbroner's strongly inertial assumptions about the constancy of human nature, specifically, the persistence of what he refers to as its myopia and political dependency. My view of selfhood as an open-ended project at least provides the basis for hope—hope that warrants and maybe enables committed effort—though it cannot justify sanguine optimism. (In my lexicon, hope is a blessing, optimism a mistake!)

Looking back, in conclusion, on what I have been saying, I have been urging, and trying partly to exemplify, the further incorporation of humanistic perspectives in the large and various family of psychological studies—scientific, theoretical, and applied (Koch, 1976). If psychology can come to deal more directly and coherently with the phenomena of human selfhood, it should gain in competence to play an essential role in interpreting humankind to itself and in supporting people in their struggles to gain a measure of self-direction in their lives. As an endangered species and an endangering one, we need, collectively, all the self-understanding and self-direction that we can muster.

Notes

1. See Chein's (1972) provocative account of the Jewish theologian Rosenzweig as an essentially disembodied self as he neared total paralysis (pp. 188–90).
2. This section is adapted from Smith (1978c).
3. I am exercising restraint in adding to contemporary speculation about the evolutionary origins of selfhood. No such restraint has inhibited Jaynes (1977), who has speculated brilliantly about the origins of modern consciousness in a late transition from what he calls the bicameral mind. I remain skeptical about his grand hypothesis, but his close and imaginative analysis of historical sources convinces me that the constitutive metaphors of selfhood have been profoundly transformed in historic times. This analysis considerably enriches and complicates the Meadian account, but I think it does not supplant it.
4. See Langer (1967, 1972) for an evolutionary-humanistic view of mind that uses music more than language as its paradigm of symbolization.
5. For another example, see Levy (1973).
6. Clifford Geertz has called to my attention the fact that Trilling's last major essay (Trilling, 1976), published posthumously, refers at length and sympathetically to Geertz's cross-cultural analysis of selfhood. The concordance that I sensed between Geertz and Trilling is thus acknowledged by them both.
7. Jane Loevinger's (1976) scholarly and imaginative treatment of "ego development" is a major contribution toward integrating the psychoanalytic and developmental traditions. I have misgivings, however, about the cross-cultural generality of her stage theory. (see chapter 1.)
8. The case for a dialetical approach in psychology is discussed by Riegel (1976) and Rychlak (1977). See, also, Smith (1977).
9. Levinson (1978), in a richly suggestive account of the lives of a rather special sample of American men in middle adulthood, argues that the stages and eras he describes have general cross-cultural validity. That remains to be seen.
10. Paralleling psychological attribution theory is sociological labeling theory, a perspective that seems to me to have parlayed an important partial truth to the

point of absolute error. See Murphy (1976) for key references and a critical evaluation with respect to issues of mental health in cross-cultural perspective.

11. My discussion here is adapted from Smith (1978a). See Bernstein (1976) for selective and sophisticated guidance through this terrain. Geertz (1973) argues explicitly that the interpretative perspective need not and—in his view as an anthropologist of symbolic culture—*should* not be internal: Meanings are publicly displayed.

12. Freud worked on both sides of the fence, which contributes to the richness, and the inconsistency, of psychoanalysis (Holt, 1972). His great originality lay on the interpretative side; his serious efforts to deal with the causal side have dated badly.

13. Gergen (1973) launched a recent controversy in social psychology in regard to what I agree with him is its historical rather than Newtonian character, a version of social psychology that I would hold can also be scientific. See Smith (1976), which also gives a fuller bibliography of the controversy. Cronbach (1975) has recently stated his concordant version of an agenda for psychology.

3

Attitudes, Values, and Selfhood

The challenge and opportunity to give a coherent account of oneself as a psychologist, an *apologia pro vita sua,* is one that can hardly be refused by any psychologist as a self-regarding person. But I faced serious substantive questions about just *what* account to give in this contribution to a much respected series. I had drifted rather far from the focal concern with opinion-and-attitude research with which I began, and, since near the beginning, I had been marginal to the mainstream tradition in experimental social psychology. At the time of writing, I was in the midst of trying to accommodate ambivalent commitments to both humanistic *and* scientific psychology in the arena of selfhood—that is, personality theory. My concurrent involvements in the American Psychological Association (APA) made it impossible for me to take a responsible sidewise look at the state of research on beliefs, attitudes, and values. By my schedule of inner readiness, it was hardly the right time to look back on my earlier investments in the psychology of attitudes. But is there ever a right time?

This essay is in two parts. The first is a venture in metapsychology. After making explicit my discontent with the framing assumptions of recent social psychology, it goes on to develop a perspective on selfhood as a positive alternative. The second part examines the psychology of attitudes and values in some historical depth from this perspective.

A Metapsychological Stance

Before I can talk about how social psychology has dealt with attitudes and values from a perspective that takes the phenomenon of selfhood seriously, I need first to make explicit my reservations about the metapsychology—the philosophical assumptions, sophisticated or naive—underlying mainstream experimental social psychology in the years since World

War II, and sketch the quite different stance that I have come to, which highlights a conception of selfhood. There has been much armchair debate about the "crisis of social psychology," in which, with sharp prodding especially from Gergen (1973), many of these ideas have gained currency. So I can be brief on the critical side. But I cannot appropriately omit the criticism, even if it is old hat by now, because for the most part experimental social psychology seems to be going right on as if the criticisms had never been made.

What Is Wrong with Mainstream Social Psychology?

The main current of American psychology, and postwar experimental social psychology as it joined the mainstream, has always aspired to the goal of cumulative, systematic, ahistorical, unified science, on the model of Newtonian or post-Newtonian physics. True, the grandiose aspirations of American neobehaviorism were abandoned as premature and unrealistic; general experimental psychology had moved on to the era of minitheories and models, now predominantly within the quasi paradigm of cognitive behaviorism, by the time that experimental social psychology emerged with its own minitheories and models: dissonance theory, equity theory, exchange theory, reactance theory, attribution theory, and the like. But these were all seen ahistorically, usually as pieces of a larger imagined jigsaw puzzle, pieces that with enough reshaping and replacement could eventually be fitted together into a general Newtonian or Einsteinian account. The old goal had not been abandoned; it had simply receded. Cumulative progress toward the receding goal had to be assumed if we psychologists were to justify the activity of our laboratories and the content of our journals.

I can quickly recapitulate the criticisms I have made elsewhere (Smith, 1976) of this way of viewing our common enterprise:

1. After three decades of industrious and intelligent (which is not to say wise) effort, the case for cumulative advance in experimental social psychology remains open to reasonable doubt. Brilliant pedagogical integrations like Aronson's *The Social Animal* (1976) hold together by selection and conceptual sleight of hand. It has sometimes seemed to me that the near-simultaneous publication of the five-volume Lindzey-Aronson *Handbook* (Lindzey & Aronson, 1968–1969) and the nine-hundred-page *Theories of Cognitive Consistency* (Abelson et al., 1968) in fact precipitated the "crisis": without benefit of a year in jail, no one could get abreast of the field. *Pages* cumulated; what else?

2. So far as the domain of personality and social psychology is concerned, it seems to me to require a heavy dose of dogmatic blindness not

to agree with Gergen (1973) and Cronbach (1975) that the central problems and relationships to be dealt with are heavily cultural and historical. The putative ahistorical generalities that have been proposed are either almost empty of specific content or lie very close to the psychophysiological or sociobiological poles. (Harry Triandis [1978] convinces me more than anyone else, but even his cross-cultural universals are not outside human history.) Or, like exchange theory, they are reasonably good fits to the historically given preoccupations of our own society—and thus are descriptors of it.

3. The "classic" contributions to our field—studies by Asch (1951), Festinger (1957), Lewin (Lewin, Lippitt, & White, 1939), and the Sherifs (Sherif & Sherif, 1953), for example—that we are proud of, and ought to be, have been valuable as exemplifications and demonstrations of important processes and relationships, more than as starting points for cumulative parametric exploration. What cumulates from them is sensitization to and enlightenment about aspects of contemporary human, social process that we had not previously seen so clearly. The attempts at parametric exploration, when they have been valuable, have added to and clarified the enlightenment rather than filled in a firm composite of bricks in a systematic structure.

4. Sensitization and enlightenment for the guidance of human action through enriched understanding are congruent with humane values as we inherit them and continue to reshape and refine them in the dialectic of participant human history. The ideal of an ahistorical science of people, built upon manipulative (and often deceptive) experimentation, and applied through manipulative technology, is a very bad fit indeed.

5. As things now stand, Koch (1976) is surely right that our scientific and applied concerns are best characterized as a diverse family of psychological studies, not as a single, inordinately ambitious but indifferently successful science. Our prevalent ideal self-image as a would-be unified science and profession surely has some productive consequences, pressing us to make useful connections, but it is hard for me to envision its realization in any conceivable run, short or long. Such a view of what we are up to is largely a distraction from what we do well and might be doing better. It is a source of vulnerable pretense and needless self-castigation.

6. At least in personality and social psychology, our masochistic love affair with the physical sciences seems to have led to faddishness rather than unification. If we are determined to find our models in the harder, more successful sciences, we would do better to seek them in meteorology or biology. But we should make a more serious try to find models that better fit our own historical, cultural, meaningful domain.

A First Look at My Topics

The topics of this essay—attitudes, values, and selfhood—identify facets of social psychology that made it a refuge from and an alternative to the mainstream in psychology during the periods of classical Watsonian behaviorism, the neobehaviorism of Hull and Spence, and, potentially, the cognitive behaviorism of today. During the first two of these periods, the old *Journal of Abnormal and Social Psychology,* which I once had the arduous honor of editing, was the respectable vehicle for unrespectable psychology. In an early handbook chapter, my teacher Gordon Allport (1935), a previous long-term editor of the journal, had declared the psychology of *attitudes* to be the central topic of social psychology. So, in a way, it was—with some technology of measurement, the beginnings of a descriptive taxonomy, but little indeed that could pass as theory in the most tolerant sense. Attitude research gave some psychologists in the twenties and thirties an excuse for attending to otherwise excluded topics of cognition and affection, and for involving themselves in social issues: the minimal technology of measurement was legitimizing.

It was Allport, too, who introduced the topic of *values* into American social psychology, bringing back from his *Wanderjahr* in early Weimar Germany a strong interest in the *Geisteswissenschaftliche* (cultural, humanistic) psychology of Edouard Spranger (1928), and a lifetime agenda of defending this interest against and accommodating it to American empiricism. The *Study of Values* (Allport, Vernon, & Lindzey, 1951), a measure of individual differences corresponding to Spranger's ideal *Types of Men,* was the successful product of his accommodation; it kept the topic of values conspicuous in personality and social psychology until Milton Rokeach (1973) gave it a new lease on life.

As for selfhood, after William James's (1890) prescient introduction of the modern treatment of the self and Mary Calkins's (1906) abstract attempt that had no sequels, the concept thus labeled found its home in the sociological wing of social psychology launched by C. H. Cooley (1902) and G. H. Mead (1934)—the symbolic interactionist wing that had little interaction with psychological social psychology until Newcomb and others began to knit the two traditions together. Psychologists including Allport (1943) and Sherif and Cantril (1947) preferred the term *ego.* Only recently has *self* returned as a term of choice for socially and humanistically oriented psychologists of personality. Now the term is taking new hold even in psychoanalysis (Kohut, 1971).

In the years immediately preceding World War II, thus, social psychology was the forerunner of a humanistic science that didn't quite happen. So was the psychology of personality under the leadership of Allport

(1937), Gardner Murphy (1947), and Henry Murray (1938)—the first two of them strongly identified with social psychology. Kurt Lewin (1951), the acknowledged patron saint and founding father of modern social psychology, also contributed importantly to the psychology of personality. At its inception, Division 8 of the new postwar APA, Personality and Social, reflected this common ground of a psychology that sought to be at once scientific and humanistic, an alternative to the behavioristic mainstream. But postwar developments, expanding social psychology exuberantly along scientistic lines and cramping personality psychology into a narrow situationism of experimentally manipulated variables, aborted the promising venture.

As I now reconstruct my own participation since World War II, I see it as an attempt to hold onto the ideal of a personality-*and*-social psychology that is both scientific *and* humanistic—and also relevant to our continually changing perceptions of our human predicament and historically given concerns. But it is not good enough just to regress to my origins with Gordon Allport and Henry Murray. Having raised my objections to the dominant tradition in personality and social psychology, I need now to sketch the grounding of my positive alternative, before recurring to examination of attitudes and values from the perspective of selfhood.

An Evolutionary and Historical Perspective on Selfhood

I will not repeat here the perspectives on our social/cultural/historical human nature that I developed in chapter 2. The relevant gist follows from a broadly evolutionary approach that merges with a historical perspective and even an existential one. I take seriously what we have learned from our colleagues in anthropology about our human distinctiveness as technologists and as symbolizers, as creators and creatures of material and symbolic culture. Two decades ago, Washburn (1959) had speculated that the selective advantages given to early prehuman bipeds by tool use and toolmaking had participated in the evolution of our large brains, and of the behavioral complexities and competences that depend on them. The early date of prehuman toolmaking (back several million years) and the large cortical projection area for the human hands make this interactive view of the role of material culture in human evolution plausible, but by itself it can hardly be sufficient since there was very little change in toolmaking technology over the past million years until, well within the past hundred thousand, our own big-brained species had already appeared after a rapid evolutionary spurt of cranial development.

So it now looks as though precursors of our other distinctive human feature, virtuosity in symbolization, may have played the more central role in selecting us to become biologically human—through the advantages that even primitive symbolization gave in social organization to survive and exploit the competitive ecology of the savannahs in Africa or elsewhere, to use tools to greater effect, and eventually to make better ones. Our symbolic functions, too, are built into the brain in ways that must have a long evolutionary history. Certainly, since the dawn of true language among early *Homo sapiens* genetically virtually identical with us— the best conjecture now seems to be as recently as forty or fifty thousand years ago (Harnad, Steklis, & Lancaster, 1976)—it is to symbolization and its consequences that we must turn to understand the emergence of humanness, of selfhood as we take it for granted.

In chapter 2, I applied the familiar ideas of G. H. Mead (1934) in this speculative evolutionary-historical context. Mind, self, and society entail each other and emerge together, he held. Only the quantum leap of attaining true language on what is now the universal human model seems adequate to account for the rapid proliferation of the species beginning about forty millenia ago and the rapid elaboration and diversification since then of what, for a million years and more, had been a remarkably uniform and stable material culture continued by tenuously small populations. I also suggested that our language-given capacity to be social objects to ourselves, to be aware of ourselves and of our mates and kin with forethought and afterthought, brought with it the distinctively human existential predicament as an unwelcome but inherent side effect: we are all too aware that none of us can avoid miseries and that we must die. Much of the symbolic culture that we have elaborated is intelligible as creative ways of denying or transcending or somehow coming to terms with this disastrous fact, of avoiding or reducing a natural anguish that could otherwise disrupt our lives. Elsewhere (Smith, 1978c), I have followed out that line of thought in an attempt at a bird's-eye view of the human adventure. Here, the idea I want to emphasize and develop is the radical degree to which our symbolic formulations are actually constitutive of our selfhood, as well as of the culturally interpreted world that we inhabit.

G. H. Mead's armchair account of the emergence of reflective selfhood with role-taking and language was essentially unhistorical, both in the framework of the individual life (we are beginning to learn a good deal more about the origins of selfhood in infancy) and in the history of our species. Selfhood as we know it cannot have burst forth in full bloom all at once. We can be sure of that if only because, as the anthropologist Geertz (1973, 1975) shows us, selfhood as *we* know it is substantially unlike selfhood as it is known in Bali, in Java, and in Morocco. Selfhood as *we* know it is clearly only one of very many cultural and historical versions, actualizations of human potentiality.

I have found a toehold toward an understanding beyond Mead's schematic generalities in the brilliant but extravagant speculations of Julian Jaynes in *The Origins of Consciousness in the Breakdown of the Bicameral Mind* (1976), a mind-boggling title. I am not persuaded to accept his grand hypothesis that our predecessors of Homeric times and earlier, even the partially literate Sumerians and Egyptians, were walking automata who hallucinated the voices of the gods. But he makes a strong case, along the way, that the self-consciousness of the Homeric heroes and of the bards who sang about them was different from ours. On this matter, Jaynes's conclusions independently converge with those of the German classicist Bruno Snell (1953) two decades earlier. The English classicist Onians (1973) had offered generally similar analyses.

On close examination, what at first glance seems to be the psychological language of the Iliad does not translate accurately into such terms of our common language as *spirit* or *soul, mind, thought, consciousness, emotion, will,* or their reasonable equivalents in the Greek of classical times. In fact, though some of the words (like *psyche*) that later became psychological occur in Homeric context, Jaynes and Snell agree that for the bards of the Iliad, these words were not psychological at all. When they occur in Homer, they stand rather for concrete bodily organs or functions (like the lungs, the breath, the blood, the stirrings of the gut, the movements of the limbs). For the Homer of the Iliad, there is no subjectivity or introspection. So it follows, as Lionel Trilling (1972) observed, that it would be quite meaningless to speak of Achilles as *sincere*.

Snell traces the emergence of unmistakable subjective reference in the remnants of post-Homeric but preclassical Greek literature. In justifying the title of his book, *The Discovery of the Mind,* he writes,

> The discovery of the intellect cannot be compared with the discovery of, let us say, a new continent. America had existed long before Columbus discovered the New World, but the European way of thinking did not come into being until it was discovered; it exists by grace of man's cognizance of himself. All the same, our use of the word "discovery" can, I think, be defended. The intellect was not "invented," as man would invent a tool to improve the operation of his physical functions, or a method to master a certain type of problem. As a rule, inventions are arbitrarily determined; they are adapted to the purpose from which they take their cue. No objective, no aims were involved in the discovery of the intellect. In a certain sense it actually did exist before it was discovered, only not in the same form, not *qua* intellect. (vi)

Slightly later in his discussion, Snell goes on to say,

It must be obvious to anyone that we are here using a metaphor; but the
metaphor is unavoidable. . . . We cannot speak about the mind or the intellect
at all without falling back on metaphor. (vi)

In Jayne's view, too, developed in his introductory chapter in more
abstract detail than I can do justice to here, our consciousness, our
subjective world of inner "space" and serialized biographical "time," is
fundamentally metaphoric, a realm of "as-if." It is a symbolic construction
historically developed and culturally transmitted.

I fear I have drawn us into a realm of extreme ambiguity, in which
empirical difficulties are complicated by all sorts of philosophic traps, and
I certainly do not regard myself as the all-qualified guide to lead us firmly
forth on the one true path. But I see alternative directions of interpretation
at this point, all the same, and I have a clear preference between them.
The choice depends upon the valuation one puts on metaphor, on "as-if."
To use a metaphor to clarify metaphor, is it half empty or half full? Is
consciousness of self *merely* metaphoric, or is it creatively, comically,
tragically, and sometimes even gloriously metaphoric?

The tradition of positivism would say "merely." Sarbin (1977) takes
radical issue with the positivist tradition in ways that I find thoroughly
congenial, but has on other occasions espoused the "merely" view of
metaphor in his analysis of a variety of psychological problems. According
to Sarbin, hypnosis, for example, is not a "real" state of consciousness as
implied by the term *trance;* it is "merely" role taking that is highly
accomplished and imaginative, deep investment in "as-if" (Sarbin & Coe,
1972). Schizophrenia is a myth (a metaphor mistakenly taken as reality);
so is anxiety. Calling psychological concepts metaphors and myths in this
"merely" vein becomes a kind of debunking. It is implied that we are
getting beneath phony appearances to tougher realities. Yet, I wonder,
doesn't this appraisal come down to whether one evaluates metaphor and
myth as half full or half empty? It is a distinction that may be more a
matter of affective connotation than of conceptual difference, but it has
important consequences all the same.

To return to the problem of the origins of selfhood, and the light thrown
on them by Snell and Jaynes in complicating and enriching the Meadian
account. Of course, I am urging the path, one congenial to artists and
humanists, that regards myth and metaphor as creating peculiarly human
realities, constitutive of human selfhood and of the humanized, interpreted
worlds in which all human beings in fact have lived. Through their
symbolic capacities and resources, people early and late have always (that
is, ever since they can be described as people) created the *macrocosm* of
the world they inhabit and the *microcosm* that characterizes each of its

inhabitants. Not surprisingly, there have always been strong symbolic correspondences between their formulations of microcosm and macrocosm. What we learn from Snell and Jaynes, if we take their inherently uncertain findings on this point seriously, is that our own prized version of microcosm, reflexive selfhood with its metaphorical inner space that we think of as "inside our heads" (though Aristotle didn't), may be a much more recent attainment than the crucial, nearly miraculous achievement of true language on which it is built.

The role taking that Mead said was required for language—ourselves reacting to the signs we produce for our partners in conversation *as if* from the perspective of their receivers—is necessary but not sufficient for generating human subjectivity as we think we know it. The microcosms of the Homeric heroes surely contained "I" and "Me," just as Mead would have it, but reflective inner conversation between the heroic "I" and "Me," if it occurred, would have been severely limited before the "invention" of the metaphorical language of subjectivity that permitted the "discovery" of mind. Alfred Schutz's (1967) brilliant phenomenological analysis of intersubjectivity (which he found congruent with Mead's differently based ideas) applies to Schutz and Mead and to thee and me, but it would not make sense applied to Achilles and Agamemnon. It lacks the universality to which it makes claim (with no empirical basis for doing so). Selfhood is not just a matter of role taking, of adopting the perspective of a "generalized other"; its structure depends upon specific metaphoric content. This content has its historical origins and partakes of symbolic culture. It takes different shapes in different cultures—and is changing even today, in part under the impact of scientific psychology.

What leads positivists to debunk metaphors and deny the minds and selfhood that people have attained is their commitment to the very special veiw of the macrocosm that is the product of the physical sciences. There is a perspective on the scientific worldview, one that I understand Claude Lévi-Strauss espoused at least on occasion, that regards it as only one more mythic macrocosm on all fours with the myriad others. For the unsophisticated person in the street, that is probably pretty much the case: atoms and black holes may be even less real from the commonsense perspective than the angels and hells of former times. Certainly for scientists themselves in their own fields of competence, however, the particular scientific version of the macrocosm that they accept (limited, as they know, by the state of development of the sciences) has a very special status. It is the product of the remarkable cultural invention of scientific inquiry as a collective and public enterprise, with rules of evidence and customs of conceptualization that foster abstract, generalizable, and corrigible formulations. They know, and so do the rest of us, that the scientific macrocosm has paid off by powerful pragmatic tests. Scientific constructs and theories are not brute reality in itself, and as cognitive schemes for selection from the plenum, they have their metaphoric aspect. They are framed and modified under a very different discipline, however, from the formative metaphors of everyday life.

Like everyone else since time immemorial, scientists are uncomfortable unless their macrocosms and microcosms are symbolically consistent. The problem, as it affects the challenge to personality-and-social psychology, arises when scientists set out to construct a new microcosm on the model of the specially privileged macrocosm of the physical sciences. In important respects, this agenda has obviously been productive. We have discovered much that is factual and intellectually, even humanly, important about muscles and nerves and the biochemistry of the brain and body as it relates to behavior, and we draw on computer theory and information science for metaphors of mind that fit its phenomena and mysteries a good deal less restrictively than the mechanistic metaphors that previously attracted us.

All the same, the common human microcosms of metaphoric intentionality and subjectivity elude the attempt at reconstruction on scientific macrocosmic lines. It has been a high drama. The first stage of it was the "warfare between science and theology" (White, 1896), the scientists' successful attempt to establish firmly their own view of macrocosm to replace the religious one that was in tune with ordinary people's prevailing versions of the microcosm. By now the arena of battle has shifted to formulations of the microcosm, our own territory as psychologists and, indeed, as people. A good instantiation of the terms of the debate can be encountered in Skinner's (1971) *Beyond Freedom and Dignity* and Chein's (1972) *The Science of Behavior and the Image of Man*.

From my side of it, the same as Chein's, it is a critical consideration that our personal myths and metaphors of the microcosm, of selfhood, have a standing, a *reality* if you agree with Lewin that what is real is what has effects, that has no parallel on the macrocosmic side. True, our mythic or scientific conceptions of the macrocosm also have subjective reality for us as human actors, but Heisenberg notwithstanding, these conceptions do not change the reality they conceive, except as they guide human actions that alter it. In utter contrast, our metaphors and myths about the microcosm of personhood enter intrinsically into constituting who we are as persons as well as providing the ground for our valuing (the physical macrocosm knows no values) and for our actions toward ourselves and others. As my quotation from Snell caught the point, our metaphors make us who we are, insofar as we care about ourselves.

The tension toward "cognitive consistency" that pushes the scientist to invent a congruent but dehumanized microcosm has its counterpart with respect to the microcosmic worlds of ordinary people. The impressive technological success of the scientific worldview has left very many of us bereft of the symbolic support of a congenial, metaphoric world, a macrocosm imagined along meaningful, value-rich human lines and actually believed in. That is a crucial part of what the cultural and personal crises of modernity have been about. Strains toward consistency with the scientific-technological worldview that has entered common sense even begin to undermine our views of our own microcosmic selfhood that we formerly took for granted, a trend augmented by the rapid cultural change catalyzed by technological "progress" (which leaves all of us unsure of our footing), and by the depersonalized relationships increasingly characteristic of urban mass society. The problems come close to home as it becomes apparent that psychologists and other would-be scientific theorists of human nature are adding to the problems of living a truly human life as some of their dehumanized, macrocosmically based versions of the microcosm get disseminated in the general culture. It was Hannah Arendt (1958) who observed that the danger is not that the positivist view of human nature *is* true but that it might *become* true, if people were to come to believe in it. Our vital metaphors may be an endangered species.[1]

Naturwissenschaften *and/or* Geisteswissenschaften

Selfhood, then, is a metaphoric realm. If personality and social psychologists are to study *people* in their relationships, not just as human organisms, they must somehow find ways of dealing with this realm on its own terms, not just in imposed terms that essentially deny it. So to assert may seem to be regressing to the old view of Dilthey at the turn of the century that distinguished between the explanatory natural sciences (*Naturwissenschaften*) and the interpretative cultural or mental sciences (*Geisteswissenschaften*), a conception that has since occupied many pages in the literature of social thought. Or an even deeper regression may be suspected: to a distinction shared by Wundt, the founding father of scientific psychology, and Durkheim, the founding father of modern sociology, the distinction between the individual realm of "physiological psychology" and the separate collective realm of *Völkerpsychologie* (or, for Durkheim, sociology), where Wundt placed the study of the "higher mental processes," and has traditionally been criticized for doing so. (From my present perspective, I think he had a point.) Of course, Wundt himself tried to contribute on both sides of this dichotomy.

I believe that the distinction is indeed pertinent, but we need not descend into a regression. Psychology, following Wundt's precedent, has been working on both sides of the fence ever since, and this is both a problem for our field and one of its strengths. By now, many of us do not want to accept the dichotomous choice of either-or: a dehumanized science of people or a disembodied and maybe ineffectual humanism. As I have suggested elsewhere (Smith, 1978a; chapter 2), I think we are already partly engaged in a dialectic process that may actually be a better match than dichotomies to the puzzling realities that we are trying to deal with. I shall not elaborate on that suggestion, since it seems to me that there is still much mystification in the conceptions of a dialectical psychology. Two of the connotations of *dialectics* do seem to me to give us appropriate directives, however. For one, if the competing and seemingly complementary perspectives can really engage with each other in their continuing conflict, more comprehensive and valuable insights may result. A second connotation with important general implications for social and developmental psychology is advocacy of the sort of radical interactionism-in-process that has been only weakly represented in psychology since the days of John Dewey (see Riegel, 1976).

The prescription for a dialectical psychology does seem much easier to pronounce than to carry out. A more conventional strategy, with ample precedent in the psychology of personality, would seek to apply the conceptual and evidential rigor of science to the symbolic phenomena of selfhood closely described in their own terms. This, as I understand it, is essentially the advice that Geertz (1975) gives to his anthropological colleagues when he suggests an ideal interplay between "emic" and "etic" modes of analysis.

Some Linkages to a Metaphoric Conception of Selfhood

My emphasis on selfhood as a symbolic, metaphoric emergent in evolution and history makes ready contact with some notable sources of insight that have as yet been little drawn upon by the academic psychology of personality: proposals from the first great generation of rebel disciples in the psychoanalytic tradition. One such source is Jung's evocative panorama of dynamic archetypes of the collective unconscious (Jung, 1966). The archetypes are constitutive, metaphoric symbols of selfhood that could be fitted quite congruently into the account I began with G. H. Mead but elaborated with the help of Jaynes and Snell—to the extent that they are substantiated by research and scholarship more disciplined than Jung's.

We need not be bothered by the ambiguous and probably unsatisfactory metaphor of the "collective unconscious." Archetypal formations like animus and anima and, indeed the Jungian Self, may perhaps be based on templates that are passed on genetically: as I see it, this is no longer ruled out as a scientifically acceptable possibility in light of what we now know about the time frame of human evolution and the inherited basis, for example, of universal language learning in humans. Or, rather, they may be quasi universals of human culture, evoked as recurrences of symbolic response to universals of the human condition. The rich but untidy Jungian corpus has yet to be mined for testable insights about the role such metaphoric structures play in the transformations and vicissitudes of selfhood. Not surprisingly, students of literature, for whom such "humanistic" speculations have become a stock in trade, have paid closer attention to Jung than have psychologists.

Adler, too, has been relatively neglected, in spite of sedulous efforts by the Ansbachers (1956) over the years. Since, as they point out, he was deeply influenced by Vaihinger's (1925) *Philosophy of As-If,* a metaphoric perspective pervades Adler's psychological thought, especially in his conception of fictional goals. A renewed interest in human subjectivity should turn more of us back to Adler.

I have already echoed major themes in Rank (especially, 1932), in my imagery of microcosm and macrocosm and my taking note of symbolic culture as an accommodation to the human existential plight. For those like me who find Rank's own writings in translation hard to penetrate, Becker's (1973) enthusiastically appreciative overview may prove helpful.

Note that all three of these early psychoanalytic rebels broke with Freud on essentially humanistic grounds: the inadequacy of psychoanalysis to meaning and purpose. As Holt (1972) has pointed out most clearly, Freud had both a humanistic and a mechanistic side, but he insisted heavily on the latter: the abstract constructions of libido theory. It was Freud's insistence on libido theory (as he expounded it in metapsychological terms that were rooted more in the First Law of Thermodynamics than in clinical observations) and, of course, the *group* dynamics generated by a leader who required his followers to be "true believers," that drove Jung, Adler, and Rank out of the fold.

From early in the century, psychologists have always been interested in Freud, though they have always found him hard to digest. The early rebels got initial attention from psychologists, too, but their attention was soon co-opted by the second generation of "neo-Freudian" rebels in the thirties, whose grounds for revolt depended rather on ripening concerns, shared by many psychologists and anthropologists of the time, about sociocultural factors in the formation of personality and in the origins of personality disorders. Karen Horney (1937), of the neo-Freudian generation, reissued Adler's ideas without attribution, probably for reasons that were compelling in the politics of the psychoanalytic movement. Carl

Rogers (1942) drew substantially on Rank, at one remove by way of the Pennsylvania School of Social Work. Murray (1938) merged themes from Freud and McDougall with those of Jung, who carried on with his own voice, surviving the opprobrium of involvement in Nazi Germany, but few psychologists besides Murray listened to him. In general, the work of the first generation of psychoanalytic rebels, who were carrying forward diverse humanistic agendas, has received rather little close attention from psychologists of personality. Now a new generation of Freudians, trained by the earlier generation of Freudian "ego psychologists" who had tried in principle to accommodate aspects of academic psychology ("ego psychology" was the Freudian counterreformation contemporary with the neo-Freudian revolt), are engaged in a project to resurrect and build upon the humanistic side of Freud's own work. The humanistic rebels of the older generation also surely deserve our renewed interest.

A symbolic psychology of selfhood also makes contact with one of the most satisfactory general interpretations of psychotherapy and personality change, one that also takes into account the social psychological literature on attitudes and attitude change: Frank's (1973) *Persuasion and Healing,* which over more than a decade has gone through two editions. Frank draws on Cantril (1950) for his central concept, the person's "assumptive world": the "highly structured, complex, interacting set of values, expectations, and images of oneself and others, which guide and in turn are guided by a person's perceptions and behavior and which are closely related to his emotional states and his feelings of well-being" (p. 27). As befits the problem context with which Frank is concerned, his conception is focused individually rather than collectively, unlike my discussion that followed from Jaynes and Snell. I note it here not only because of its continuity with Adler's "as-if" formulations but also because of Frank's explicit reference to the psychology of attitudes, in a broad view that brings experimental research together with an examination of coercive persuasion and "brainwashing" (Lifton, 1961). Apart from Rokeach's (1973) experimental work on values, the psychology of attitude change has paid in superficiality for slighting the changes, such as those induced during psychotherapy, which depend upon reconstitution of a person's metaphors of selfhood. (See also Sarbin & Adler, 1970–1971.)

Frank's reasonable and informed discussion offered bridges between the laboratory-based formulations of social psychology and the humanly more consequential concerns of the clinician, bridges that I am surprised have not drawn more traffic from social psychologists. Our compartments of thought are sufficiently rigid that it seldom dawns upon us that much clinical psychology *is* social psychology in principle, if not in the way differently specialized psychologists have come to talk about their conceptual problems. The Skinnerian experimental analysts of behavior and the social learning theorists have done better than social psychologists in crossing these arbitrary boundaries, as the booming behavior modification movement attests.

Finally, the general approach that I am urging links directly with attribution theory in recent social psychology, and with its sociological counterpart, labeling theory. As Jones and Kelley extracted it from the richer and still to be fully exploited phenomenological formulations of Fritz Heider (1958), attribution theory took shape as a partly formalized set of guiding ideas—rather different ones stemming from Jones and from Kelley—that provided a useful perspective on a surprising variety of social psychological problems (see Jones et al., 1972). One is tempted to dismiss the surge of attribution research in the journals as only another of the fads and fashions that sweep through social psychology whenever a new idea or a new technique appears, a sign of the field's lamentable lack of a reasonably stable and productive guiding paradigm. I think this would be a mistake. The appeal of attribution theory, and its fertility, it seems to me, follow from the fact that the attributionists have been grappling with fundamental symbolic processes by which people assign and therefore create meaning—in the crucial human realm of self and the interpersonal world.

From the angle that I am following here, the power and enduring promise of the attributional approach is especially evident in the way that it has assimilated Rotter's (1966) concepts of internal and external locus of control, which he had developed in the very different context of his social learning theory. In result, we have the beginnings of a psychology of self-concep*tion*, embedded in causal-functional-explanatory propositions about conditions and consequences, that has far more psychological and human interest than the sterile old tradition centering on the self-concept (Wylie, 1961, 1974). The attributional analysis of "locus of control," and De Charm's (1968) slightly different phrasing in terms of people's self-confirming views of themselves as "Origins" and "Pawns," deal frontally with the critical juncture between symbolic-meaningful-interpretative and causal-functional-explanatory modes of conceptualizing human experience and behavior. They deal, as I have put it (Smith, 1978a), with selfhood as the prime arena in which the "self-fulfilling prophecy" becomes a causal mechanism (see Jones, 1977). They bring together ways of conceiving the task of psychology that, as we have seen, well-respected metatheoretical traditions have insisted *cannot* be joined. The juncture has nevertheless been made, with results that seem to me to give it ample pragmatic justification. An especially promising theoretical-empirical development is Seligman's extension, in attributional terms, of his theory of learned helplessness (Seligman, 1975; Abramson, Seligman, & Teasdale, 1978). We had best readjust our metatheoretical assumptions accordingly.

Attribution theory is concerned with the meanings, the causal interpretations, that the human subject or actor ascribes to the actions of self and others, and their outcomes. Sociologists of the symbolic interactionist tradition have advanced complementary notions about how society at large or particular "alters" provide or impose meaning for the actor by the labels they apply to the actor and his or her behavior, so called labeling theory (Murphy, 1976). Weinstein's (Weinstein & Deutschberger, 1963) "altercasting" is a cognate conception. The ideas involved seem to me to be the other side of the same coin that attribution theory has been concerned with. The value of these sociological ideas is not diminished by their frequent abuse by both sociologists and psychologists in social criticism, according to which the essence of such problematic phenomena of "deviance" as delinquency and mental illness is exhausted by the condemnatory labels that get put upon the people who exemplify them. Here again, as in the debunking of psychological concepts by labeling them metaphor and myth, I think we need to show more discernment in how we employ some important and useful ideas.

The view of human selfhood as a symbolic production, thus, makes potentially useful contact with a variety of lines of psychological thought that deserve continued exploration. To epitomize the stance from which I will be looking at the topics of attitudes, values, and selfhood in the second part of this essay, I remain committed to the collective strategies of science insofar as they fit the phenomena of human personality and social behavior. For this area, I forgo the goal—a mirage, I think—of a structure of universal ahistorical laws on the Newtonian model, and proclaim that a frankly historical and cultural science is greatly preferable to one that aspires to universality but is historically limited and culture-bound by default.

Attitudes, Values, and Selfhood: A Selective Retrospection

My attempt to make sense of where we have been and to try to discern promising and less productive lines of development, opportunities missed or bungled in the past or opening in the present, will not hinge on exact definitions.

Dispositional Concepts in Personality and Social Psychology

I start with the domain of beliefs, attitudes, and values as social psychologists have actually dealt with these and related topics, a traditionally identified area of interest within a subdiscipline, with the usual degree of historical, nonfunctional autonomy fostered by courses and textbooks and academic inertia. When I ask myself, What is the functional job of this traditional area? my answer is that it has the job of developing and elaborating *dispositional* concepts and principles to account for social behavior, in this respect joining the psychology of personality. When I ask myself further, What is our best account of productive grand strategy for so employing dispositional concepts and principles? where else should I turn but to Kurt Lewin's (1951) old formula, B = f (P,E): Behavior is a joint function of the Person and the psychological Environment. Putting aside Lewin's important distinction between the geographical and the psychological environments as not immediately relevant, I want to stress that this familiar formula is in no sense a "law" or an empirical conclusion from research. Rather, it is a declaration of intellectual strategy for the guidance of research and of theory building, and even of social analysis for public enlightenment. It says that if we are going to work with dispositional concepts, we should not expect them to do the whole job; we need to relate them to concepts specifying the situation of action. Of course, we have given lip service to the strategy much more than we have actually followed it in practice.

Note that it is by no means the only strategy open to us in accounting for social behavior. For instance, radical behaviorism, with its commitment to avoid dispositional concepts entirely, has never accepted it. Skinnerians want to achieve an input-output analysis of behavior under environmental contingency that bypasses inferred dispositions. This is a perfectly reasonable option. It entails two problems, however, from my point of-view. One is the empirical, pragmatic question as to whether, in the realm of the complex social behavior of everyday life and politics, we can attain a degree of explanatory power that is at all satisfactory without reference to dispositions of personality, beliefs and attitudes, and the like. I doubt it. The other is metatheoretical but also has its pragmatic aspects: the radical behaviorist account does violence to the conceptions of human personhood that I spent the first part of this essay developing, whereas the dispositional account does not.

A variety of compromise strategies have been tried that also avoid, in one way or another, a direct treatment of person-environment interaction. In the days of Hullian neobehaviorism, for example, Doob (1947) identified attitude with habit strength. The attitudinal disposition got translated into a little behavior, an "implicit" behavior, a readiness to behave. Building the behavior to be predicted into the disposition from which it was to be predicted might lack theoretical elegance or even acceptability from some points of view (those were the days when it was customary to condemn R-

R psychology in contrast with the approved S-R model), but it had some pragmatic justification when psychologists were not geared to deal with PE interactions effectively.

Nonbehaviorist theories in the functional tradition seem to me to have made a similar accommodation to duck the implications of the Lewinian strategy. Katz and Stotland (1959), for example, wrote of the "behavioral component" of attitudes as complementing the cognitive and affective components. The behavior to be predicted gets built into the formulation of the structure of the attitude itself. Fishbein and Ajzen (1975) deal more satisfactorily with the problem, it seems to me, by introducing behavioral intention as a separate concept that intervenes between attitudes and their expression in behavior, but they give up much of the ambition of the dispositional strategy.

If we turn from the academic theorists to the one arena in which the study of attitudes was being conducted in "field" settings for practical purposes—survey research in the opinion polling tradition—it is quite clear that asking people how they were going to vote or what they were going to buy provided a much better predictor of behavior than could be obtained from any conceptually guided attempt to deal jointly with attitudinal predispositions and situational constraints and pressures (see Smith, 1954). But commercial polling had a practical job to do without the scientific obligation to understand or explain. It was quite all right to let people be their own predictors, and skimp this challenge to social science. Angus Campbell and his collaborators at the Michigan Survey Research Center (Campbell, Converse, Miller, & Stokes, 1960), who were committed to such an obligation from a primarily psychological perspective, came forward with their "funnel" causal model to account for the voting act—a kind of conceptual path analysis conceived before the statistical techniques to match this way of thinking were available—in which attitudinal dispositions toward party, candidate, and issues, each with its own determinants, converge in determining voting intention and thus the act of voting. But their research problem, too, did not require them to face up to the PE interaction.

From where we are now, it seems to me that psychologists who continue to be interested in beliefs, attitudes, and values are almost bound to be committed to the dispositional strategy, whether they are thoughtful about it or not. Within this strategy, beliefs, attitudes, values, self-attributions—the whole family of related concepts—seem to me to fit under the more inclusive rubric of personality. That was the assumption of my early work in the field (Smith, Bruner, & White, 1956), which participated in the "functionalist" episode in the study of attitudes to which I will recur later. It was certainly the assumption of Allport (1935) in his *Handbook* chapter that summarized the premodern period of attitude research, and in his book on personality (Allport, 1937), which launched this as a legitimate subfield of academic study. In Allport's treatment, "social" attitudes are coordinate with "personality" traits. Attitudes are dispositions organized around a psychological object: they are attitudes *toward x*; in phenomenological language, they are structural stabilizations of "intentionality." The coherence of stylistic or motivational personality *traits* does not depend upon an object as the focus of organization. The close linkage between the two concepts is illustrated in one of the early topics of attitude research. Measures of such social attitudes as those toward the church, toward war, toward conventional morality tended to intercorrelate positively. Following ideas that were part of the common culture, psychologists therefore extracted a dimension of radicalism versus conservatism from this clustering—at first informally, then by the laborious new technique of factor analysis. But radicalism-conservatism has no specific object; in other contexts we would regard it as a personality trait. As Allport wrote, *"The more generalized the attitude becomes the more it resembles a trait"* (1935, p. 838; his italics). The two concepts are of the same ilk.

I have gone into this bit of history not for its own sake or because I subscribe to Allport's old version of trait psychology but to call attention to the basis for a strict parallelism between central methodological issues that have bedogged attitude research and personality research respectively during the past two decades: the attitudes-and-behavior issue, on the one hand, and the trait-versus-situation issue on the other. Both inhere in the strategy of deploying dispositional concepts, and both find their resolution, it seems to me, in returning with new sophistication to Lewin's formula.

In retrospect, the position of Allport and his contemporaries was vulnerable in both domains. We have seen that social psychologists tended to expect attitudes to predict behavior directly, without taking situations of action into account. The same charge can be fairly made of Allport's conception of personality, a relatively encapsulated or "integumented" (Chein, 1972) one. In spite of Allport's awareness of the essential contribution of other social sciences to understanding a concrete social problem like the nature of prejudice (Allport, 1954), even in his postwar years of involvement in the new Harvard Department of Social Relations he did not find it comfortable to step outside a rather self-enclosed conception of the personality system. Psychoanalytically oriented psychologists of personality did no better, making them, too, vulnerable to the incursions of the behavioral approach with its situational emphasis.

The years since, until just yesterday, have been unfriendly to the dispositional strategy in personality and social psychology generally. In this period, which appears to some of us as a dark age for personality research (Carlson, 1971, 1975), the emphasis became overwhelmingly situational, and personality holistically conceived as organized dispositions and processes almost vanished from view. Quite apart from the intrinsic vulnerability of a one-sided dispositional approach, it is easy to reconstruct why. These were boom years for laboratory experimental research in personality and social psychology. The brave new style of research fitted the prevalent ethos of self-confident positivism, and it thrived in the expanding university laboratories where funds were readily available. The published results needed for career advancement could be more quickly attained in small laboratory studies than from intensive "explorations in personality" in the Murray (1938) tradition or intensive forays into the personality roots of consequential attitudes and ideology, like the Berkeley studies of prejudice and authoritarianism (Adorno, Frenkel-Brunswik, Levinson, & Sanford, 1950). Observe that in laboratory experimentation, it is situational variables that can be directly manipulated; personality traits can only be measured and selected for, without experimental control.

In spite of the fact that possible trait-situation "interaction effects" could be highlighted according to the logic of analysis of variance that had come to dominate experimental design, the prevalent experimental style encouraged theoretical attention to situational effects singly or in combination, and to "states" rather than "traits" on the dispositional side. If your research is focused on the effects of situational variations that you are laboring to produce, that is what you will naturally come to believe is most important.

The pendulum had swung so far in the situational direction by the seventies that a corrective reaction was obviously called for, and it has happened. There seems no doubt that an interactive view is finally beginning to prevail in personality theory (Magnusson & Endler, 1977). My side comment—my *snide* comment—is: About time! The resurrection of the view that personality and situation interact (as in Lewin's formula) finally legitimizes a dispositional psychology of personality as once again deserving serious attention in research and theory. The same counterswing of the pendulum, I hope, should affect our treatment of attitudinal dispositions. Once some pseudoproblems identified by Smith (1954), Campbell (1963), and Fishbein (1967) years ago are swept aside, the hoary problem of attitudes versus behavior ought to yield to the interactive treatment.

The Psychology of Attitudes as a Venture in Social Psychological Understanding

My first theme, just concluded, bore upon whether psychology has room for attributing causal significance to the person (by no means inherently an "attributional error," as some writers in attribution theory seem to assume, joining forces with the extreme situationism in personality theory that is becoming outmoded). My second is concerned with the extent to which the psychology of attitudes has been prepared to deal with substantive issues of human meaning, and has actually contributed to a psychological understanding of our participation in current history. If social psychology has dubious claim to success as a "Newtonian" science, how good has it been at the tasks of a historical discipline?

With a few notable exceptions, I will argue, social psychologists have not been at all good at it, because we have not been interested in the assignment. Even Allport (1935) sought to anchor attitudes in the hard-science side of the discipline. His *Handbook* chapter developed what I can regard only as a legitimizing pseudohistory of the concept, linking it to the ideas of the Würzburg school of experimental psychology such as set and determining tendency but especially *Bewusssteinslagen,* which got translated as "conscious attitudes." The word *attitudes* was there, but the issues of the imageless thought controversy had nothing to do with how the concept was to be used by social psychologists.

With the lead of L. L. Thurstone, who initiated formal measurement of attitudes with his article "Attitudes Can Be Measured" (Thurstone, 1928), attitudes as they came to be measured were narrowly conceived as having pro-or-con *direction,* and maybe also *intensity,* with respect to a social object, but no analyzed cognitive content. (The source of Thurstone's use of the term traces through the sociologist W. I. Thomas, who used it in the methodological introduction to *The Polish Peasant* [Thomas & Znaniecki, 1918] to refer to *any* object-directed personal disposition, with the linked term *value* referring to any object toward which an attitude is directed, a very different usage from Allport's, Rokeach's, and mine.)

If we are seeking a more cogent historical source for a conception of attitude appropriate to a humanized social psychology, one that is congruent with a dispositional view of personality, we should turn back to the brilliant, much-maligned, and indeed often wrongheaded psychologist of vitalism and purposivism William McDougall (1908), whose ideas (if stripped of naively hereditarian, racist, and Lamarckian fallacies, some but not all of which were typical of his time) now seem like a remarkably good attempt to develop a psychological framework congruent with the concerns of my metatheoretical introduction. To the extent that McDougall's ideas have survived, it is mainly in their amalgamation with Freudian and Jungian concepts by Murray (1938).

McDougall did not talk about attitudes; his equivalent term was *sentiments,* which he adopted from the Scottish armchair characterologist Alexander Shand (1914) who conceived of sentiments—integrations

around a psychological object of readiness to experience the prime emotions—as the building blocks of character: in present language, personality. For Shand, love and hate were prime examples. Love is not a simple
emotion but a readiness to experience joy, fear, anger, and so on, depending on the context relating the subject, the loved object, and the environing
situation—already a dispositional concept with interactional implications.
For McDougall, too, sentiments were the main structural components of
personality: in his case, integrations of the "instincts" around objects.
Mostly, psychologists today remember McDougall only as an instinct
theorist, and condemn him for that. Actually, the famous list of instincts
provided only the abstract foundation for his purposive psychology, and
emphasized not preprogrammed actions but integrations of cognitive,
affective, and conative tendencies (matching Katz and Stotland's [1959]
three aspects of attitudes). Minus the imaginary biology, McDougall's
"instincts" translate to Murray's (1938) "needs"—in a longer, more
comprehensive list, to be sure. The whole emphasis of McDougall's
account of people as social beings, however, was not on instincts but on
sentiments, which as integrations of instincts also had cognitive, affective,
and conative aspects.

An interesting feature of his scheme, which puzzled me when I first
encountered it before I had had any contact with symbolic interactionism,
was his conception of the *self-regarding sentiment* as the keystone of
personality organization, the explicit agency of volition. Now I see it as
one more example of McDougall's prescience. Of course, it echoes William James's (1890) discussion of the "I" and the "Me," and parallels
G. H. Mead's (1934) doctrine that "I-Me dialogue" is the locus of creative
self-direction: our symbolic reflexiveness is the source of such contingent
human freedom as we enjoy. McDougall's treatment of the will by means
of the role of the sentiment of self-regard in the hierarchy of personality
resembles Chein's (1972), in that he sees our ethical evaluation and
sanctioning of volitional moral behavior as depending on philosophical
determinism. His account of the social development of the self-regarding
sentiment, and of the steps in the development of moral volition that
accompany it, may be couched in language harking back to James Mark
Baldwin (1897) rather than to Piaget (1932), but the ideas have a distinctively modern ring to readers familiar with Piaget and Kohlberg (1969).
(Piaget was himself explicitly indebted to Baldwin, of course.)

McDougall's theory of sentiments was indeed rich and suitable in
principle to the description and analysis of actual human lives, though his
interests did not lead him in that concrete empirical direction. Murray and
Morgan (1945) picked up McDougall's concept for their descriptive, somewhat abortive monograph from the Harvard Psychological Clinic. Both

McDougall's ideas and Murray and Morgan's example were sources for
the approach taken in *Opinions and Personality* (Smith, Bruner, & White,
1956), though we decided to use the more prevalent terminology of
opinions and attitudes.

During the postwar decades, the substantive psychology of attitudes fell
on evil days, like those of personality theory—at least in regard to its
adequacy for contributing to an account of historical human actors. (I will
return to two major exceptions shortly.) One might think otherwise, given
the initial burst of interest in attitude change exemplified and stimulated
by Hovland, Janis, and Kelley (1953). The focus of their progammatic
research is best described, however, by the title of their book: *Communication and Persuasion*. A good deal was learned that is properly sensitiz-
ing, if not definitive, about the variables involved in communication effects
on beliefs and attitudes. But the dependent variables in their research were
given little attention. The beliefs, expectations, and attitudes selected for
study were chosen because pilot work had showed that measurable
changes in them *could* be produced by very brief communications or minor
manipulations in the laboratory. So the topics were mostly inconsequential
to the experimental subjects. The measures employed were also *ad hoc*.
The emphasis, like that of postwar experimental social psychology generally, was on discovering lawful relationships of process, not on understanding the psychology of particular classes of attitudes, or the attitudes of
particular categories of people.

With the early death of Carl Hovland, interest in persuasive communication, which had been guided by his rough map of the communication
process that accommodated research suggested by quite disparate theories
about the psychological processes involved, generally gave way to interest
centered on the theories themselves—theories, for example, concerning
reinforcement, social comparison and social judgment, and, especially,
cognitive dissonance. If measures of attitude happened to be employed as
dependent variables in the research that followed, that was incidental.
Typically, the measures used remained *ad hoc*. (It is remarkable that
sophisticated experimental design and theoretical analysis were usually
accompanied by the most casual and amateurish psychometrics.) So it has
mostly been with the treatment of attitudes in mainstream experimental
social psychology, up to this day.

Eddies in the Mainstream: A Substantive Focus

The two major exceptions that stand out against this account are, on the
one hand, the Berkeley studies of anti-Semitism and authoritarianism (with
them, also, a whole minor tradition of research on prejudiced attitudes and

behavior), and survey research, particularly that focused on political attitudes and the act of voting, on the other. Each had strong substantive, content-oriented concerns that fit squarely the conception of social psychology as a historical science, and in this respect each deviated from the process-oriented, content-free mainstream. It should be instructive to examine both.

I have thought for some time that the history of research on the authoritarian personality, after its splendid beginning, is one of the more scandalous episodes in our discipline. A recent occasion to rereview *The Authoritarian Personality* (TAP; Adorno et al., 1950), together with Allport's *Nature of Prejudice* (1954) only confirmed my judgment (Smith, 1978b). The *Authoritarian Personality* reported a major program of interrelated studies, purporting to show first that anti-Semitic attitudes are correlated with ethnocentrism as a more general attitudinal structure; then that ethnocentrism in turn is related to an ideology—a psychologically coherent though, it appeared, logically inconsistent structure of beliefs— that the Berkeley authors saw as underlying antidemocratic or protofascist political orientations; and finally that the antidemocratic ideology seemed congruent with a particular defensive structure of personality, which they accounted for in generally psychoanalytic terms. The research drew upon a rich background of speculative theory about the origins of German Nazism, as developed by members of the Frankfurt school, and upon the technical resources of attitude measurement, clinical interviewing, and projective techniques. It employed a number of special samples to check the generality of the findings and to provide independent tests of some of the implications of the theoretical structure that emerged. Presenting a serious model of the relationship between family relations in childhood, personality, political ideology, and more specific social attitudes, *TAP* was a major contribution to social analysis and criticism. It was no small study. Of course, it had major flaws.

What happened afterward bothers me. To be sure, Rokeach (1960), who got his start at Berkeley in the aftermath of this research, reacted to one of the flaws—the one-sided focus on right-wing authoritarianism—in an appropriately constructive and programmatic way, in his important studies of "dogmatism." But his work stands by itself in this respect. For nearly a decade, social psychologists were fascinated by *TAP*'s technical deficiencies, mostly those of the "F-Scale," the pencil-and-paper measure of fascistic tendencies that emerged from the Berkeley studies but was far from their sole or central focus. By the time that this flurry of methodologically directed activity had subsided (which for a while made the alphabetically first but substantively marginal Theodor Adorno among the most frequently cited though least known names in the social psychological literature), interest had moved in other directions, mostly captured by the wave of laboratory experimentalism, without adequate resolution of the serious substantive claims of *TAP*, the claims that made it relevant to the social psychology of contemporary history.

The substantive, analytically descriptive research on "authoritarianism," like the experimental demonstration studies of Asch (1951) and the Sherifs (Sherif & Sherif, 1953), did serve a useful sensitization function. People familiar with it are bound to take a different view of such historical episodes as McCarthyism, antigay and antiflouridation outbursts, and the present reactive yearning for a "macho" U.S. foreign policy that President Carter was unwilling to present. All the same, I see this stream of research as a missed opportunity to stay with the substantive, essentially historical problem until firmer conclusions could have been drawn.[2]

At almost the same time that *TAP* appeared, Allport (1954) published *The Nature of Prejudice,* not *a* theory of prejudice and discrimination but a collation of theories and research bearing on them, judiciously appraised and brought to bear on recommendations about what ought to be done to ameliorate them. This classic of the applied psychology of attitudes and values is currently being revised—more probably, rewritten—by Pettigrew and Kramer. That they need to do so follows from the fact that the historical context has substantially changed over the quarter century (*justice* more than *mutual liking* is now a central value in ethnic relations), and also from the fact that a good deal of relevant research has continued to go on in the years since Selma and *Brown v. Board of Education.* This work has participated competently in "social psychology as history" along the lines I am urging, but it has been only a minor current in the social psychology of the time. Prestige in the discipline lay elsewhere.

The development of survey research is a clearer success story, paradoxically, but survey research has been essentially marginal to the social psychology of beliefs, attitudes, and values as pursued by psychologists. Survey research is historical and analytically descriptive, and the present interest in developing time series in historical depth is making it an even more powerful instrument for these purposes. But it has been done mainly by sociologists, whose discipline has probably been too dependent on this one channel of data. And even though the founder of the Michigan Survey Research Center, which has been the main site of psychological participation in survey research and analysis, Rensis Likert, got his start in academic attitude research (Murphy & Likert, 1938), and subsequent survey analysis at Michigan in the style of Angus Campbell (e.g., Campbell et al., 1960) has developed its own cognitively oriented array of concepts, there has been remarkably little back-and-forth flow of ideas and influence between attitude research and survey research. I cannot believe that this is a healthy state of affairs. (During the period when persuasive communication was a focal topic for the academics, Hovland [1959] wrote a classic paper that tried to bring the two traditions together. Mostly they have gone their separate ways.)

So the exceptions actually highlight the general thrust of my second retrospective theme: the psychology of attitudes has mostly avoided substantive issues of human meaning, and shown little interest in contributing a psychological perspective to the understanding of people as participants in current history. Yet the challenge has been there all along, and, as we have seen, a variety of relevant technical and conceptual tools have become available. If our field is to earn its keep, we need to develop a more diversified portfolio, instead of putting so many of our eggs in the basket of the process-oriented, law-seeking experimental strategy.

An Example of Conceptualized Interpretation

If we take the "sensitization" function of social psychological research seriously, moreover, we might set higher priority on organizing what we think we have learned about beliefs and attitudes into coherent conceptual maps for the guidance of analytical and critical thinking about concrete social-historical phenomena. In his contribution that originally accompanied this chapter, Triandis (1980) presented a rich example, though he conceived of portions of his map more along the lines of Hullian "mathematical" formulations than is to my taste. He wanted his map to become a quasi-Newtonian theory.

Quite a while back I developed a conceptual map of this sort—which bears some resemblance to Triandis's—as an outgrowth of trying to apply the "functional" approach of Smith, Bruner, and White (1956) to the psychology of prejudice. I thought it was more intelligibly coherent than Allport's (1954) end-to-end collation of theories and factors in the successive chapters of his book. For a series of concrete problems—McCarthyism and fertility decisions among them—I found the same general map to be a substantial help in my own thinking, calling attention to relationships to be looked for, possibly relevant factors to be considered. It functioned like a checklist for me, but—more than a checklist—it was organized in a way to suggest paths and levels of explanation. It was useful in my teaching. So I put forth a generalized version of it as a map of how attitudes, personality, and other factors enter into individual political behavior. Since then I have followed its fate with paternal interest and concern.

With the sponsorship of Fred Greenstein (1975), it has had quite a run in the political science literature of personality and politics. Every now and then, I still get requests from odd places to reprint it or to print specially adapted versions—invariably, it seems, from outside the circle of social psychology. Within my own subdiscipline, it seemed to fall with a dull thud—understandably, since it was offered as an aid to social interpretation, not as a quasi-Newtonian theory. My colleagues weren't much interested. I display it here, not just because I can be assured that it will finally get a psychological audience but because I think it illustrates several of the points of conceptual strategy that I have been talking about.[3]

For the moment, disregard the tangle of arrows in the fine structure of the map and look at only the five major panels identified by Roman numerals. Personality Processes and Dispositions (panel III) occupy the center of the stage. The behavioral payoff is in panel V, to the extreme right. It is labeled Political Behavior here, but there is no need for the political restriction. Terminating at panel V, the unbroken arrows (marked A and B) that link it with Personality Processes and Dispositions (panel III) and with Situation as Immediate Antecedent of Action (panel IV) represent Lewin's methodological premise: All social behavior is to be analyzed as a joint resultant of characteristics of the person, on the one hand, and of the psychological situation, on the other. To specify the contribution of either requires taking the other into account.

Causal antecedents can be traced back from each of these two panels that show the immediate determinants of action. To Personality (panel III) a cluster of arrows leads from panel II, Social Environment as Context for the Development of Personality and Acquisition of Attitudes. Both the environment of socialization (panel II) and the immediate situation of action (panel IV) have their own more distal antecedents, represented in panel I. That is, historical, economic, and institutional factors (panel I) have an indirect impact on individual behavior—both by shaping the contexts in which socialization occurs and attitudes are learned (arrow D) and as sources of the features of the immediate situations in which action takes place (arrow E).

The broken arrows from panel V reflect the *consequences* of behavior, which may alter the situation in which it occurs (arrow F), and cumulate across the many actions of many persons to modify the long-run social environments that shape and support the attitudes of each (arrow H), in the still longer run constituting history and shaping institutions (arrow I). Arrow G, leading back from behavior to personal dispositions in panel III, represents the effects that self-committing behavior can have on attitudes, a phenomenon emphasized by Festinger (1957) that has standing in its own right.

I will enter the internal detail of the map only on the right side of panel III, Personality Processes and Dispositions, to illustrate how the map

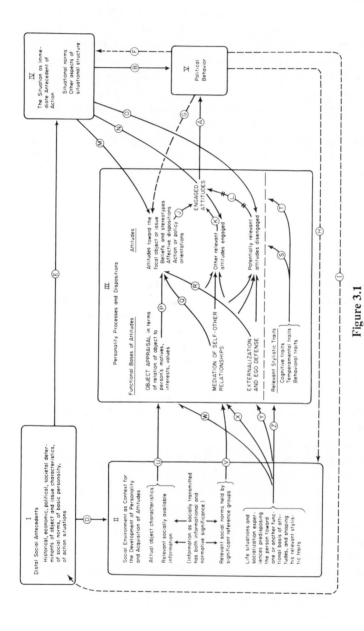

Figure 3.1

Figure 3.1 A functional map: political attitudes and behavior in their personal and social context. From Smith (1968a). Reprinted by permission of the publishers of *Political Research and Political Theory*, Oliver Garceau, ed., Cambridge, Mass.: Harvard University Press, Copyright © 1968 by the President and Fellows of Harvard College. A slightly different version appeared in *Journal of Social Issues* (Smith, 1968b).

seeks to clarify the problem of why behavior does not correspond directly to attitudes. Other features of the map are based on the Smith-Bruner-White version of functional theory, accounting for how attitudes arise and are sustained in terms of their role in the person's ongoing psychological economy, or are probably self-explanatory.

The part of the map to which I am calling attention suggests that we cannot take for granted just which of the person's attitudes will become engaged as a codeterminant of behavior in any given situation. Political scientists are probably less naive about this than many psychologists who have been perplexed by the attitudes-and-behavior issue. How people vote for one or another presidential candidate depends, as we know, not only on their focal attitudes toward that candidate but also on attitudes toward alternative candidates, toward party, and toward issues. As arrows M, N, and O are intended to indicate, the immediate situation of action plays a dual role. On the one hand, it engages with certain of the person's attitudes and leaves in abeyance others that might potentially be engaged; on the other, it serves as a direct codeterminant of behavior, together with the engaged attitudes. An example, again from the political realm: On the floor of Congress, certain of a congressman's attitudes become engaged with the issue under discussion—different ones, very likely, from those that would be engaged in discussion of the same issue with an important constituent. But what he or she says in either situation (and saying is behaving) will depend not only on the attitudes engaged but also on what seems appropriate and likely to be instrumentally effective, given the norms and contingencies of each situation. These complex relationships give us no reason to suppose that people's behavior should correspond in any simple way to their attitudes on a single focal issue or toward a single focal object—the same conclusion reached by Fishbein and Ajzen (1975) though by a different route.

Any map is a simplification, and likely a falsification, too, with trade-offs like those involved in projecting the globe on a flat page. The psychology of attitudes represented in my map is rooted in the functional perspective to which I was committed. The functional point of view is a kind of bastard cousin of the strictly causal-explanatory approach, and it has its pragmatic justification for many psychological as well as biological purposes in the empirical adaptedness that is a salient feature of evolution and development. It can be seen as a way station toward a more adequate causal analysis, as it has been in physiology, or it may be given an ambiguous quasi-teleological interpretation. What is clear, however, is that while my map has an explicit place for the role of values in what we called the "object-appraisal" function of attitudes, it has no way of representing the sort of reflective, symbolic view of selfhood that I was urging in the metatheoretical first part of this essay—for attitudinal orientations such as "Origin" versus "Pawn" that are constitutive of the self as actor and as reflexive object. Perhaps it could be jockeyed with to accommodate this more humanistic orientation; perhaps not.

Values in the Perspective of Selfhood

So far, my retrospective has dealt mainly with the psychology of attitudes. I will deal much more briefly with the topic of values, which are more fully treated in chapter 1. Rokeach (1980) has given searching attention to the concept in his paper that was originally presented together with this essay.

I find Rokeach's approach to values generally congenial. His stress on rather punctiform instrumental and terminal values—*single* beliefs—has surely paid off, though it seems to me to be tied to his own particular measuring instrument, a simple and surprisingly powerful one. (Before I had seen his results, I would not have expected findings so impressive and internally coherent from such a barebones schematic measure.) All the same, Rockeach's concepts as embodied in his instrument still seem to me only one among various possible approaches. Think, for example, of Morris's (1956) much more complex "paths of life," which I am not advocating as preferable. At this stage in our enterprise I am not enamored of definitions, but I continue to like Kluckhohn's (1951), which seems to me more general and flexible than Rokeach's. Rokeach's definition is congruent with it in the most essential respects. According to Kluckhohn, "A value is a conception, explicit or implicit, distinctive of an individual or characteristic of a group, of the *desirable* which influences the selection from available modes, means, and ends of action" (p. 395).

I agree with Rokeach that the distinction between the desirable and the merely desired, the preferable and the preferred, is difficult to maintain in practice and in empirical research since the pull toward consistency is so strong that it makes us likely to desire what we regard as desirable, and to regard as desirable what we in fact desire. But the history of moral and ethical thought is replete with instances in which this consistency breaks down, and these instances are humanly important and psychologically interesting. It breaks down for both saints and sinners. In social commentary (chapter 7), I have been particularly concerned with the now-visible tendency for our "conceptions of the desirable" to collapse into mere preferences: what we want—now! This is a response, I think, to our modern situation, in which for many of us our values are no longer legitimated by a symbolic macrocosmic order. As our criteria or standards for choice lose the phenomenal quality that Heider (1958), following

Köhler (1938), referred to as "objective requiredness," our commitments to them are likely to falter, and values that have become mere preferences cease to provide the microcosmic anchor needed for a firm sense of identity, meaning and order in the conduct of our lives. I speak as a resident of California!

Values, like attitudes, I agree with Rokeach, have a cognitive core. I don't mind calling both concepts instances of the broader class of *beliefs,* as Rokeach does, so long as we remember that both are integrations that involve much more than cold informational content. The contemporary cognitive psychology of "information processing" is not yet in a position to deal with them.

Beliefs and attitudes as we commonly use the concepts are human phenomena, symbolically elaborated in ways that depend upon our shared linguistic symbol systems. But they have obvious counterparts or precursors at the prehuman animal level in behavioral expectancies (Tolman, 1932) and "canalizations" (Murphy, 1947)—preferences, appetites, and aversions. Animals as well as people can learn about the world and take it into account, and what animals, like people, learn and take into account may be organized around objects, though not around ideal, imaginary, metaphorical, or abstractly conceptual ones. In contrast, values as standards or criteria of the desirable linked to the experience of "ought," are uniquely human. Like the elaborated symbol systems on which they depend, they are social emergents that require continuity of culture and human association in community.

Yet, with Kluckhohn, I would not restrict the concept to *shared* prescriptive or proscriptive beliefs as Rokeach does. It can be quite true, and I think it is, that we would not have standards for the desirable without social experience (initially the approval and disapproval, then the explicit requirements and prohibitions of parental caretakers), just as we would have little experience of selfhood if we were raised inhumanly as isolated animals. All the same, on this social foundation persons can and do develop value standards of their own that are not wholly shared. It is fine for some purposes to focus on the standards that *are* shared. For other purposes, including some involved in the psychology of personality, the restriction would seem to be hampering.

Values are a major, constitutive ingredient of selfhood, along the lines suggested in the first part of this essay. Some time ago (Smith, 1963), I sketched a historical, developmental sequence according to which, in the first case, that of stable, traditional societies, the requirements of the parents (given "objectively" in the nature of things from the perspective of the infant) merge seamlessly into macrocosmically sustained values. In such societies, which were the universal human setting until very recently, everyone "knows" what is right and proper in each of the finite array of life situations that the culture recognizes, and has no occasion to question why. (If there *is* questioning, there are mythic answers.) Rapid sociocultural change in the modernizing West offered tempting alternatives and also imposed stricter demands (for capital accumulation, as Fromm's [1941] neo-Freudian-Marxist analysis would have it); so new provisions emerged for the "internalization" of values, along lines such as those formulated by the Freudian superego, still with macrocosmic support (the "Protestant Ethic" *was* rooted in Protestantism, after all!). In our contemporary "postindustrial" society, the imperatives for self-discipline have slackened and the macrocosmic props have also eroded. Now we find some people's values anchored neither in macroscopic myth nor in unthinking "introjection" but in principled self-commitment—but vulnerably so, ever at risk of relapsing to mere preferences. Existential philosophy expresses and explores aspects of this predicament.

Even this schematic account should suggest correspondences with the historical characterology of Riesman (1950), based on Fromm (1947), and with Kohlberg's (1969) developmentalist ideas about moral judgment, which have the drawback of being unhistorical and I fear culture-bound in essential respects. My hope is to persuade the reader that an appropriate psychological treatment of values requires a historical and cultural perspective not only in regard to the *content* of the values to which people adhere (the main focus of Rokeach's research, as I understand it) but also in regard to the *way* in which people adhere to them (which has been Kohlberg's main concern).

How Can Psychology Participate in the Dialectic of Values?

Psychologists study values; they also participate in the advocacy of values, often without being aware of doing so. A prime example is their use of evaluative concepts like "maturity," "personal soundness," "mental health," or "self-actualization" in personality theory and in framing the goals of professional practice. In my Allport Memorial Lecture (chapter 1) I examined a number of attempts by psychologists (including ones by Maslow [1954] and by Loevinger [1976]) to provide an empirical, "scientific" justification for choice among values in this area of special psychological relevance. I concluded that it can't be done: as many philosophers have held, no magic bridge between facts and values is to be found. All the same, I further concluded that we *can* participate legitimately, *as psychologists,* in the ongoing discourse or dialectic about values, in which, in our fluid, unstable culture, values get transmitted, differentiated, and sometimes transformed. Indeed, we have been participating all along, although sometimes unwittingly and under the false colors of supposed "value-neutrality."

I used Allport's (1954) classic, *The Nature of Prejudice,* to illustrate actual ways in which psychologists participate in the dialectic of values without the need to claim access to a magic bridge that they do not have. In this careful, wise, and humane work, infused with democratic values as conceived in the context of his time, Allport drew upon the resources of psychology and social science primarily to *clarify causal and means-end relationships*—how best to proceed to attain already valued goals. Beyond that, however, his close examination of the nature and manifestations of bigotry surely made many of his readers more thoughtful and self-critical about ways in which they too had played the bigot unthinkingly: a role of *sensitization* that can lead to the emergence of new values, and a role of *encouraging Socratic self-confrontation* that can lead to the reordering of the reader's values toward more inclusive self-chosen patterns of consistency. (Rokeach's [1973] research has focused on these processes.) And Allport's own example of scrupulous fair-mindedness was surely a cogent contribution to the dialectic of values—*modeling* has a role in the dialectic, too. According to my conception of social and personality psychology as a historical discipline that also *participates* in history with its own specialized resources for augmenting human reflectiveness and self-direction, the example is a cogent one.

The Self?—and Selfhood

To bring this long excursion to a close, I return to the theme of *selfhood* as a historical, cultural, creative project in symbolization. When I agreed to undertake this essay, I offered "Attitudes, Values and the Self" as my working title. By the time I was writing chapter 2, I had come to realize that my proper topic was selfhood, as criterial features of the human condition—reflexive self-awareness prime among them. *The self* then seemed much too concrete a term for my purposes. But as I mulled and stewed about what I would do for this essay, I still held to the hope and expectation that I would somehow be able to sort out my thinking so as to resurrect a concept of "the self" as one of a family of concepts in the domain of selfhood. I stuck to the old title nearly to the bitter end. But I couldn't make a go of it, as I discovered at the cost of unusually painful writer's block. Now I attribute the snarl not to my incapacities but to the nature of the problem. (Healthy attribution, that!) I now think that I started with the wrong heading.

There are a number of terms in the domain of selfhood that give me no trouble, or seem potentially useful. There is the *person,* the actual, concrete participant in symbolically construed and governed social relations. There is *personality,* the psychologist's formulation or construction of the person, a construction of organized processes, states, and dispositions (beliefs, attitudes, and values among them). There is Erikson's (1959) rich but slippery concept of *identity*—some trouble, here, to disentangle and pin down the meanings. There is a set of terms in the reflexive mode—*self-perceptions* and *attributions, self-concepts, self-theories* (Epstein, 1973)—in which the prefix *self-* implies reflexive reference but does *not* imply a surgically or conceptually separable object of reference, other than the *person.* People—persons—may reify "I" and "Me," but psychologists shouldn't, except as they recognize the causal-functional importance of people's own reifications. There is Jung's (1966) elusive *Self-as-archetype*—an ideal of integration to be approached, perhaps a template for integration, a symbolization of it, to guide the process of "individuation." I don't see a place for *the self* in such a list. It is not a term that designates an entity or agency, except in usages that treat it as synonymous with the *person,* in which case one or the other term is superfluous.

Yet there *are* contexts in which *self* is employed in near synonymy with *person* that seem to me more justifiable. We may talk about transformations of the Greek self from Homer to Euripides, or of the Western self from Shakespeare to Proust, Pynchon, or R. D. Laing. We may talk of the fragmentation of self in role-differentiated modern society. When we use such locutions, we are emphasizing the symbolic, *self-referential* aspect of being a person (with the reflexive prefix having its usual sense as interpreted above), with the implied reminder that self-referential features in which we are interested are somehow constitutive of the person as social actor. We are not talking about an entity, conceptual or otherwise, that is distinguishable from the person. If it makes sense to talk about a fragmented or divided self, the fragmentation or division is a metaphor of metaphors: a characterization of the metaphoric symbol system that partly constitutes us as persons.

So I draw back in what I think are significant ways from the language of William James and George Herbert Mead, which I began by taking for granted. *Selfhood, person,* and *personality* remain my key terms.

Conclusion

In the first part of this essay, I developed a metatheoretic basis in which selfhood is proffered as the proper concern of a personality and social psychology that is at once scientific *and* humanistic in its aims. In doing so, I gave voice to my misgivings about the recent preoccupation of the field with the model of the physical sciences, calling rather for a view of its historical character and its potential value as a mode of participating in human history. I exemplified a historical approach and sought a kind of justification of it in a speculative account of the evolutionary and historical emergence of selfhood, an account that was nevertheless grounded on an empirical base. I proposed that a view of selfhood as substantially constituted by vital metaphors of culturally transmitted symbolism is congruent with a variety of existing clusters of theoretical insight, some of them currently neglected by the personality and social psychology of the mainstream, some of them (like attribution theory) near the center of the main current. Divergences among contemporary theorists, I suggested, partly hinge on whether they take a positive or a pejorative view of the role of metaphor in selfhood.

In the second part, I applied the perspective thus developed to the psychology of attitudes and values, in a retrospective, evaluative look at the recent history of our discipline. I applauded what seems to be our present belated rediscovery of the Lewinian principle that psychological dispositions, whether beliefs, attitudes, or personality, are relevant to the explanation of behavior only when they are taken jointly in interaction with formulations of the situation of action. The rediscovery should relegitimize the psychology of personality, the context in which a substantive psychology of attitudes belongs. I decried the inadequate attention that mainstream social psychology has given to the substantive understanding of attitudes, where a view of the discipline as historical might expect it to make more of a contribution. And I resurrected an old conceptual map, an outgrowth of my earlier participation in functional attitude theory, to illustrate, among other things, a legitimate role for social psychology in clarification and social interpretation that we have largely skimped. My brief treatment of values, differentiating my approach from Rokeach's, again emphasized a historical-cultural perspective on people's ways of relating to value standards, conceived as important ingredients of selfhood. It also took a quick look at how psychologists can legitimately participate in the modification of values—again from a perspective that regards psychology and psychologists as *participating* in history, not merely studying history with or without the knowledge that that is what they are doing.

And I ended, as I do here, with the discovery that my search for *the* self as the protagonist of this adventure was misguided. The protagonist, if there is one, is the *person,* whose selfhood is a cultural gift and a historical and personal achievement. From the point of view of this essay, psychology has a potentially proud role to play in people's enacting of their further history, through contributions it can make to collective and individual self-understanding and therefore to collective and individual self-direction.

Notes

1. Shotter (1974) has argued effectively in a more philosophical vein for a congruent metapsychological perspective, making a direct attack on the Cartesian assumptions that undergird positivism and mechanism in modern psychology.
2. Now, in 1990, as this goes to press, I am delighted to note that Bob Altemeyer (1981, 1988) has restored the topic of right-wing authoritarianism to its rightful place in social and political psychology. His programmatic studies are psychometrically sound, experimentally ingenious, and conceptually insightful. While they call the psychoanalytic assumptions of the Berkeley research into question, they confirm essential aspects of the character type, and document its social relevance.
3. This section is adapted from Smith (1968a).

4

The Metaphorical Basis of Selfhood

The volume for which this chapter was originally prepared (Marsella, De Vos, & Hsu, 1985) substituted a new label, "culture and self," for "culture and personality," the label I grew up with in the 1930s to 1950s.[1] My contribution takes this substitution seriously. As a culturally oriented (but hardly cross-cultural) psychologist, I have always thought that mainstream social science deserted culture and personality before the full potential of the topic had at all been realized. It now seems to me that the general area is due for a renaissance of scholarly interest, catalyzed in part by the new semantic auspices. This chapter is intended to further the enterprise by taking note of developments in the psychology of personality that favor it, and particularly, by carrying forward my own treatment of selfhood (chapters 2 and 3) to make more explicit its symbolic grounding in culturally provided metaphor, and therefore the necessity of cross-cultural approaches if selfhood is to be dealt with satisfactorily, in ways that avoid the destructive charge of being culture-bound (or history-bound—an equivalent but much less recognized failing). The moral of my story: good *science* of personality or selfhood requires cross-cultural *hermeneutics*. If this be philosophical treason, make the most of it! In the realm of selfhood, I have come to believe, science does not clash with interpretation but requires it.

Culture and Self/Personality

What happened to "culture and personality"? As the movement thrived during the 1930s and 1940s, "culture and personality" was mainly a temporary marriage between cultural anthropology and neo-Freudian psychoanalysis. There were some extravagances and errors, particularly in the wartime study of national character at a distance, that began to bring

73

the field into disrepute among more tough-minded behavioral scientists. By the 1960s and 1970s a cognitive focus had emerged in psychological anthropology as well as in psychology, which brought new issues to the fore. Academic interest in psychoanalysis crested, followed by a downward sweep that leaves its current scholarly reputation as undeservedly low as it was once faddishly high. In spite of some good work in continuity with the earlier tradition by scholars like Le Vine (1973) and Spiro (1967), social scientists largely abandoned culture and personality just when more adequate methodological sophistication was beginning to prevail, before the major substantive problems of the area had been dealt with satisfactorily. The abandonment coincided, too, with the emergence of less dogmatically physicalistic, more interpretative psychoanalytic formulations.

The colleagues whom I join under the new rubric obviously have not given up on the old problems, but we are attacking them from a new angle. What denotations and connotations make the terminology of "culture and self" more auspicious than that of "culture and personality," and why, indeed, is the present time auspicious for a renaissance of interest in cross-cultural formulations of the relations between self and society?

The Revival of Personality

First a word about the auspiciousness of the time. In psychology, the 1960s and 1970s were a period of sterility and despair in personality psychology (Carlson, 1971). The great academic personality theorists who were contemporaries of the culture-and-personality movement—Gordon Allport, Henry Murray, Gardner Murphy, and George Kelly—had envisioned a humane science of personality that aspired to be at once scientific and humanistic in traditional senses of both these words. In the academic psychology of personality, there ensued a period of laboratory experimentalism that emphasized experimental manipulations and situational influences rather than dispositions, and variables rather than people. The gospel of extreme situationism prevailed for almost two decades, if only because psychologists were mainly studying the impact of experimentally manipulated situational variables, encouraged by the grant system of project support that rewarded series of tightly designed studies that could readily be described in advance.

Shortly before the end of the 1970s, however, the tide had turned (see Magnusson & Endler, 1977; Epstein, 1979, 1980). Person x Situation interactionism is once more acceptable and even fashionable, at least in principle. Personality structure or organization and traits of dispositions are no longer derided. New models are needed if the revived interactionism is to be pursued fruitfully, but armchair polemics are no longer called for.

It is now respectable and even interesting to be talking about personality again.

The Decline of Positivism and Rise of Interpretation

Our choice of the term *self* or *selfhood* requires notice of an even broader set of developments. Relaxation of the stranglehold that situation-oriented laboratory experimentalism had on personality theory is part of a shift in the general atmosphere of enquiry in the human and social sciences. The heyday of culture and personality was also that of Vienna-style logical positivism (particularly exemplified in psychology by the neobehaviorism of Clark Hull [1943], a major participant in interdisciplinary ventures of the culture-and-personality movement). As we all know, the dictatorial reign of logical positivism as a philosophy of science has ended. It never did constrain the self-confident physical scientists; now, in the human and behavioral sciences, it has become much easier to follow problems where they lead us, with fewer prescriptive restraints. As the credentials of positivism declined, those of a hermeneutic, interpretative perspective with roots in the humanities gained in attractiveness and credibility (see Bernstein, 1976; Geertz, 1973). The terminology of self and selfhood fits naturally into this newer emphasis, as I will try to show more explicitly a little later on.

The broadening of our perspectives to include interpretative, symbolic considerations is critical in laying the basis for new advances in the study of personality. As I suggested earlier, the grand academic personality theorists who in their time were rebels against the behaviorist tradition saw their enterprise as both humanistic and scientific. Freud, too, had both his positivistic-mechanistic and his humanistic sides, which as Ricoeur (1970), Holt (1972), Loevinger (1976), Schafer (1976), and other recent interpreters of Freud in a more hermeneutic vein have made clear, got into considerable conflict with each other. During the 1960s and 1970s, when the positivists held the day in academic personality psychology, the attempt to sustain a humanistic psychology of personality got caught up in the irrationalist counterculture. So "humanistic psychology," as typified by the Esalen Institute and the Association for Humanistic Psychology, became more a social movement than an academic field (Smith, 1984). That movement, too, has substantially faded. We can now try to reconstruct a psychology of personality that is interpretative and humanistic and historically anchored but shares the critical, corrigible, and conceptualizing aspirations of science.

The Present Need for a Cross-Cultural Approach

A cross-cultural approach once more seems essential if the serious study of personality is to get back on track. Except for participants in the culture-and-personality movement, personality theorists have mostly been egregiously culture-bound. Maybe we can do better on this persent round! It was easy enough for the generation of Karen Horney (1939) to criticize Freud for his lack of awareness of cultural influences. It is similarly easy— too easy—for contemporary feminists to reject Freud's thought out of hand because of his history-bound views of gender and sexual repression. Perhaps we are at last in a position to conceive that Freud's psychology of gender and of the super-ego fits turn-of-the-century Vienna pretty well but is much less apt for the men and women of today. If we are to build on this dawning insight into the inherently historical component in our formulations of personality, we obviously need all the help we can get from cross-cultural studies. Even though the methodological and conceptual relevance of historical data and that of cross-cultural data are closely similar if not identical, we can pursue our questions more rigorously, with better evidence, in cross-cultural comparison than is ever possible in historical retrospect.

Some Terminological Issues

The time is opportune. And the term *self* does provide a useful change of semantic auspices, which has advantages beyond mere novelty. My own preference is for the term *selfhood,* and for *self* in the many reflexive hyphenated contexts in which it is used in ordinary language. Chapters 2 and 3 spell out my reasons for finding *the self* largely redundant with *person.* But I do not revolt against *self* in the title of the volume for which I originally prepared this chapter. I take the implied contrast with *culture and personality* to suggest that people's own formulations and theories about themselves as personal and social objects—which enter reflexively into constituting themselves as persons—ought to play a larger role in our conceptualizations of personality than heretofore. From such a perspective, it is immediately apparent that the symbolic ingredients of these formulations and theories are intrinsically cultural.

How people symbolize themselves to themselves and one another is important. Indeed, "ethnopsychology" (a term now employed rather differently) might become institutionalized as a special field analogous to ethnobotany or ethnoscience generally: How do culturally contrasting peoples conceptualize their human nature and their personal-social processes? The ontogenetic version of this question—"metacognition"—has recently opened up in developmental cognitive psychology, but the comparative cultural question seems still rather rare in the ethnographic literature. A fine example is Geertz's (1973, 1975) comparative treatment of naming as anchoring different modes of selfhood or identity in Bali, Java, and Morocco. (It was Geertz's provocative treatment of how the Balinese system of teknonomy minimizes the salience of individuality, taken together with Lionel Trilling's (1971) account of the historical vicissitudes of selfhood in European literature, that led me to see the strong parallel between historical and cross-cultural perspectives.) Another good example is Leenhardt's version of structures of the person in New Caledonia (Clifford, 1982). Before her tragic death, Rosaldo (1984) was carrying Geertz's program forward in a provocative analysis very much along the lines I am asking for, focusing on her data on Ilongot ethnopsychology. A more systematic recent consideration of "the anthropology of self," with a number of contributed examples, is provided by Heelas and Lock (1981).

From Classical Symbolic Interactionism to Constitutive Metaphor

For most contemporary social scientists, the terminology of self calls to mind the theoretical tradition extending from James (1890) through Cooley (1902) and Mead (1934) to contemporary symbolic interactionists, with a modern branching to include the phenomenological successors to Schutz (1967). As a deviant social psychologist, I enjoy watching my more experimentally oriented psychologist colleagues rediscover this tradition, as more and more of them are doing. One of its key features is the view that self-awareness and self-evaluation are social emergents.

The Meadian Account

G. H. Mead (1934) held, as we know, that mind, self, and society emerge together both in the individual life and in the history of the human species. The attainment of language involves the acquired ability to emit signs that the emitter interprets in the same way as the receiver: "significant symbols." To acquire significant symbols, we must "take the role of the other," reacting to our own behavior as our partner in interaction does. From practice in a variety of such role-taking relationships, we generalize, and become able to take *ourselves* as objects, from the perspective of the "generalized other." By the same token, we can then orient our actions as well as our talk so as to participate effectively in the complexly organized expectation-and-rule sytems of society. The "Me" is the product of generalization from the responses of others to oneself, and thought is inner dialogue between "I" and "Me." This armchair account, made the more difficult to grasp (and thus the more dogmatically received) because it was constructed posthumously from student notes on Mead's lectures, became the gospel of the so-called symbolic interactionists in sociological social psychology. For decades, it formed part of an orienting framework for research in a qualitative, participant-observer style, but it was not itself directly tested in research.

Needed Revisions or Extensions of Mead

Research is only now beginning to appear that requires us to correct or elaborate upon the Meadian formulation. The broader social science community is now becoming acquainted with Gallup's (1977) fascinating study of selfhood in chimpanzees. He raised chimpanzees in living quarters that were amply provided with mirrors. Then he anesthetized a test chimpanzee, painted a red patch on its forehead, and let the chimp come to in its own quarters provided with mirrors. Chimpanzees under these circumstances regularly grasped at their foreheads when looking in the mirror, evidently puzzled about the new red spot. Lower mammals did not show this behavior; neither did chimpanzees raised in isolation, even though mirrors were available. Appropriate understanding of one' mirror image may not reflect full-blown selfhood—say, that of a Kierkegaard or Sartre puzzled by the absurdity of existence—but it does suggest that socially raised chimps are capable of taking themselves as objects in a more conceptual way than is involved in scratching or self-grooming. This aspect of selfhood clearly does not depend upon language, though the fact that only the socially raised chimps showed this behavior agrees with Meadian assumptions.

Michael Lewis and his collaborators (Lewis & Brooks-Gunn, 1979) are engaging in studies of mirror behavior among human infants, and Kagan (1981) infers the emergence of self-awareness, self-reference, and self-evaluation from the close observation of infants' and toddlers' behaviors in a variety of cognitive tasks in the laboratory. Selfhood, we now see, does not emerge suddenly, all-or-none; and the role of language and role taking in its ontogenesis needs to be worked out in detail. Now that the details of how selfhood emerges have become problematic and methods have been devised for studying the problem, we can expert rapid progress in enriching the Meadian account.

The infant studies just cited were done in the United States (though Kagan incorporates Fijian data), but it seems likely that they concern developmental processes that are essentially panhuman. Language and self-reference are human universals. Cross-cultural studies are desirable to confirm this presumption, but I would be surprised if they showed much cultural variation in the steps toward attainment of selfhood in the first two years. The case should be different for the later years, especially with respect to what might be referred to as the *content* of selfhood: to use Kelly's (1955) language, how do persons in different cultures come to construe themselves? Competent reviews of the development of selfhood in infancy and childhood have recently been provided by Damon and Hart (1982) and by Harter 1983).

A Focus on the Symbolic Content of Selfhood

How do culturally provided symbol systems affect people's self-conceptions and therefore their distinctive ways of relating self to interpreted world? Currently fashionable miniature theories—"labeling theory" in sociology and "attribution theory" in psychology—have recently focused attention on some of the *processes* by which participants in society acquire interpretations of themselves, which therefore are likely to result in self-fulfilling prophecies. Labeling theory has mainly been used as a blunt instrument for cudgeling traditional accounts of deviant behavior (Murphy, 1976, 1981), and attribution theory in the hands of experimental social psychologists has characteristically assumed a framework of causal explanation, not of intentional, meaningful interpretation (cf. Shotter, 1981).

A prominent attribution theorist (Ross, 1977) has called inappropriate attribution to personal dispositions "the fundamental attribution error," a position that is readily misinterpreted as asserting that the error includes any attribution to personal dispositions whatsoever. Harvey, Town, and Yarkin (1981) have recently and I think appropriately questioned the "fundamental" label. There *are* problems in how attribution and labeling concepts have been deployed. All the same, attribution theory and labeling theory are focusing attention on social psychological processes that contribute to the content of selfhood.

I am particularly taken by how attribution theory has been used by Seligman and his colleagues (Abramson, Seligman, & Teasdale, 1978) in extending and enriching his theory of learned helplessness (Seligman, 1975) as a dynamic of depression and other self-defeating reaction patterns. As he and his colleagues have been saying, a vicious circle of self-defeat can be sustained by the learned tendency to attribute failures to the self, the pernicious self-attributions being global rather than specific, and stable rather than temporary. That is, "I failed the math test not because the test was too hard but because of my own inadequacies, and it's not just a matter of my poor mathematical ability or the fact that I had a hangover—I am just stupid, so there is no point in trying."

This kind of dynamic, as formulated in attributional terms, goes well beyond the static and sterile work that predominated under the rubric of "self-concept" research (Wylie, 1974, 1979). Psychologists do have a disciplinary bent toward preoccupation with abstract process, however, and different approaches are needed to enrich our understanding of the *content* of selfhood. In which respects is our experience of selfhood panhuman, and in which is it historically and culturally specific? This question is of great human interest in its own right, and we need at least an approximate answer before we can have any confidence in our strategies for developing personality theory. My hunch is that much theory in personality and social psychology, and related research, has been misdirected by the assumption that we are dealing with timeless human universals rather than with historically and culturally specific phenomena. I believe that psychology in its personal-social aspect will be more humanly useful, and also be sounder science, if we give up the aspiration to an ahistorical, quasi-Newtonian science. (See Gergen, 1973, 1982; Smith, 1976, and chapter 3 above.) But these issues are themselves pragmatic and historical, and cannot be settled from the armchair.

Enter Constitutive Metaphor

My own thinking about selfhood in historical/cultural perspective was much stimulated by Julian Jaynes's (1976) brilliant but extravagant speculations in *The Origins of Consciousness in the Breakdown of the Bicameral Mind.* Jaynes had the idea that consciousness as we know it originated rather recently. He drew on evidence from Egyptian and Sumerian inscriptions, some biblical writings, and Homer to suggest that people originally went through their lives unconsciously (un*self*-consciously?), unreflectively, receiving guidance when they were puzzled by hallucinating the voices of the gods—through some kind of right-left hemispheric shunt in the brain. He suggested that in the second millennium B.C., the folkwanderings and catastrophes in the eastern Mediterranean made this way of life untenable, giving rise to modern consciousness. The book is fun to read, both because of the outrageousness of the hypothesis, and because of its ability to integrate a wide range of phenomena including ancient oracles, modern mediumship, hypnosis, and schizophrenia.

I call upon Jaynes here not because I give credence to his main hypothesis; he is so centered on the traditions of Western civilization that one immediately asks for better cross-cultural evidence. I am not persuaded that the ancient Sumerians and Achaeans were walking automata who continually hallucinated. But Jaynes's analysis of the language of the *Iliad* converges with independent analyses by the German classicist Snell

(1953) and the English classicist Onians (1973) to suggest strongly that the Homeric bards conceived of self-consciousness in terms quite different from ours.

As we hear from Jaynes and from Snell and Onians, what at first glance seems to be the psychological language of the *Iliad* does not translate accurately into terms from our common language like *spirit* or *soul, mind, thought, consciousness, emotion, will*, or their reasonable equivalents in the Greek of classical times. Some of the words (like *psyche*) that later became explicitly psychological occur in contexts indicating that for the bards of the *Iliad*, they were not psychological at all. In the *Iliad*, they appear to stand rather for concrete bodily organs or functions, like the lungs, the breath, the blood, the stirrings of the gut, the movements of the limbs.

There seems to be little if any subjectivity or introspection in the *Iliad*. Passages that imply deceit and complexity of intention can be argued to represent later interpolations. Certainly, the voices of the gods are constantly intruding when courses of action are in doubt. At the very least, Lionel Trilling's remark seems well justified, that it would be quite meaningless to speak of Achilles as *sincere* (1972, p. 2). Sincerity implies reflective scrutiny of intention and behavior—sophisticated but integral selfhood—that simply does not apply to the Homeric hero.

Snell and Jaynes converge in suggesting that modern self-consciousness depends upon the metaphors that people use to construe their experience. Snell goes so far as to entitle his book *The Discovery of Mind*, though he goes on to note the ambiguity as to whether one should speak of invention rather than discovery: mind as we know it requires our contemporary conceptualization to be what it is for us. To speak of the *discovery* of mind, says Snell, is to engage in metaphor, but he notes in passing that we must inevitably fall back on metaphor if we are to speak at all about the intellect or mind. This is a serious point that warrants elaboration.

The language of subjectivity *is* inherently metaphoric. The point was well recognized by the behaviorist critics of the older introspective psychology, who regarded subjectivity as a disqualification of any psychology of consciousness. It is a standard defense of objectivism in psychology that only when we are comparing one another's discriminations in the public world are we able to check our denotations by pointing, by ostensive definition. In the child's acquisition of language, no such check is available for the vocabulary of emotion or, for that matter, for the *qualities* of our experience of external stimuli. The language of phenomenological description stumbles at evoking qualities as such, and has to be satisfied with what the Gestalt psychologists called "isomorphism": formal, structural correspondences. All of this was old hat in the heyday of behaviorism.

Given the impossibility of direct denotation in the realm of the subjective, we inevitably fall back on metaphor, which is the language of isomorphism.

Jaynes (1977) bases his treatment of consciousness—with its "as-if" inner space, its serialized time, its narratively interpreted plot-structure of intentionality—on his own version of a theory of metaphor. One can agree with him that the substance and perhaps some aspects of the structure of our reflective consciousness are heavily metaphoric without following him to his caricature of walking automata. His account of the metaphorical nature of mind is worth close consideration to which I will return. Here, however, I draw instead on the recent formulations of Lakoff and Johnson (1980) as further elaborated by Lakoff (1987) and Kövecses (1986; Lakoff & Kövecses, 1987). Metaphor is a complex and currently stylish topic, for which there are many competing treatments. (For a representative recent sampling, see Fernandez, 1974; Sacks, 1979; and Ortony, 1979.) In *Metaphors We Live By* (1980), however, Lakoff and Johnson provide a framework that seems to me ideally suited to my purposes. Encountering their book was a major intellectual discovery for me, so I sing its praises.

Lakoff's Treatment of Metaphor

"*The essence of metaphor is understanding and experiencing one thing in terms of another*" (Lakoff & Johnson, 1980, p. 5; their italics). Like most of us, I was accustomed to think of metaphor as a "figure of speech," a linguistic phenomenon belonging to the minor ornaments of expression and not to the essential nature of thought. I was also educated to believe that our language is thickly sedimented with "dead metaphors": expressions that were once vividly evocative but have mainly lost their connotative metaphorical meanings. The first novel idea with which Lakoff and Johnson confronted me was that although literary metaphors may lose their poetic vitality in common use (they do not discuss this), ordinary prosaic human thought processes are largely metaphorical and the human conceptual system is metaphorically structured and defined. The metaphors are far from dead.

To illustrate the potential power of their metaphorical approach, I turn to Lakoff and Kövecses (1987), whose treatment of "the cognitive model of anger in American English" has explicitly psychological content, whereas the rich examples in Lakoff and Johnson (1980) do not. I can only suggest the nature of a long and complex analysis by quoting selectively from a small part of it:

> In our overall conceptual system, we have the general metaphor:
> THE BODY IS A CONTAINER FOR THE EMOTIONS
> He was *filled* with anger.

She couldn't *contain* her joy.

. . . .

The ANGER IS HEAT metaphor, when applied to fluids, combines with the metaphor THE BODY IS A CONTAINER FOR THE EMOTIONS to yield the central metaphor of the system:
ANGER IS THE HEAT OF A FLUID IN A CONTAINER
You make my *blood boil.*
Simmer down!

. . . .

She was seething with rage.

. . . .

When there is no heat, the liquid is cool and calm. In the central metaphor, cool and calmness corresponds to lack of anger.

. . . .

Let us refer to the HEAT OF FLUID IN A CONTAINER as the scource domain of the central metaphor, and to ANGER as the target domain. . . . A conceptual metaphor can be productive [by carrying] over details of . . . knowledge from the source domain to the target domain. We will refer to such carryovers as metaphorical entailments. Such entailments are part of our conceptual system. . . . The central metaphor has a rich system of metaphorical entailments. For example, one thing we know about hot fluids is that, when they start to boil, the fluid goes upward. This gives rise to the entailment:
WHEN THE INTENSITY OF ANGER INCREASES, THE FLUID RISES
His pen-up anger *welled up* inside him.
She could feel her *gorge rising.*

. . . .

We also know that intense heat produces steam and creates pressure on the container. This yields the metaphorical entailments:
INTENSE ANGER PRODUCES STEAM
She got *all steamed up.*

. . . .

I was *fuming.*
INTENSE ANGER PRODUCES PRESSURE ON THE CONTAINER

. . . .

I could barely *contain* my rage.
A variant of this involves keeping the pressure back:
I *suppressed* my anger.
He *turned his anger inward.*
He managed to keep his anger *bottled up* inside him.
When the pressure on the container becomes too high, the container explodes. [So:]
She *blew up* at me.
We won't tolerate any more of your *outbrusts.*

. . . .

In an explosion, parts of the container go up in the air. [So:]
I *blew my stack.*

. . . .

He *hit the ceiling.*

. . . .

When something explodes, what was inside it comes out. [Thus:]

His anger finally *came out*.

....

(pp. 197–200)

Metaphors, Lakoff and Johnson assert, enable us to understand one domain of experience in terms of another. The domains organized by metaphoric relations comprise "experiential gestalts" that are "natural kinds of experience" such as products of our bodies, our interactions with the physical environment, and our interactions with other people. Some of these kinds of experience may be universal; others will vary across cultures. The concepts that are used metaphorically to characterize other concepts also are asserted to correspond to kinds of experience that are natural in this sense. The meaning of some basic concepts, like that of love in our culture, inheres primarily in the network of its metaphorical affinities, which characteristically can be described as connotationally coherent rather than logically consistent. Since metaphors organize our experience through their entailments, they thus create social realities for us, and become guides to action. In this sense (congruent with my conception of the consequences of our self-understandings), metaphors can involve self-fulfilling prophecies.

To be fair to Lakoff and his collaborators, I should add that they are careful not to overwork their central concept of metaphor. In their usage, metaphor does do double duty to include what would otherwise be labeled *analogy*. But they give explicit treatment to *metonymy*, the general case in which one entity is used to refer to another, as in letting the part stand for the whole (*synechdoche* in traditional rhetoric), the producer for the product, the institution for the people responsible, and so on. In their view, metaphor and metonymy are different kinds of processes:

> Metaphor is principally a way of conceiving one thing in terms of another, and its primary function is understanding. Metonymy, on the other hand, has primarily a referential function, that is, it allows us to use one entity to *stand for* another (Lakoff & Johnson, 1980, p. 36).

Yet in the relationship chosen for metonymic reference, understanding is also involved, and, as in the case of metaphor, metonymic concepts are systematic and contribute to the coherence of thought and action within the framework of the cultural symbol system. A historically minded commentator cannot help noting that, between them, metaphor and metonymy cover the ground of the old psychological principles of association—similarity and contiguity—and of Frazer's (1951) conceptualization of "primitive" thought and action in terms of homeopathic and contagious magic.

Lakoff and Johnson embed their view of the basic concepts with which metaphor and metonymy operate in terms of prototypical instances rather than neatly bounded logical sets. At a more complex level, metaphor merges with myth in giving meaningful structure to self and world.

I hope this brief selection conveys some of the persuasive attractiveness of the approach. In the present context, it is essential to note that Lakoff and his colleagues are only incidentally concerned with the role of metaphor in framing concepts of selfhood, and hardly at all with the comparison of metaphorical construction across languages and cultures. In a word, they do not do *our* job for us. But they provide us with powerful tools that can be adapted to our purposes. Further, by their insistence, well-exemplified, that the entire texture of human conceptualization is inherently metaphorical, they demystify what now appears to be the smaller claim that consciousness is metaphorical (Jaynes) or that metaphorical thinking is constitutive of our selfhood, as I have been asserting. The metaphorical texture of our views of self is part and parcel of our metaphorical construction of the world—necessarily so, since our interpretations of self and world emerge together in our infancy. Presumably, cultural interpretations of self and world have been linked in tandem ever since they emerged in human prehistory.

Metaphoric Consciousness Further Considered

With the conceptual equipment provided by Lakoff and Johnson, we can now return to Jaynes's (1976) treatment of the metaphoric nature of our self-consciousness. Spatialization metaphors are central, for the mind-space of our experience has no literal location in geography; its spatiality is entailed by metaphoric linkages to such things as seeing with the eyes or moving along on the road. Thus we talk, and find ourselves thinking, in such terms as "the mind's eye" and "seeing the solution clearly." And we assume a mind-space in which these metaphorical events occur—for us, somewhere "inside our heads," though not for Aristotle, who thought the brain served to cool the blood, and put the mind-space somewhere near the heart. As Jaynes observes, we do use our brains in thinking and being conscious, but we also use them in riding a bicycle. No more than our bicycle riding is our consciousness "really" located inside our heads.

Consciousness is an especially complex metaphoric construction, which, once attained, provides a framework for interpreting our remembered past, our anticipated future, and the world around us. Jaynes proposes several key features of consciousness as metaphorically structured: among them, spatialization—very widely applied, even to temporal relationships; narratization—the interpretation of our own activity in the plot structure of intentionality; and the presence of a metaphoric "I" and "Me" in this spatialized and narratized construction of experience. Such a grandly ambitious view of reflective consciousness seems in tune with modern rejections of traditional dualism like Gregory Bateson's (1972) "ecology of mind" and the radical functionalism of Egon Brunswik's (1956) and James Gibson's (1950) different interpretations of perception.

It hinges on a *respectful* view of metaphor, in which "as if" is not regarded pejoratively as a reason for debunking. Our value-laden human world is richly metaphoric; therein lies its tragedy, comedy, and glory. It is not to be disparaged as "merely" metaphoric. Locke's doctrine of "primary" and "secondary" qualities, filtered down to become part of our common sense, involves just such disparagement. The Lockean distinction is itself a preemptive metaphor.

The metaphorically constructed microcosm of reflective selfhood and the linked, constructed macrocosm of an interpreted world—in the immense variety of their culturally differentiated versions—have presumably been supportively congruent throughout the previous course of human history and prehistory. One interpretation of the underlying crisis of modernity is that the accelerating trajectory of scientific culture and technology with its preemptive metaphors has produced a dehumanized macrocosm for most people—not just for scientists—that seems incompatible with the metaphoric microcosm of intentionality and value in which most of us still live our lives (chapter 2).

Second Thoughts about Metaphor and Science

Having gone so far toward making salient, even celebrating, the role of metaphor in human thought and in the constitution of selfhood, I had best draw back momentarily. Is *everything* metaphorical? Is even science metaphorical? If so, the term loses meaning. This is not the place for a thorough discussion of matters that concern the most fundamental issues of epistemology and philosophy of science, but it may be helpful to sketch briefly the context in which I understand *constitutive* metaphor.

There is a sense in which even scientific concepts are metaphorical. They impose coherence upon the plenum from which they select; they interpret "similarities" within an observed "reality." But they are distinctive from the metaphors of everyday life and of literature in regard to the discipline of evidence, logic, and public scrutiny that has arisen in the scientific subculture to make them as corrigible and cumulative as possible. Scientific concepts and laws are a special case, a spectacular cultural emergent, the ideal goals of which inspire efforts like the present one.

At the most encompassing level I would place *generative* metaphors, what Stephen Pepper (1942) called "world hypotheses": frameworks like mechanism, organicism, and contextualism for "modeling" the macrocosm and microcosm, and—in a world dominated by science and technology—for providing the metatheories within which scientific paradigms are nested. (But see my reservations in chapter 10 about Pepper's particular formulation.) Generative metaphors are never tested directly, but whole structures of thought and evidential formulation that are based on them may continue to grow in empirical power and human relevance, or may become sterile and peter out; there is a long-run pragmatic control over their fate.

Constitutive metaphors that contribute to the composition of human consciousness and selfhood would be the next in comprehensive import. Here is where my concern has been primarily focused. These metaphors participate in the formation of emergent human nature. This is the special realm of self-fulfilling prophecy.

Then I would add, with some ambiguity, a class of *expository* metaphors: those embedded in the continually reconstructed narratives of our own lives (Gergen & Gergen, 1983), and in the continually reconstructed formulations of personality theory. Narratives are more complex structures than metaphors, and merge into theory and myth. We all have our own theories and myths about ourselves, our "self-understanding," which is under continual revision. The general import of this chapter is that our expository metaphors about ourselves tend to become constitutive metaphors: there is no clean line between the two classes. The case is similar, I think, for the expository metaphors of personality theory. In this respect, psychoanalysis has been particularly rich. The metaphorical institutions of the person—id, ego, and super-ego, in the Latinate perversion of Freud's good German—became for a while more identifiable functionally in people at large, one can speculate, because psychoanalysis reified them metaphorically.

These considerations pose complex problems for personality theory. Within our assumed generative metaphorical frame, we aspire to formulations that meet the tests of science. But because people's and psychologists' narrative metaphors may become constitutive metaphors, the formulations we can arrive at that seem to meet the scientific test may lack the stability and transcultural validity of formulations in the natural sciences.

Culture and the Content of Selfhood

What, then, of the cultural content of metaphors of mind and selfhood? Jaynes suggests that symbolic culture is radically constitutive of consciousness, but he relies too exclusively on the written records of Mediterranean civilization. The serious challenge is to pursue the question in cultures that have remained distinct from the modern Western model. Of course, the "psychic unity of mankind" may be far greater than Jaynes's radical view assumes: an important conclusion if it is sustained. Our experience a quarter century ago in trying to break out of the closed circle of language in attempts to test the Whorfian hypothesis should leave us warned of the methodological traps and difficulties likely to beset such research.

Whatever the outcome with respect to basic psychic unity, we can be sure that differences in how people are culturally disposed to interpret themselves make a difference in their lives. Consider, for example, the cultural analogue to a concept popular among personality psychologists, "implicit personality theories."

Implicit Theories of Personality and Psychology

During the dismal recent period when psychologists were skeptical about the very notion of personality dispositions, yet found that when they asked people to rate other persons on a series of adjectival traits they got stable predictable patterns of correlation, it became fashionable to attribute such patterns not to possible real personality structures in the persons rated but to the implicit personality theories held by the raters (see Schneider, 1973). Implicit personality theories include the basis for "halo effects," the assumption that good qualities go together, likewise bad ones. They include assumptions about the relations between physique and temperament—the jolly fat man, the lean and hungry look—that have the possibility of becoming self-confirming.

People's implicit personality theories are obviously partly idiosyncratic, but there must also be strong historical and cultural components. For a recent example, as Freudian psychology permeated Western culture, commonsense theory about the interpretation of human action was clearly affected. For another, stereotypic conceptions of male and female personality have obviously undergone changes in the past in our society, and are currently under strong feminist attack that is producing further rapid change.

George Miller's (1969) often cited remarks about how psychologists contribute to human welfare by "giving psychology away" bear on the diffusion of *explicit* psychological theory into the general culture. I am more skeptical than Miller about the social value of psychology's contribution thus far: we would be hard put to demonstrate a favorable cost-benefit balance for this indirect impact of contemporary psychology. In this connection, Hannah Arendt's (1958, p. 322) passing comment comes to mind, that the danger in the positivistic/behavioristic view of human nature is not that it is true as a description of the empirical world but that it might *become* true in the mode of self-fulfilling prophecy if people were to come to believe in it consensually.

In general, once we escape from the dogmatic situationism that dictated an empty personality, the question becomes pertinent once again as to how, and to what extent, culturally shared implicit personality theories may actually be formative of personality. The narrower scope implied by "implicit personality theory" and the broader concerns suggested by Miller and Arendt both fall short of Jayne's grand speculations about how metaphoric thought is constitutive of the entire realm of self-consciousness. The full range of relationships suggested by these examples would be encompassed in the kind of ethnopsychology that I am calling for.

Transformations of Selfhood and Transformative Metaphors

Under the influence of contemporary cognitive psychology, there is a danger of overemphasizing conscious interpretations of selfhood, of who we are as persons. Less conscious, more tacit and affect-laden aspects are evoked in a literary critic's classic of western ethnopsychology: Lionel Trilling's *Sincerity and Authenticity* (1972), to which I have already referred. In this memorable book, Trilling traced the trajectory of selfhood as reflected in Western European literature since the Renaissance. He started with the ideal of *sincerity* in Shakespeare's poetic formulation:

> This above all: to thy own self be true
> And it must follow, as the night the day,
> Thou canst not then be false to any man.

Through literary sources, Trilling followed the subsequent course of selfhood toward a skeptical view, in which sincerity, as an attribute of the well-integrated person, becomes hard to conceive, and gets replaced by authenticity to the possibly chaotic impulse. Trilling's account is supplemented by the critic Bersani (1976), who celebrates the fragmented selfhood that Trilling deplored. I see Gergen (1971) as taking a similar position, in theoretical social psychology, as does Lifton (1976) in his concept of the Protean self. The very concept of integral selfhood underlying the ideal of sincerity is coming to seem an illusion. The old, metaphoric concept of the Christian soul is being replaced by less integral concepts—I fear to be our considerable loss.

Although integral selfhood is important and good in my personal scheme of values, as a social-cultural scientist I cannot propose *the* self as a central concept. It is one of the problems of modern life in contemporary Western society that integral selfhood is relatively rare and difficult to attain. With Trilling as a guide, I find it attractive to believe that sensed unity of selfhood may have been more accessible to persons of the advantaged classes in the Renaissance. The cult of the individual in Montaigne, Cellini, Rembrandt, Dürer, and Shakespeare is strongly persuasive. But Trilling and Laing are obviously right: many features of modern society make integral selfhood harder to attain today.

Any review of the treatment by psychology of metaphoric ingredients in the constitution of selfhood must attend to the mythopoeic writings of Carl Jung (e.g., 1966). Jung was not a scientist, and his writings need to be read in the interpretative humanistic vein rather than in a scientifically critical one. All the same, Jung gave a sensitive meta-metaphorical formulation to metaphorical processes that a science of persons must eventually come to terms with. As I try to read Jung, I find myself reformulating one set of his "archetypes of the collective unconscious" as proposals for relatively panhuman metaphors of recurrent experiences and relationships in the human condition, including metaphors provided by the seasonal cycle of the natural and agricultural world and by the life cycle inherent in the lives of individual persons and families. These archetypes are the stuff of thematic recurrences in world folklore. Another set of Jungian archetypes—Animus, Anima, Persona, Shadow—are presented as dynamic symbols of aspects of being a person that he claims are formative of personhood. His archetype of the Self appears as a metaphoric ideal that supposedly provides a template for "individuation": the emergence of personal integrity. Is such a Self archetype a human universal, as Jung implies? What indeed are the cultural limits to his formulations?

Selfhood and Cultural Change

From the standpoint of cross-cultural studies, change in culturally shared self-conceptions should be an interesting ingredient in the study of acculturation and modernization. In the classic study *Becoming Modern* by Inkeles and Smith (1974), the sense of efficacy and the belief that the world is benign and supportive of human effort emerged as parts of the syndrome of modernity. In spite of the limitations in value perspective that follow from the rootedness of this work in the development policies of the 1950s and 1960s, it still makes sense to regard self-conception as *agent* rather than *patient* as an aspect of modernity, and, indeed, as an attribute likely in the long run to be valued in a way that transcends cultures. It is involved in Lévi-Strauss's contrast between "hot" and "cold" cultures.

To study how culturally supported self-conceptions result from and mediate transitions into the modern homogenized world is a large agenda. For those who worry about the very fact of homogenization from either a principled or nostalgic standpoint, a close look at how peoples in transition actually conceive themselves should be very relevant.

Conclusions and Summary

When as a staff member of the Social Science Research Council a generation ago I assisted in launching Whiting's (1966) cross-cultural studies of child rearing and socialization, we liked to view the array of still surviving nonliterate cultures as a natural laboratory. (That rhetoric would get aspirants to cross-cultural research nowhere today!) Our stance was objective and positivistic. Cross-cultural comparison allowed the consequences of a wide range of child-rearing practices to be studied under conditions in which even the extremes of the distribution were normative. Many of the old problems linking socialization, modal personality, and cultural coherence remain interesting today, but they are bound to look different from the new perspective in which meanings as well as causes require consideration, and in which the "subjects" of our research require a different kind of respect. Our present stance, embarking on the study of "culture and self," is different from that of participants in the "culture and personality" movement—toward the task of the human sciences, toward the nature and significance of data, and toward ourselves.

We are all too aware of problems in the modern world that put at risk the future of humanity, and indeed of life on earth. How we construe ourselves and one another is a crucial aspect of determining what we will make of our future, complementary to the more obvious issue of how we construe the world.

Like our predecessors in human history and prehistory and our contemporaries in other cultures, we live as metaphoric actors in a metaphoric reality, a reality of *as if*. Yet this is the only world we know; it is not a pseudoworld. Our interpretation of it undergoes continual change as its relation to our enterprises alters; the changes in our interpretations are constrained and disciplined by feedback from our actions, and to some extent by the special discipline of scientific enquiry. Our cultural interpretations of our human nature also change, and here the constraint of ineluctable fact is looser, or at least different, because our assumptions about ourselves and one another have some of the causal force of fact in a way that is different from our assumptions about the physical world. Comparative cross-cultural studies should illuminate how people's views of themselves interact with their concepts of the world, and deeper knowledge of these relationships might inform our own attempts to find a new footing in a world that has increasingly come to seem unfriendly.

In summary: the study of "culture and self" furthers a renaissance of interest in problems abandoned with the demise of the culture-and-personality movement of a generation ago, with differences in metatheoretical orientation, especially involving new concern with reflexive self-regard in terms of cultural symbol systems. I have argued the need for a better-developed "ethnopsychology" displaying and analyzing how culturally contrasting peoples conceptualize thier human nature and their personal-social processes.

The standard Meadian account of the emergence of selfhood in symbolic interaction needs correction and refinement in terms of psychological research now in progress, and it needs supplementation with respect to how culturally transmitted symbol systems inform the content of selfhood. We need richer data on people's self-understanding—the self-concepts, self-formulations, and self-theories upon which they draw—and on how these aspects of self-interpretation affect the terms and content of personality organization, as inferentially constructed by the outside observer. Progress on this front is essential if we are to advance in our intendedly general theories of personality beyond the collection of disparate and culture-bound theories bequeathed us by the theorists of a generation ago.

I drew on the recent conceptualization of metaphor by Lakoff and his collaborators to provide what seem to me promising underpinnings for the analysis of symbolic culture as constitutive of selfhood. They illustrate richly and systematically how, for speakers of English, metaphorical linkage provides the coherent structure of thought in everyday life, whether in conceptualization of self or of world. I referred also to Jaynes's analysis of the metaphoric basis of consciousness as posing the most extreme version of a view that strongly demands cross-cultural testing. At a more modest level, compatible with conventional assumptions about the "psychic unity" of humankind, culturally provided "implicit personality theories" call for study.

How people construe themselves and how their constructions are culturally phrased should interest us not only because they are humanly interesting for their own sake, and scientifically interesting for their bearing on general personality theory, but also because reflexively conscious creatures, people are influenced by their self-conceptions. Their metaphors of selfhood become in part self-fullfilling prophecies. A fuller understanding of this process would seem to be high in priority as knowledge that potentially contributes to human liberation.

Note

1. I have modified the original version of this chapter by substituting an example of metaphorical elaboration from Lakoff & Kövecses (1987) for one from Lakoff

& Johnson (1980). The example I now use, unlike the former one, has psychological reference so bears more directly on the treatment of selfhood that I am advocating. I also have eliminated some repetition of matters discussed in chapters 2 and 3.

II

Humanistic Psychology and Human Science

5

Toward a Secular Humanistic Psychology

In March 1985, the Division of Humanistic Psychology of the APA joined the Association for Humanistic Psychology and the Saybrook Institute in sponsoring a conference in San Francisco, celebrating "A Quarter Century of Humanistic Psychologies." Those attending came to hear from Carl Rogers and Rollo May as founding fathers, yes, but also to share in the thinking of virtually all the leaders in the movement, early and late, who were still around, and to participate in the consideration of what next. I begin with an important point that was taken for granted in the title chosen for the conference: Our real situation, for better or for worse, involves a diverse congeries of humanistic psycho*logies,* not a single, monolithic "humanistic psychology." Far from lamenting that diversity, I think it is appropriate to the nature of the terrain to which humanistic psychologists have staked a claim. I agree with Sigmund Koch (1976, 1985) that for the most part the will-o'-the-wisp of *a* science of psychology has only distracted psychologists from their proper tasks. So, also, with the humanistic side of the field: the "psychological studies," to adopt Koch's useful term, cannot be coerced into the confines of a single coherent "discipline," scientific *or* humanistic.

When, as a long-term observer and more or less friendly critic of the humanistic psychology movement I was astonished to find myself elected to the role that puts me before you, I found that in order to get my bearings, I needed to map for myself the main dimensions around which the concerns of humanistic psychologists are organized. I came up with something like the statistician's fourfold table, a cross-classification in terms of two dichotomies (Smith, 1985). On one hand, humanistic psychologists can be sorted according to whether or not they are primarily identified with clinical practice. (Later, I encountered Coward and Royce's [1975] classification contrasting the practically oriented humanistic psy-

97

chologists who seek to alleviate the human condition with the theoretically oriented ones guided by a "desire to elaborate on the definition of man." I like their version better.) On the other hand, humanistic psychologists can be sorted according to whether their version of humanism is primarily worldly or whether it is committed to religious or spiritual sources of meaning. On this axis, transpersonal and religiously oriented psychologists are distinguished from "secular humanists."

Secular Humanism Underrepresented in Humanistic Psychology

In the humanistic psychology movement, the quadrant in which I feel at home—theoretically oriented secular humanism—is sparsely populated. Surely the considerable majority of psychologists who identify themselves as humanistic have been involved in psychotherapy, growth centers, or perhaps organizational development, on the practically oriented side, and it is the context of therapy that has given most of the theorists their privileged window on human experience. The academic study of personality is underrepresented, and the window provided by the arts and literature is hardly represented at all. It is also my impression that the mainstream of the humanistic movement has been considerably more likely to find affinity with mysticism and Eastern religion—or with ESP as watered-down mysticism—than with secular humanism. I hope, therefore, to give secular humanism more prominence than it now has among the alternative humanistic psychologies. Of course, my motivation is not just to promote better "balance" and more representative variety. My commitment to secular humanism is serious, and I am convinced that its absence from the humanistic psychology movement has had unfortunate consequences.

I will return shortly to some of the consequences. First, however, I should proclaim another reason for featuring my identification with secular humanism: my abhorrence of the tactic by which Jerry Falwell and other socially reactionary "prime time preachers" (Hadden & Swann, 1981) of Christian fundamentalism have tried to make secular humanism an evil label. Look: Here I am, a secular humanist! I don't have horns or a tail! Indeed, I hope to illustrate that a secular humanistic perspective can have its own myths that bestow meaning, that it can be as mindful of the human need for transcendence, as capable of wonder, even of reverence, as the mystical and transpersonal psychologies.

The disregard for secular humanism in the humanistic psychology movement has contributed, I am convinced, to the movement's lamentable estrangement from the academic psychology of personality. It is a historical fact that the great theorists of the age of classical personality theory—

Gordon Allport, Henry Murray, Gardner Murphy, and George Kelly— were all major participants in the 1964 conference at Old Saybrook that launched humanistic psychology as a third force, along with Carl Rogers, Abraham Maslow, and Rollo May of the next generation of leadership. While Allport was privately a deeply religious man and as a psychologist contributed importantly to the psychology of religion, and Murphy had a lifelong interest in psychic research, all four classical theorists proposed psychologies of personality that sought to recast scientific psychology to deal more adequately with human experience. These early humanistic psychologists were variously involved in debate with the doctrines of behaviorism and psychoanalysis then prevalent in American psychology, but their aim was a humanistic science of people, not an antiscientific humanistic psychology. Their psychologies of personality were in the spirit of secular humanism. (See Smith, 1984, for the historical account I draw on here.)

By fateful historical coincidence, humanistic psychology was being founded just as the counterculture of the flower children and drug-oriented hippies emerged as a phenomenon of the 1960s. Especially as typified by Esalen and encounter groups, the humanistic movement was essentially captured by the counterculture with its irrationalism, its hedonism and emphasis on the here and now with minimal baggage of moral commitments, its extreme individualism. Some survivors among the older generation of founders dropped out in dismay. And the irrationalist, mystical tendencies pressing from the counterculture found even the fuzzy boundaries of humanistic psychology confining, leading to the differentiation of transpersonal psychology, which just now is making its claim for status as an APA division. So when I urge the case for secular humanism, I am also calling for humanistic psychology to find common cause once more with the psychology of personality, now rising from the ashes of Mischel's (1968) situationism.

The omissions and exclusions from the humanistic psychology movement during the past quarter century are really quite surprising, given the movement's openness to a wide variety of approaches. Together with Henry Murray (1981), a surviving Saybrook participant now in his nineties who exemplifies more than anyone else a humanistic psychology in equal touch with biological science, psychodynamics, and creative literature but who is seldom regarded as within the humanistic movement, I think also of Isador Chein (1972), whose *Science of Behavior and the Image of Man* was among the most eloquent refutations of a mechanistic psychology, Skinnerian or otherwise. For all his Talmudic proclivities, Is Chein was very much the secular humanist but, again, he was never identified as a humanistic psychologist by those in the movement's mainstream. And I think of Erich Fromm, who as a "revisionist" in both Marxian and Freudian traditions won more popular attention than academic, but who offered in *Escape from Freedom* (1941) and *Man for Himself* (1947) a version of secular humanism that was as well articulated as any that has yet been put forward. (*Revisionism* is a good term in my lexicon, in contrast with dogmatic orthodoxy.) He too lacked recognition and honor in the humanistic psychology movement.

From a world perspective, the total neglect of Marxism by mainstream humanistic psychology is indeed an astonishing state of affairs. The publication in the 1930s of Marx's early, partly Hegelian manuscripts was a major intellectual event (see Bottomore, 1964), one that launched a major Marxist tradition of secular humanism, especially in Europe. Marx's dialectical conception of how man creates his own human nature in the process of acting in the world has an especially modern ring—in all respects except the sexist language.

And our recently gained sensitivity to sexist language calls attention to another major exclusion or omission from humanistic psychology: a female perspective, let alone a feminist one. This gap was particularly conspicuous at the San Francisco conference, at which women were a majority of the audience but only slightly visible on the platforms, except briefly in protest at the final plenary session. The feminist critique of implicitly male perspectives in mainstream psychology—and in humanistic psychology as it currently exists—is surely relevant to attaining understanding of what it is to be human. This-worldly secular humanism as a stance for humanistic psychology would foster concern for the experience and perspectives of both genders—and of gays too.

What It Means to Be Human: A Secular Origin Myth

Thus far, I have declared myself as a secular humanist, and pointed to serious omissions in humanistic psychology entailed in the underrepresentation of secular humanism. I will use the remainder of this occasion to sketch a framework for secular humanism that underlies my own sense of meaning, my personal response to the challenge of being human in our unique historical moment. The route I take is historical and speculative. A sophisticated Catholic colleague once branded it as my own "origin myth." So be it. As a view of our challenge and predicament, it is far from original, but for me, and perhaps for some of you, and for now, I think it is right.[1]

From the standpoint of a secular humanism, what does it mean to be human? This is surely the oldest, most central question known to human self-consciousness, and the core of any serious attempt to answer it must be that we are the sort of creatures who can frame such a question about ourselves.

In the dawn of self-consciousness in individual infancy and, speculatively, in the evolution of our species, self and interpreted world emerge together. Questions about human origins, about human nature, and about human fate have "always" been linked indissolubly with questions about the human significance of the world in which people live their lives. Or, rather, the content of human symbolic culture—the rich web of myth and ritual and folklore, then of religion and philosophy and the "humanities," and, just recently, of the natural, social, and psychological sciences—has "always" provided *answers* to these two kinds of questions of meaning. The questions themselves probably stayed implicit for the most part until urban civilizations developed conditions in which people became so complex cognitively that they could not take traditional answers for granted. When the culturally available answers become open to choice or doubt, the questions themselves become salient as, in our Western tradition, they did in pre-Socratic Greece, and as they have become especially salient for us today, with new force. In regard to questions, answers, and perspective, our present position is both unprecendentedly privileged and exceptionally vulnerable.

Privileged: As never before, we have ever-increasing stretches of the historical and cross-cultural record spread before us. As Malraux (1953) put it dramatically for the realm of art, those of us who have enjoyed a good education have access to a remarkably wide range of visions of human meaning—as never before. We are potentially free from the previously universal human condition of being *culture-bound,* of treating our own limited perspective in culture and history as the only right one, maybe the only possible one.

But vulnerable: Such freedom entails heavy costs and frightens us, as Kierkegaard (1944) put it most poignantly and Fromm (1941) and Rollo May (1977) have reminded us in more recent contexts. You and I share in the general plight. So many meanings! How is one to choose among them? By what charter can any particular answer to the perennial questions be taken as more persuasive, more valid, than the others? Science, the most modern myth, has deepened our predicament. It has eroded the older, anthropocentric meanings cast in an appropriately human scale, and in the view of many, it has not provided a satisfactory replacement. It is hard for us when the new answers to questions about the world, answers by Copernicus, Newton, and Darwin, dethrone humankind; it is worse when scientific accounts of human nature reduce humanness to terms no longer "anthropomorphic."

But our position of cross-historical, cross-cultural sophistication, at once privileged and vulnerable, contains at least the possibility of transcending the demoralizing relativism and attrition of meaning that it breeds. If we can only face the historical, cultural nature of human nature squarely, we might get beyond the static view of what it means to be human that fits a particular time and place but is bound to be wrong from any timeless, universal perspective. We might arrive at a view of what it means to be human in terms of process and context, one that still has a special place for what it means for *us* to be human here and now.

We know that wherever and whenever we find them, human beings seek meaning and create it, individually and collectively. To be human is to be engaged in a life infused with meaning. In the long eons of human prehistory spent in hunting-gathering bands—man, the hunter; woman, the gatherer—and in the dozen millennia of village or pastoral life, slowly evolving systems of unquestioned cultural meaning endowed individual lives with significance, made them livable in the face of unpredictable adversity and inevitable death. Over the past few centuries, these traditional frames of meaning have been shattered, and their successors in the brief episode of modernity seem too transient and humanly inadequate to save us from meaninglessness and cultural crisis. The thoughtful and articulate among us are well acquainted with meaninglessness by now, and we know that it is dehumanizing (see Bellah et al., 1985). If we take the fact seriously that people are intrinsically seekers and creators of meaning, we must regard the meaning of being human as intrinsically open, an unfolding, creative human project. In Clifford Geertz's (1973) happy phrase, *homo sapiens* is "the unfinished animal." In history and culture humankind participates in shaping its human nature.

Origins of Humanness

The perspectives that we have recently gained on human evolution make the boundary between the prehuman animal and the truly human more ambiguous for us, and make the distinctive features of humanness more remarkable. We have pushed our divergence from our closest primate cousins back some five million years or more. We have learned that our Pliocene ancestors could already walk bipedally and were first using, then making crude tools to help them as hunters and gatherers in the savannah long before they developed the big brains that underlie our present complexity of experience and behavior. We speculate (Washburn, 1959) that tool use and toolmaking—incipient material culture—gave evolutionary advantage to neural complexity. It is now plausible that material culture and distinctive human biology evolved interactively.

These speculations involving one feature of distinctive humanness—our technology—rest on the factual basis of dated sequences of bones and hearths and artifacts. The beginnings of language and symbolic culture leave no such traces until late in the game, dramatically with the flower-lined Neanderthal graves of about fifty thousand years ago, dating from about the same time that our own subspecies of *homo sapiens* was gaining prevalence. Human language, such as we now know it, must date from about then (see Harnad et al., 1976).

A date that recent—in evolutionary perspective only yesterday—fits the sudden efflorescence and diversification of Late Paleolithic culture, after the million years and more in which the simple Acheulian tool kit of crudely flaked stones was shared by all early human beings. About fifty thousand years ago, something extraordinary indeed happened, launching a process of cultural innovation, population expansion, and artistic-aesthetic objectification of human experience, with the high religious art of the Magdalenian cave paintings attained by nineteen thousand years ago. A new dynamic prehistory began that sweeps in its headlong trajectory to our own historic present.

The late date of the takeoff in human cultural development is a matter of fact, although the link to language remains conjectural. It is easy to imagine, however, that the attainment of true language by a few intercommunicating bands of hunter-gatherers must have struck the speakers as a quantum leap, akin to what Helen Keller experienced when it dawned upon her that *everything* has a name and can be talked about. Whenever and however it occurred—and occur it did, however miraculously—humanness as we know it was essentially established.

Let us consider the emergent situation of people newly possessed of true language. For more than a million years, the bands of Acheulian hunter-gatherers had been poised at the juncture of Nature and Culture. They had been part of Nature. Their slowly evolving culture of tools and fire and, at the boundaries of the last glaciation, of clothing and constructed shelter—also surely if conjecturally of social organization and protolinguistic communication—fed back to give a selective advantage to those whose bigger brains made them more adept at first using, then inventing culture. But this cultural adaptation within Nature was stable, with a universal sameness that approached the stereotyped behavior of other animal species.

Language, once attained, brought immense advantages. It facilitated the coordination of group activities. It provided the symbolic basis for distinctive human social organization in family and kinship. It made deliberate instruction of the young feasible in new depth, taking fuller advantage of the long period of human infancy and childhood. And with its culturally transmitted symbol system, it provided the framework and tools for thought, including "time-binding" in Korzybski's (1941) apt phrase: fore-thought and afterthought. People could now make plans, undertake commitments, and recognize and correct errors—all essential adaptive ingredients of human social life as we know it.

But there were inherent consequences of becoming a speaking, thinking creature—side effects, if you will—that provided no obvious evolutionary advantage yet are central to the situation of being human and our experience of it. One is an aspect of the elaborated experience of selfhood. Our understanding of the emergence of selfhood in individual development is becoming more firmly based in fact and more differentiated than George Herbert Mead's (1934) classic speculations, but Mead was surely right in emphasizing the *reflexiveness* of language—we hear and interpret our own words as others do—as crucial for the human capacity and propensity to take the self as object, figuratively to look at the self as if through the eyes of others. Mead argued persuasively that reflective selfhood is "functional," in that the implicated ability to "take the role of the other" is essential for our participation in the coordinated activities of organized social life. So it surely is. But consider the costs: human self-consciousness breaks the unity of human beings and Nature and, when forethought and afterthought are added as gifts of language, the human existential predicament emerges in full force. As self-conscious human beings talking to one another and ourselves, we and our forebears for some fifty thousand years or more have faced the cognitive puzzles of whence we came into the world, why we are here, and what happens when we die. Of course, this is not just a matter of curiosity released by our newfound ability to formulate questions. Primarily through language, we have become *persons*, linked to other persons whom we love and care for in a web of "intersubjective meaning" (see Schutz, 1967; Berger & Luckmann, 1966). The inevitability of eventual death for self and loved ones, and the unpredictability of death from famine, disease, accident, predation, or human assault become grounds not for momentary animal terror but for potentially unremitting human anguish. The search for meaning gains the urgency of a life-and-death matter.[2]

Culture, Selfhood, and Existential Terror

Yet this mainly familiar account is wrong in one obvious respect: Contrary to the old myth, our forebears cannot have been cast out of Nature's Garden of Eden in one sudden event of "birth trauma." Even if in broad evolutionary perspective the final full attainment of language competence happened rapidly once the unique structural/generative principles of human language had been hit upon, self-conscious selfhood with its new urgency to find supportive meaning in the face of creature mortality cannot have appeared all at once. If so, the symbolic resources of language-bearing human communities could be developed to meet the need for meaning as it arose. Thus emerged the myriad cultural worlds of myth, ritual, and religion, which provided the traditional answers to the question of what it means to be human. They were good answers, proclaiming to each communicating tribal group its value as The People; legitimizing the group's way of life as ordained by the ancestors; giving intelligible meaning to the exigencies of life and death; providing appropriate ways in which individual and community could participate in the encouragement of auspicious outcomes and the avoidance of ominous ones. The traditional mythic answers could not eliminate anguish and terror, but they could give it intelligible shape; they could make the blows of fate more bearable to the victim and more endurable to the members of the victim's kindred and community. They allowed life to go on quite satisfactorily between emergencies.

These mythic systems typically drew a distinction between the commonplace objects and meanings of everyday life and *sacred* objects and meanings of transcendent power and value. The commonplace and everyday seemed to be sustained in their human significance by their contact with and participation in a realm of the sacred and numinous.

I have stressed common features of these cultural systems, but, in fact, we know that their accounts of the meaning of being human, and the ways of life to which they lent significance and support, were enormously various. For millennia each self-enclosed system provided a secure, unchallenged interpretation of human life. Each system was open to such novelty and change as altered circumstances might call for, yet was conservative of tradition, the source of its authority. The wide divergences among these cultural worlds occasioned no problem. The Babel of language differentiation helped to isolate the meaning systems of the local tribal groups. And when significant contact did occur, each cultural group had the ethnocentric self-confidence to reject foreign conceptions and lifeways as barbarous or subhuman (while borrowing or accepting culture features when convenient or unavoidable).

The Fact of Progress and the Idea of Progress

Over the millennia what can only be described in retrospect by the unfashionable terms *progress* and *cultural evolution* manifestly occurred. Throughout the world people came to cultivate food crops and domesticate animals. With agricultural surpluses came towns and cities, more complex social and political organization, civilization. And as we look back on the last half millennium of Western history—a tiny fraction of human evolution that began parochially but came to engulf the whole human world—there was indeed dramatic progress, according to the value standards of the major actors in the course of events. (To be sure, other peoples and their ways of life were regarded as expendable and fell disastrously by the wayside.) Knowledge increased, first in the recovery of the texts of the Ancients and in the invention of printing for the many, then in the new takeoff of scientific discovery. Technology developed, first in its own independent trajectory, then increasingly as a by-product, and then again as an explicit goal of progress in science. We are all acutely aware of the mixed blessings that have ensued in a globe that has shrunk as "life-space" for humankind, in which (in regard to population growth) our very success as a biological species raises doubts of impending failure, and in which previously unimagined human powers for destruction put the species and the entire biosphere in acute jeopardy.

The era of Progress—of headlong change that the principal actors consensually regarded as for the better—leaves humankind in a common worldwide predicament, sharing as never before a common fate, although divisions of rampant nationalism and ethnic conflict continue unabated. The old sheltered plural worlds of culture-boundedness are fading away in every quarter. But while Progress was undermining the parochial, timeless certainties—the traditional mythic and religious worlds—for a time it provided an alternative source of hope. People who were caught up in Progress lost touch with the sacred, but for the time being they hardly needed it. Progress itself served for them as a source of *transcendent* meaning that they could take for granted: a source of meaning beyond the desperate trivialities of everyday life and death and disappointment. The future came to justify the present; human essence was interpreted as human *potentiality*, whether individually or collectively. In grand social theory, both Hegel and Marx found meaning in history as progress toward an idealized state: the self-realization of the Absolute for Hegel; the classless society for Marx. Darwinian evolutionary theory not only installed the doctrine of progress in biology, it provided a brilliant account of the purposeful, beautifully designed world in terms of nonpurposeful processes in keeping with mechanistic science. And businessmen and politicians could take faith in economic growth, "the bigger the better," a crasser version of Progress.

Now, of course, we know better—or the more thoughtful among us do. The horrors of two world wars, the Holocaust, the human costs of totalitarian utopianism, the preview of nuclear catastrophe at Hiroshima and Nagasaki, the foreshadowing of a closed, exhausted, polluted planet, the cheapening of traditional ethical and aesthetic values in commercial mass society—these products of "progress" have brought the idea of Progress into ill repute.[3] We can no longer share the secular faith that the future will continually be better for our offspring and for theirs in turn. Our science fiction gets morbid and bleak.

What it means to be human, I have been trying to suggest, has been an open venture, a developing human project. The core of what it has continually meant is a matter of process rather than of essence. It lies in the endless human quest for meaning and its creation in symbolic culture. Hitherto, the meanings that have sustained people in the self-awareness of their mortality have transcended the mundane. People have attributed their sources of meaning to a sacred realm of human values and purposes read into the supposed general scheme of things. But the traditional mythic world in its countless versions is no longer accessible to many of us, at least in a state of traditional innocence. When even the idea of Progress fails us as a source of hope, we find ourselves to our dismay back in the original position of the First People, Adam and Eve, contemplating their mortality. We face a new set of dangers and opportunities, to be sure, but we are also blessed with new resources for understanding and coping.

Responses to Our Predicament

In this predicament, social scientists and humanists and prophets of popular culture would variously lead us in all possible directions, urging upon us a cacophony of competing meanings. Some social critics in the humanistic camp see the very enterprise of civilization as itself a disease (e.g., Mumford, 1967, 1970; Brown, 1959, 1973). The regressive route seems to have a strong appeal to post-Freudian romantics. Humankind is out of touch with Nature, and, even at its best, our life of reason leads us toward destruction of the texture of natural life. We should retreat from the city and the machine, retreat from our delusory self-consciousness, and trust the animal life of instinct. The theme has been familiar at least since D. H. Lawrence.

But just where did people get off the track? There has been tension in human transactions with Nature ever since Paleolithic times when we began talking with one another and ourselves. The dawn of language *was* a portentous, risky break with Nature, and the myth of Original Sin does symbolize something deeply problematic about our footing in the world. Yet our very nature as "incomplete animals" requires culture for our viability, let alone our fulfillment. Once we set out on our remarkable course, agriculture, villages, cities, civilization, industry, and science all seem steps in a trajectory toward greater power in the world and greater understanding of our place in it. Even if we could turn back from our adventure in humanness, few of us or our offspring could survive the trip.

Some prophets, such as B. F. Skinner (1971), deify the natural sciences. According to Skinner, our time-honored interpretation of our own humanness in terms of a life of intention, purpose, and commitment—a drama of good and evil and human responsibility, of tragedy and comedy—is just as mythical as our former vision of the environing world in these human terms. To gird ourselves for survival, he says, we must conquer these illusions and program our own behavior with the same dispassionate intelligence that Skinnerians apply to the training of animals. But in asking us to forsake our conceptions of human freedom and dignity, Skinner would have us give up the very aspects of our self-conception that many of us have come to value most in our humanness, aspects that help *constitute* our humanness, given the reflexivity of our nature. There is nothing in the scientific strategy that forces this denial of meaning upon us. Skinner's dehumanized reinterpretation of human nature, if it gains acceptance, contributes to our cultural crisis of meaninglessness rather than to its solution.

Meanwhile, a great many ordinary citizens in the relatively advantaged Western world, especially members of the affluent middle class, go their own individualistic way seeking success, pleasure, and self-development. Robert Bellah and his colleagues (1985) have recently made a detailed analysis of the pervasiveness of this pattern, according to which we account for even our more altruistic or principled acts by straining our utilitarian vocabulary of cost-benefit payoffs. They see our contemporary "expressive individualism" as a pathological reflection of our modern loss of embeddedness in community, in historical tradition, and in mythical structures of meaning. What is especially relevant to us as psychologists is that they see psychotherapy and the human potential movement as expressing and accentuating this state of affairs, setting a model for value-free, uncommitted human relationships justified in terms of self-interest. Insofar as selfhood can flourish only in a context of committed human ties within a tradition of shared meanings that anchor individual lives in goals and projects beyond their own immediate interest ("transcendence" in a sense that I firmly believe people require), the individualistic "solution" does not really work. We consequently see it as having to be bolstered by all manner of narcotics, distractions, and palliatives.

In the recent proliferation of cults and the occult, in the charismatic movement in the established churches, in the new appeal of Christian fundamentalism, it is not hard to see the equivalents of the Ghost Dance of the Plains Indians at the end of their cultural tether, or the cargo cults of the beleaguered Pacific Islanders: messianic bursts of nativistic revival, desperately reasserting traditional meanings that are felt to be in mortal danger. To the nonbeliever, these too smack more of symptoms than of cure, although we should remember that our Christian era began with the emergent predominance of just one such messianic cult among many competitors in the faltering days of the late classical world.

Religious and Secular Alternatives

Indeed, the religious alternative has to be taken seriously. We have no evidence that human beings as a species and in the long run are capable of living coherent human lives without a religious frame of meaning. It seems to me close to certain that we are stunted and thwarted unless the meaning of our individual lives can be interwoven with a cultural system of beliefs that has strong social support, probably traditional, a system of beliefs that establishes "objective" values for us beyond our individual self-interested preferences. Only saints and heroes can build meaningful lives all on their own, and even that is dubious.

The criticism of American expressive individualism that I cited from Bellah and his colleagues points implicitly toward a major role for religion in the restoration of community and commitment in modern life. The philosopher Alasdair MacIntyre (1981) writes from a similar though more pessimistic diagnosis in his justly acclaimed book, *After Virtue*. After a closely argued exposition asserting that our fragmented individualistic society has lost the intellectual and social base in tradition and community that makes coherent moral discourse possible, MacIntyre (1981, pp. 244–45) concludes by drawing a cautious parallel between our times and

the epoch in which the Roman empire declined into the Dark Ages. . . . A crucial turning point in that earlier history occurred when men and women of good will turned aside from the task of shoring up the Roman *imperium* and ceased to identify the continuation of civility and moral community with the maintenance of that *imperium*. What they set themselves to achieve instead—often not recognising fully what they were doing—was the construction of new forms of community within which the moral life could be sustained so that both morality and civility might survive the coming ages of barbarism and darkness. If my account of our moral condition is correct, we ought to conclude that for some time now we too have reached that turning point. What matters at this stage is the construction of local forms of community within which civility and the intellectual and moral life can be sustained through the new dark ages which are already upon us. And if the tradition of the virtues was able to survive the horrors of the last dark ages, we are not entirely without grounds for hope. This time however the barbarians are not waiting beyond the frontiers; they have already been governing us for quite some time. And it is our lack of consciousness of this that constitutes part of our predicament. We are waiting not for a Godot, but for another—doubtless very different—St. Benedict.

Actually, it is unfair to identify MacIntyre so closely with the religious prescription. His emphasis is on the desperation of our plight, and on the need for radical reconstruction of the basis for moral community. It would not be surprising, however, for the "very different" St. Benedict for whom he says we are waiting also to arrive under religious auspices.

Maybe our moral plight is as desperate as MacIntyre asserts. Certainly his book, like Bellah's, is a good piece of consciousness-raising. For my part, I continue to hope without much optimism that aspects of our almost physical plight—the prospects of nuclear Armageddon and planetary depletion and pollution—may conceivably provide humankind with the challenge to transcend its historical shortsightedness and collective stupidity. In this very realistic context, one wholly without historical precedent, I fear that the meanings of being human that have served us so long and so well—the mythic and religious ones handed down to us by tradition—no longer give us good guidance or dependable support, even though they symbolize important truths of human life. The problems of the real world can surely provide enough high drama to engage us and make our lives meaningful, if our imaginations can only be sufficiently aroused to get us involved.

And herein lies the main reason for my promoting a secular humanism. I see it as a mode of collective self-conception that potentially empowers us to cope more effectively with our awesome problems of *this* world. The historical reconstruction of how we got into our present jam, the main subject of this chapter, *can* serve as a meaning-bestowing myth, at least for some of us. The story of human life thus far reads like a long picaresque novel. Now the plot thickens, and it is hard not to believe we are moving toward a denouement. This time, we cannot count on Progress. Our fate depends, and more and more of us know it, upon our own human actions, intelligent and compassionate or the contrary. *If* we can manage to solve the interrelated ecological and human problems defined by exponential trends that seem to be carrying us to catastrophe and *if* we can avoid nuclear holocaust and find real peace, we will have transformed human nature as we know it—a transformation that the early Karl Marx would have understood.[4] Commitment on the part of each of us to do our utmost toward meeting the momentous challenge would indeed be a giant step toward the adult, responsible conduct of our lives.

Some Grounds for Hope

In rising to this challenge, which is also a challenge to critical, self-conscious social and personal reconstruction, we can take heart in remarkable recent changes in how we conceive of our humanness, changes that are still at an early stage of being worked out in actual social life: gains in the recognized humanness of women, of minorities, and of Third World peoples, both in the humanity that they claim and espouse for themselves and in the humanity they are accorded by others in what had been the mainstream of Progress. Enormous injustice remains, but we have certainly gained the basis for *hope* in the substantial advance in our conception of what justice requires.

I say "our" conception, but the grounds for hope lie especially in the transformed meaning of "our." In times past, the "we" in such discussions were the more or less enlightened passengers on the train of Progress, who sometimes exhorted one another toward more inclusive definitions of humanity. Today, "we" include those who were formerly "others," who for some time have been making their own—our own—claims and, in gaining self-respect, have earned the respect of all of us.

The times may be bleak—at the petty concrete level, I'm appalled at the enormous success Mr. Reagan has achieved in most of his regressive ideological objectives—but we have the privilege of being participants in what may be a profound revision of the meaning of being human. We have become the people we are by a long hard road. The reconstructed "scientific" story of this journey is just as miraculous and awe inspiring as the accounts of Creation in religious myth. The tragedy and comedy, the pathos and glory of our earthly life include the fact that our common human project of self-understanding is also one of collective self-development and reconstruction. There is so much to do! Let us get on with the agenda.

Notes

1. What follows is adapted from Smith (1978c), probably a safe bit of self-plagiarism since it was obscurely published in Australia. I have refocused and updated the discussion.
2. See Becker (1973) for a brilliant account of how this search has participated in the creation of human culture. What follows is in accord with his story, and partly indebted to it.
3. For the rise and fall of the idea of progress, see Bury (1920) and Nisbet (1980).
4. The biophysicist and polymath John Platt (1966) made this point two decades ago.

6

Metapsychology, Politics, and Human Needs

Can the study and criticism of politics be based on psychology? Or, in important respects, ought we to look at the relationship from the other end of the tube? My intent in this somewhat fragmentary essay is to help to clarify our thinking about this perennial arena of controversy, as it is focused on questions of human motivation. The volume for which it was written (Fitzgerald, 1977) is only one more round of discussion of the topic felicitously named by Graham Wallas (1909) in the first decade of the century in his book *Human Nature and Politics,* a title resurrected (with a minor variation) by Davies (1963) about a decade ago. What has happened in the intellectual development of our disciplines since Wallas and Davies to change the terms of discussion? *Have* there been developments that warrant reconsideration?

The New Context for Theorizing

As a social psychologist, I am keenly aware of two major developments from the outside that affect my field, each of which requires, I think, a fundamental reorientation of its agenda. I am still very much caught up myself in the attempt to digest them; many of my colleagues seem to remain blissfully unaware of the changed context. Both call for a reformulation of our questions about human needs and politics. One is the decline of positivism as a prescriptive, even dogmatic philosophy of science. The other is the opening of radically new perspectives on the emergence of human nature in the biology of evolution—now a "sociobiology" (Wilson, 1975). The first development, a liberating one, is abstract and metatheoretical; the second, also liberating to the imagination, is empirical though still highly speculative. It has taken me much working through to realize, partly, the far-reaching implications of each of these developments; I can only begin to suggest their implications for our present topic. The substantial task of making the implications explicit, and elaborating them in relation to evidence and to critical thought, is for the future.

First, very briefly, about the collapse of positivism as a consensual, prescriptive frame for the human sciences. This shift in basic assumptions has been so widely heralded and so often discussed that I can best help the reader who seeks to catch up by calling attention to four representative recent works that among them cite the relevant theoretical and critical literature in its bearing upon psychology from somewhat different perspectives: an article by Buss (1975) that summarizes the attack on positivism in psychology in very short compass; a book edited by Israel and Tajfel (1972) critical of modern social psychology from European perspectives, especially those influenced by Marxism; another by Harré and Secord (1972) reflecting for social psychology the British tradition of analytic philosophy that stemmed from Wittgenstein; and the widely read synthesis by Berger and Luckmann (1966) of ideas from the European phenomenological tradition and the American symbolic interactionist one.

A generation ago, when I shared in launching the political behavior movement in political science, positivism—especially in its Vienna variety—was the regnant assumptive framework in the social and behavioral sciences. But it was a peculiar feature of positivism that it *denied* that it was an assumptive framework at all, let alone one among many conceivable and potentially legitimate ones. Cleaving to the model of the physical sciences as they understood it, the positivists thought to eliminate metaphysics as "meaningless," and to pursue questions of human behavior in the spirit of the physical sciences, with an apparatus of operational definitions and the so-called hypothetico-deductive method.

We have since learned that the positivist interpretation of physics was essentially mythical, and that there is no avoiding prior assumptions or stipulations of one kind or another (including, possibly, positivist ones) if we are to formulate scientific questions, constitute scientific data, and establish criteria according to which we let our data help us answer our questions. To recognize the arbitrariness of positivism's dogmatic exclusions is especially liberating for our treatment of such inherently human topics as politics. If we wish the advantages of quasi cumulativeness and corrigibility that science often has to offer, of course, we are not liberated from evidence (as some neohumanists in psychology would have it). We are alerted, however, to the importance of our assumptions in determining what we will regard as evidence, as data. We are alerted to the importance of metatheory. After introducing the new evolutionary perspective on human nature, I will return to examine how "needs" and related motivational concepts are entangled in our metatheoretical commitments.

The new perspective on human evolution radically undercuts the previous sharp distinction between Nature and Culture that social scientific theory shared with mythic thought (Lévi-Strauss, 1966), and requires of us a novel, essentially dialectic view of the nature of human nature. I am thinking, of course, of the great expansion of the time span of human evolution, as we now understand it, to as much as three million years when our short, small-brained forebears arose on two feet and began to find rocks useful to help them get their livelihood. I am thinking especially of the prevailing interpretation that it was *because* using rocks (and presumably more perishable sticks) as tools made having a bigger, brighter brain pay off—there were now clever, useful things to be done with it—protopeople evolved rapidly to become the big-brained, behaviorally complex creatures that we know today. Protohumanity's capacities and performances as tool users (and thus as bearers of culture) entered into the constitution of biological human nature.

So much seems reasonably firm. More speculatively (here I find Geertz's [1973] reinterpretation helpful), it seems plausible that along with tool use, people's symbolic capacities and performances were also evolving in parallel, powered by a similar selective advantage. But the relics that remain for us to observe are stones and bones and fire hearths, not indicators of symbols and beliefs and rituals—until just the day before yesterday, some fifty thousand years ago, when late Neanderthal burial sites show persuasive evidence of belief in an afterlife (Marshak, 1976). Along with symbolism and, specifically, language evolved self-conscious awareness and, presumably, the complexities of selfhood-in-community. My point is that our standing as a social, even a political animal is as much part of our distinctive animal nature as it is of our human nature. We have evolved as organisms over the eons because emergent culture helped shape our biological human nature. One used to have to be a Lamarckian or a mystic to believe such things; now such speculation seems called for by the findings of hard science, and is made the more plausible by the great expansion of our time scale. People have participated in the creation of their biological human nature in a dialectical process of spiraling interaction with their worlds.

The distinction between Nature and Culture remains useful as a polarity, if not as a dichotomy. In the course of the biological evolution catalyzed by Culture, people's biology came ever increasingly to depend upon cultural learning to fill in the content provided for by biological templates. A good example is the case of language, in which, after Chomsky and his successors, we seem to have to think of each human toddler in every known society as predisposed to *invent* a language for him or herself constructed on a limited set of universal organizing principles, resembling in its specifics the features prevalent in the language community in which the child is immersed. Again a melding of Nature and Culture, presumably the result of long evolution. But the structural propensity, the reaching out to develop childish language and to use it creatively, has become part of our Nature, whereas the particular variant symbol system each child acquires is a matter of Culture.

The Concept of Human Needs

What do these considerations, philosophically abstract or phylogenetically remote, have to do with our topic of human needs and politics? I think they affect the very terms of our discussion. Let us begin with a look at the concept of human needs, where clean semantics are hampered by the accretions of long and loose employment in psychology.

If we try to keep the word *need* close to its everyday meanings, we use it to refer to *requirements* of the person as a biological and human system for substances or relationships or states of affairs, in the absence of which the person fails to develop or to function normally and may even falter or die. Developmental psychologists do speak of the needs of children in this vein; Harlow (1962) taught us about the monkey need for contact comfort, the absence of which leads to specifiably defective development.

Note that this narrow and I think proper use fits well with a causal-functional, "objective," natural science context, and that, further, the reference is not inherently "motivational"; it does not necessarily have to do with the organization and direction of action. I can need things that I do not want: thus particular vitamins. I can want and seek things I do not need: thus, the sweetness of saccharine or maybe the highs of a psychedelic drug. Over a considerable range—just how big a range is important, moot, and a matter for empirical clarification—needs *are* linked to motives, as a result of long stabilities in the context of biological evolution. In regard to most of the familiar biological essentials that require effective directed behavior if the species is to survive and thrive, we have come to be creatures that for the most part want what we need. Otherwise we wouldn't be here. But it is dangerous to extrapolate uncritically to the "farther reaches" of human motivation that touch on politics. Perhaps it may help to remind ourselves of Fromm's (1941) equally simplistic though provocative conception under the rubric of "social character": we are also creatures that, in some other respects, have come to want what "society" needs.

Henry Murray's (1938) familiar and useful catalogue of human needs, on which I cut my eye teeth as a psychologist—n Achievement, n Sentience, n Sex, n Aggression, n Dominance, n Succorance, and the rest—

does not use the word in the foregoing strict sense. He offered rather a general taxonomy of classes of human *motives,* similar to McDougall's (1908), on whose doctrine of instincts he drew, but more differentiated and with the biological claim explicit in the term *instinct* now disavowed. In the present context, Murray's choice of the term *need* seems purely arbitrary. As with "needs" in the strict sense, however, Murray's list of motives is to be understood for the most part in a causal-functional, potentially positivistic framework. He wanted a chemistry of human action that amounted to a causal analysis. But he also wanted to assimilate Jung and Freud, and was an artist in psychological *interpretation.* As a confirmed holist who emphasized the proactive rather than the reactive aspects of human nature, he fought positivism valiantly, and it would be grossly unfair thus to pigeonhole his motivational concepts.

In contrast with objective need is subjective wish, desire, or want, all of which are motivational terms that find their home in a metapsychological framework of meaningful human action. They assume the peculiar human property of *intentionality* that May (1977) has emphasized in interpreting the European existential tradition to American psychology. They are terms from everyday language that many of us want also to use in our more formal psychological theorizing because they seem to provide a natural phrasing for the self-direction of action among the thoughtful yet passionate symbolizing creatures that we have in fact become. But how are such terms to be employed in the causal-functional framework that many of us wish also to retain even after the passing of its monopolistic predominance with the era of positivism? The philosophical and psychological puzzles here are far from resolved; they are just beginning to be clarified.

We now see, thanks particularly to Loevinger (1966, 1976) and Holt (1972), that Freud was thoroughly confused and ambivalent on this matter. Throughout his long intellectual career, he appears to have been torn between clinical formulations in terms of wish and meaningful conflict (to which his addition of an unconscious dimension was invaluable) and "metapsychological" formulations cast in mechanistic metaphors drawn from the first and second laws of thermodynamics, with which he became enamored in his early physiological training in the antivitalist school of Helmholz and Du Bois-Reymond. The mechanistic and humanistic sides of Freud do not fit comfortably with one another.

In light of modern information science and of developments in physics, the nineteenth-century view of mechanism on which Freud drew is definitely outmoded and no longer useful even for metaphorical psychological purposes (the concept of psychic "energy" is a snare). So we need to give some care to sorting out Freud's important clinical contributions to the interpretation of meaningful action if we are to reconstruct a psychoanalytic psychology that is useful in the study of politics. Freud's concept of instinct *(Trieb)* was an unanalyzed amalgam of mechanism and meaning. We are still struggling to bring these two frames together; Freudian metapsychology does not give us a solution.

To review the terminological spectrum in metatheoretical perspective, human needs in the strict sense are a matter for empirical determination that is objective in principle but difficult in fact. The version of need theory that has seemed most attractive for application to politics is that of Maslow (1954), whose concept merges the notion of motive with that of require- ment. The patron saint of humanistic psychology, Maslow was no positiv- ist, but he was quite confused about how to relate the biological and the humanistic aspects of his thinking. We will return to his views later on. The term *drive* has been customarily used for biologically given motives like those involved in hunger, thirst, and elimination, but drives so con- ceived and emphasized as fundamental by positivists lie far from the realm of politics.

Needs, Wants, and Politics

Politics as its practice is understood by participants, and as it has been formulated and criticized in normative political theory since Plato and Aristotle—politics as political relations and political action, not just "polit- ical behavior"—requires primary reference to human wants, desires, and wishes, and their conflict and/or mutual adjustment in the context of culturally transmitted but humanly modifiable institutions. Politics as a significant component of human history, and political theory as a major perspective on it make sense only within an assumptive view of human action that has room for intentions and meanings. The positivist assump- tions tended to reduce politics to mere power and manipulation, a cynical view that can be self-confirming. Our liberation from positivist dogmatism gives us the freedom to take other possibilities seriously, and perhaps to encourage their development in social life.

But I am a psychologist, not a philosopher or professionally a political advocate. Causal and functional analysis are my stock in trade, not interpretation or "hermeneutics" (a term I encountered more recently than I like to admit). I see the primary context for political analysis as falling toward the latter pole: first and foremost, politics is to be regarded as meaningful historical action. So for me the great puzzle is the one on which Freud stumbled, and as I will argue, Maslow, too: how to link causal and functional analysis in psychology (to which the term *need* belongs) with a view of people as potentially responsible political actors. Elsewhere (Smith, 1973b), I have dealt with parts of the problem more concretely, less self-consciously and owlishly. Here I must admit to persisting puzzlement. The challenge is to find a metatheoretical stance that meets the pragmatic test of putting our thoughts and findings in some defensibly consistent order and allows us to bring evidence to bear on understanding and in humanizing politics.

Let me venture a provisional attempt at linkage in midstream, which will also serve to reintroduce the evolutionary perspective that as I asserted is a second reason for fundamental revision in our thinking. When we inquire about need, we are adopting an *extrinsic* perspective on the human actor. The actor may be pushed by drives or pulled by wishes and wants; naively he or she does not *know* about needs, although individual or cultural conceptions of need may have a part in the formation and in the justification of wants. The technical concept of need belongs to the biological or social scientist, not to the motivated person.

There are two ways in which needs *sensu strictu* can educate wants. One is the slow, enduring way of biological evolution: the feedback process that governs genetic selection. Creatures that go on wanting things that interfere with fulfilling their needs or do not come to want the things they need are likely in the very long run to have their genes dropped from the genetic pool of the species. The other is the much more rapid and flexible joint process of individual learning and collective cultural change that became possible on a grand scale when protopeople crossed the divide to become selves linked in shared systems of symbolization. It is hard to imagine how any human needs that did not remain constant over the long eons of eolithic and possibly paleolithic time—the Pleistocene—could have got translated into drives or wants embedded in the genetic code: people ceased living as dispersed bands of hunters and gatherers so recently, and biological evolution is so slow. Most needs that have characterized human beings distinctively as peasants for some ten millennia and as citizens or subjects in historic times must be mediated by culture and only indirectly by biology (insofar as our biology now requires for our survival that we remain culture-bearing animals).

Entirely new needs (system requirements for human survival) are emerging that as yet have very little psychological representation as motive, wish, or want. Given unprecedented and absolute new powers of mutual destruction, we *need* to learn to live more peaceably with one another than ever before in the course of human history—but we have not sufficiently learned to want to. Now that our technological culture has given our species equally unprecedented short-run biological success in populating the earth (the preprogrammed objective of every species), we need to discover ways of calling a halt before we spoil everything for ourselves and many other species with which we are interdependent; we also need to learn to live within the limited means of our planet. But for the most part, the motives, the wants, even the knowledge required remain to be developed. Because we are not just biologically programmed behaviors but, rather—thanks to the special cultural biology of human evolution—conscious actors, there remains the possibility, the *hope* (a legitimate word, even in social science, when we are talking about people) that we can develop the knowledge, wishes, and intentions that might save us, and find ways of carrying them into effective collective action.

Of course, this becomes a matter of politics. The human needs are there, but it will take politics and luck for them to be translated into motives, knowledge, and action. Because we are symbolizing, sometimes thoughtful creatures, and because, collectively, we have so recently invented the cultural mutation of science, of systematically collaborative evidential thought, we have a chance of meeting our novel and urgent needs. We have a chance denied to our forebears of using the immediate and powerful informational feedback that is now available to us. That is what the polymath John Platt (1966) was talking about in a powerful polemic.

There is a much-bandied Marxist concept that has always bothered me by its presumption: "false consciousness." What Marx had in mind, of course, is the situation that has made Marxist prophecies go so far awry. The proletariat do not know their own *needs*. They do not recognize their "objective" class interests, at least as Marx and Engels had diagnosed them. Marcuse (1964) has carried this idea much farther in his portrayal of the extent to which contemporary American society has seduced and co-opted people to participate in their own alienation.

I am ambivalent about "false consciousness" in two respects. First, it presupposes a "correct" diagnosis of need and interest, which is likely to be a dogmatic diagnosis. Even with the best scientific input, the diagnosis of need is bound to be approximate, fallible, and debatable. Democratic process recognizes this, and gives priority to people's own wishes and wants, while leaving channels open for persuasion and the infusion of evidence to bring wishes and wants more in tune with needs. Marxist societies mostly do not.

And, second, some manner or degree of "false consciousness" would seem to be the normal human condition. Freud taught us that much of our reasoning is also, or maybe only, rationalization. We know that for eons people lived in culturally evolved worlds of myth and magic that comforted them in and lent meaning to their predicament as mortals become vulnerably aware of their mortality (Becker, 1973). "False consciousness"? There was a very real emergent human need for comfort and meaning, which the lost magical world supplied. I do not think that our privileged scientific worldview is just one myth on all fours with others, but it has its mythic aspects. The concept "false consciousness" suggests a "true consciousness" as the norm. It is rather a shifting ideal, a moving target, to which we can aspire. If we think we have reached it, we have fallen into the trap of becoming "true believers."

The evolutionary perspective leads us to a cross-cultural one, since the cultural evolution that first paralleled biological evolution, then largely (because of its much greater flexibility) superseded it, occurred in separated groups of people who were in little interchange with one another. Can we talk sensibly—cross-historically as well as cross-culturally—about panhuman needs? We should try, but clearly there are limits. We have already seen one source of limits: needs arise as much from the historical situation of people as from their biological nature. We can see new human needs emerging today. Needs once valid have lost their relevance. For example, the Plains Indian culture that flowered between the arrival of the horse with the Spaniards and the arrival of the locomotive with the Yankees depended on the numberless buffalo herds. The herds once gone (in Murray's language, *n* Buffalo?), all the needs intrinsic to this heroic way of life collapsed, with the setting in which it was possible to meet them for a while. The culture, and the needs of people in *that* culture, can never be resurrected.

Cross-cultural immersal led the great humanistic anthropologist Dorothy Lee (1959) to raise in a classic paper the question "Are basic needs ultimate?" Her quarrel was with functional anthropologists who followed Malinowski in seeing culture as an answer to a list of needs, a controversy quite akin to the issues addressed in this chapter. She did not admire the borrowings of anthropologists from psychology, especially of the behaviorist variety then prevalent, and her complaint took the form of challenging two assumptions that she found widespread: "(1) the premise that action occurs in answer to a need or a lack; and (2) the premise that there is a list" [of basic needs to replace the old lists of instincts] (p. 70).

We have already encountered grounds for both objections: the loose or absent linkage between need, want, and action (and the different assumptive frames in which these terms are most at home), and the dubious stability of human needs across historical settings. Her proposed alternative introduces a concept that is new to our discussion: that of diverse cultural *values* pursued for their own sake with no sense of lack, as orienting features of an intact way of life. Cultural—and personal—values pose an alternative to "need" that, like other intentional terms such as want and wish, fit with a proactive, humanistic interpretation of human life as meaningful. At least in Lee's writing, *value* more than *wish* or *want* connotes commitment to a desirable, not merely desired, order of things that seems entirely objective to the participants in an intact culture.

Like many anthropologists, Lee valued as good in itself the diversity of value realized among human cultures. She embraced cultural relativism as a kind of absolute: one should admire and cherish each culture on its own terms, not analyze or criticize it in terms of external standards. Aesthetically, that is an admirable stance. Ethically, it doesn't quite work; in the test case for the previous generation, we cannot bring ourselves to appreciate Nazi Germany on *its* own terms. And conceptually or pragmatically, there are also problems. Think once more of the Sioux, or of the other vanishing unlettered peoples from among whom she draws her own examples. In a Platonic eternity, these cultures remain admirable as each expressing one variant of human potentiality. In the real, conditional, historical world, some of these variants remain viable, others have become obsolete, while new possibilities for human valuing are emerging.

In a dialectical view of emerging human nature, we can accept the critical message of relativism (to be cautious about the blinders entailed in our own ethnocentrism) but note that real limits on the range of conceivable human values that can be realized by actual human groups are set by historical contingency, by human genetics, and by the particular interactive historical process by which each culture-bearing group has arrived at its pattern for living. Values conceived in Lee's terms are both intentional and motivational concepts, whereas needs are not. As Rokeach (1973) has particularly emphasized, values can be a unifying concept in the social sciences, playing, I think, a role much more central than that of needs.

I bring our discussion to a more concrete focus by looking briefly at two recent conceptualizations of human needs that have been applied in political analysis: Maslow's (1954) proposed hierarchy of needs, which has been brought to bear on political theory and data by Knutson (1972) among others, and the need for personal control, which Renshon (1974) has recently related to political efficacy and participation. The first uses a broad brush to sketch a general framework for human motivation; the second treats a more limited topic of direct political relevance, one that draws upon an active area of research interest in contemporary psychology. Both are representative of contemporary need theory as it is being applied to politics.

Maslow's Theory of Human Needs

Maslow's theory is very widely known and cited, often loosely applied, and almost never tested. This is a frustrating state of affairs. His conception makes explicit his view of the linkage between need, intended in the strict sense, and motivation. When needs are satisfied, they are not motivating. Only when they are unfulfilled do they become motives. Since needs are human biological requirements, moreover, their satisfaction is essential for normal psychological development and mental health. A further specification is distinctive of his theory: needs fall into a natural hierarchy of preemptiveness, such that only when needs more basic in the hierarchy are met does or can the person attend to higher needs; only then do the higher needs become motivating.

The need hierarchy is composed of five ordered categories: physiological needs, safety or security needs, needs for affection and belongingness, needs for esteem, and needs for self-actualization. The first four groups Maslow regards as "deficiency needs." The person driven by lacks in these areas is short of full humanity or mental health; he or she *is* driven. When a person's deficiency needs are satisfied, a variety of further potentialities for self-actualization open out, which emerge in what Maslow calls B-motives (for Being) in contrast with D-motives (for Deficiency). It is his elaboration on these "farther reaches of human nature" (Maslow, 1971) that has made Maslow the patron saint of the humanistic movement in psychology.

The scheme has the attractiveness of plausibility. Maslow's classification of human requirements and motives makes intuitive sense, though the fact that a need for personal control does not fit neatly anywhere in the scheme should give one pause. And the idea of hierarchy must have some factual basis. People struggling desperately for subsistence are not likely to devote themselves very much to the refined arts that appeal to a self-actualizing leisure class. (But they may produce a high art, nonetheless, in the service of ritual.) All the same, Maslow's classification of needs is loose, and the claim for any strict hierarchy lacks support. It is easy to imagine circumstances in which a need for safety takes priority over physiological needs, at least in the short run; or instances in which needs for affection or for esteem become modes of "self-actualization" and at the same time may eclipse physiological and safety needs. Maslow's proposal has the appeal of satisfying simplicity, but facts of human motivation are surely less orderly.

Elsewhere (Smith, 1973a), I have discussed in some detail why I cannot accept Maslow's interpretation of self-actualization. Here I will note some of the main difficulties, putting my criticism more explicitly in the context of a view of his entire need hierarchy and also of my now clearer view of the evolutionary perspective. My objections center on the conviction that Maslow's metapsychology is too biological, or at any rate, inappropriately biological, and that it is also too individualistic, too much a captive of the present moment in our own culture in this respect.

Too biological. Consider the following passage:

> Man demonstrates *in his own nature* a pressure toward fuller and fuller *Being*, more and more perfect actualization of his humanness in exactly the same naturalistic, scientific sense that an acorn may be said to be 'pressing toward' being an oak tree, or that a tiger can be observed to 'push toward' being tigerish, or a horse toward being equine. . . . The environment does not give him potentialities or capacities; he *has* them in inchoate or embryonic form, just as he has embryonic arms and legs. (Maslow, 1968, p. 160)

Putting aside the traps that lie in Maslow's metaphorical portrayal of the interactive process of epigenesis (no modern biologist could write like that), we cannot accept as plausible the suggestion that people's guiding commitments to engage with their historical, cultural worlds of work, play, religion, art, and politics, and, generally, their relations with themselves and one another can be usefully conceived as unfolding from some pre-formed biological potential, except from the multipotential for feeling and symbolic thought.

The situation is worse, because Maslow has definite ideas about the direction toward which biologically rooted self-actualization points. In an extremely informal "study" (Maslow, 1954, pp. 199–234) that he asks to bear much more weight than it can possibly support, Maslow looked at what seemed to be the common and distinguishing characteristics of notable people whom he regarded as self-actualizing. These were, of course, people whom he saw as exemplifying *his* values: humanitarians, artists, and saints, not generals, rogues, or captains of industry. For the most part, Maslow's heroes happen also to be mine. But I cannot accept his surreptitious attempt to find bogus support for one set among the conceivably infinite directions in which human potentialities can be realized. His faith in a fictitious biology blinds him to the human drama of consequential choice among alternatives; to the perennial problem of good and evil; to the human context in which politics is significant; to the potential for tragedy and the grounds for comedy in the human condition. This "humanistic psychologist" is not sufficiently humanistic.

Too individualistic. Maslow's individualistic assumptions are evident even at the level of his Deficiency needs. Take, for example, parental care and love, or "altruistic" concern for the safety of one's family, band, or in-group, not represented by Maslow's theory. Modern primatology gives good grounds for regarding such social motives as preexisting human culture, and modern evolutionary theory (Wilson, 1975) suggests selective mechanisms by which they probably gained a firm genetic foothold in human biology. Mother love and paternal aggressive defense of family may get integrated into motivational elaborations that are in some sense self-actualizing, but to place such fundamentals at a rarified level of the hierarchy seems dead wrong. When these needs are activated, as by a child in danger or distress, they have the driven quality of the most urgent D-motives—and may lead to the sacrifice, not the "actualization" of self. They are missing from Maslow's scheme.

At the level of B-motives, Maslow's doctrines of self-actualization have fitted comfortably into the ideological platform of the counterculture (Aron-Schaar, 1977). Hippies talked of "doing your own thing," and idealized a kind of "careless love" that somehow evades the effort demanded by caring love among mutually responsible persons. They combined extreme individualism with shallow communion and communalism, and ignored or despised humankind's historical discoveries about the necessity for ethics and politics and the important consequences of different political forms—mostly with chaotic, antihuman results.

Maslovian theory, as it was developing around the time of his death in 1970, has the same defects, which make it peculiarly irrelevant to politics. Self-actualization as an ethical goal is individualism writ large, with a pseudobiological sanction. It is a glorification of "doing one's own thing," even though Maslow did note that the "own thing" of his hand-picked sample of self-actualizing people was mostly altruistic. In the humanistic psychology movement, interest has substantially shifted to a so-called transpersonal psychology, the emergence of which had Maslow's sponsorship. Transpersonal psychology is mystical and religious in emphasis. It is the latest attempt to balance the excesses of Western individualism by borrowing from the wisdom of the East, whether Hindu, Tao, Zen, Sufi, or some grand ragout of them all. It provides a haven for "true believers" in which rational appraisal of evidence is frowned upon, and ESP, *est*, and tales of flying saucers are welcome. Maslow himself cannot be held personally responsible for all this foolishness, but the wholly individualistic cast of his conception of human needs does seem to call for a magical counterpoise. What is missing, of course, is any psychological base for politics, for the management both of conflicts and of common interests among complex, partly responsible people in the real world.

Personal Control and Efficacy

If our discussion of Maslow's theory has involved us in mind-boggling issues of Weltanschauung, current interest among psychologists and political scientists in the need for personal control and allied concepts is much more down to earth and, at least for the moment, more relevant and useful. Renshon (1974) has recently provided political science with a competent summary and integration of relevant research and theory in both disciplines, along with some suggestive data of his own. But interest in the topic goes back at least two decades, during most of which its political relevance was apparent. In Renshon's phrasing, people have

> a basic need to gain control over [their] physical and psychological life-space. A person's life-space can be as varied as human experience, but generally refers to those aspects of the environment that are perceived by the individual to be important in the on-going pursuit of his goals, values, and needs. Very often this will include neither politics nor the political system. . . . When politics is perceived to be a control-relevant aspect of the individual's psychological life-space, the link is forged between psychological needs and political life. (pp. 1–2)

The background for this interdisciplinary agenda goes back to an important theoretical paper by Robert White (1959) on the concept of competence, which was mainly concerned with marshaling evidence and arguments against the view, then predominant in psychology, that motivation can be understood fully in terms of lacks, drives, and "tension reduction" (also, remember, of concern to Dorothy Lee and to Maslow). White drew evidence from many sources that people share with other mammals an intrinsic motive to produce intended effects on their environments, and that the sense of competence in one's ability to produce such effects is intrinsically gratifying. A little later, Rotter (1966) showed that people— well, college students—differ from one another in the degree to which they attribute the outcomes of their endeavors, their successes and failures, to their own abilities and skills (internal control) or to fate and chance (external control). Others were not slow to point out that blacks' feelings of impotence in face of "The Man," and alienated youths' similar feelings vis-à-vis "The System," were also instances of external control. The motivation for personal control or competence then became a *variable* of individual differences to be explored in its correlations, not just an assumption about human nature.

De Charms (1968) gave a slightly different phrasing to the variable in his distinction between "Origins" and "Pawns." "Origins" are people who feel themselves to be the source of their actions; "Pawns" are those who feel constrained or manipulated from without. Whether one is more an "Origin" or a "Pawn" makes a difference in the extent, in actual life, that one exercises initiative in shaping one's world, or merely reacts as a "patient," not an agent. (A self-fulfilling prophecy is activated when concepts or theories of the self are involved.) Nearly a decade ago, I discussed this developing perspective on the empirics of human autonomy or "free will," including notice of its relation to the concept of "civic competence" featured by Almond and Verba (1963) in their classic comparative study of political systems.

By now, what began as simple has become more complicated. Conceptualization and measurements, both of the motive for personal control and of the sense of efficacy (personal *or* political), turn out to be difficult and controversial. And the ready availability of Rotter's original and now badly antiquated instrument, along with a parcel of others (MacDonald, 1973), has led to the proliferation of fashionable but mindless research that has muddied the waters more than it has clarified them. All the same, as in the case of the spate of research on authoritarianism two decades ago, I think it is clear that we are dealing with an area of psychological dispositions that is genuinely relevant to politics.

The relevance is clearer than in the case of Maslow because the ambitions of all concerned have been more modest. True enough, White and others have tried rather persuasively to legitimize the need for competence or control through some kind of general mammalian charter. But research has been concerned mainly with personal control and the sense of efficacy among real people today, living under democratic political systems or in modernizing ones that provide a reasonable foil for comparison. Further, no claim is made that personal control is *the* primary human motive; only that it is an important one, in terms of which people now vary, and one that has transparent relevance to the workings of politics. After all, "personal control" is only a slight variant, with different conceptual associations and connotations, of Hobbes's old concept of power as a rational prerequisite for the satisfaction of the whole range of other human appetites.

And the relevance in this case involves a two-way street. As a sometime student of alienation and protest among American youth (Smith, 1969c, Smith, Block & Haan, 1973), I have been impressed with the extent to which young people's sense of hopeless powerlessness in relation to a national politics of which they disapprove may feed back to leave them feeling like pawns in their personal lives. The badly eroded capacity of the young to *hope* in regard to national issues of war and peace, justice, and planetary survival surely has much to do with the spread of privatism among them and with their vulnerability to irrational and occultist messages that seem to offer avenues of escape. We may need to improve our politics before our psychology regains its morale. (See chapter 15.)

Epilogue

This may be a good note to end on. Traditionally, theorists have looked to doctrines of human needs for a sound psychological base on which to build a theory of politics. The available doctrines, beginning with instinct theories, tended—wrongly—to conceive of human nature as independent of political life but setting its terms. From the perspective that I have been illustrating, human nature has emerged in political life; the relationship is reciprocal or interactive. Psychologists ought not to look mainly to rats and pigeons but to the records of political history and thought (along with art and literature) for the phenomena of human nature that it is their task to formulate systematically. Psychological views of human nature should meet the test of whether they can give an intelligible account of human triumphs and failures in polities; social scientists are in no position to cast doubt, as some have, upon the possibility of democracy because its prerequisites appear not to correspond to their impoverished assumptions about human nature.

Human nature, including human needs, values, motives, and wishes, is an emergent—the self-transforming product of an interactive, dialectical process in which human actions on the world, first in evolution, then in history, have created conditions that keep bringing new needs, values, motives, and wishes into being. *Of course*, social psychology and the other human sciences are historical, as Gergen (1973) has recently been arguing to the shocked response of many of his colleagues. It should be a source of strength, not an admission of weakness, to grasp this understanding. Let social psychology and the social sciences also point forward to an open, not a closed, future.

7

Encounter Groups and Humanistic Psychology

From one angle of regard, the 1977 symposium to which this essay was presented is retrospective, a requiem for a social movement of the 1960s that is well past its peak. In California, the traffic from San Francisco down Route 1 to Big Sur has declined, and in the programs that continue at Esalen, encounter groups dissolve into an ever-new mix of bodily and spiritual disiplines and delights. From a more inclusive perspective, however, the ecological niche that encounter groups occupied for a while in contemporary American culture is still there, a persistently aching void that a parade of successor movements, some touchingly innocent, some crassly commercial, vie with one another to fill. The void seems never to get filled, and the social, psychological, professional, ethical, and maybe religious problems raised by the encounter-group movement are still very much with us.

My discussion of encounter groups and humanistic psychology must therefore attend also to the broader "human-potential movement" of which encounter groups formed a central part, and to the still more inclusive half-world of somewhat therapies and somewhat mysticisms into which it shades off without clear boundaries. With respect to humanistic psychology, I will likewise need a dual referent: to the humanistic psychology *movement* with which encounter groups and "growth centers" became identified, and to a conception of humanism in psychology that the movement has seemed to me largely to desert.

In this necessarily cursory venture, I am acutely aware of the lack of the kind of *data* that could contribute to a more solidly based understanding of the role of encounter groups in recent social change. We now have some information about the effects of encounter groups on participating individuals—measurable effects that are by no means spectacular (Lieberman, Yalom, & Miles, 1973; Kilmann & Sotile, 1976). We have no good information, so far as I know, about the shifting clientele of seekers for intensive group experience—their social characteristics, their motives, their hopes and expectations, their movement among alternative providers of packaged love, communion, and human meaning—or about the heterogeneous company of leaders, facilitators, and gurus, some from within the established mental health professions, most probably not, who offer these commodities (cf. Rosenbaum & Snadowsky, 1976). So our consideration of encounter groups as a social movement—in the longer run, probably the most interesting aspect in which to view them—has to be essentially speculative.

Two Views of Encounter Groups

A good starting point is provided by two quotations that put before us the widely divergent value-laden appraisals with which encounter groups have been greeted. The first is from Carl Rogers, one of the founders of humanistic psychology as a movement, and, in his earlier years, a staunch and imaginative innovator in bringing scientific methods to bear upon the fragile interchanges of counseling and psychotherapy. The second is from Sigmund Koch, initially an experimental psychologist, then an integrator and critic of systematic scientific psychology, still later a humanist in psychology who has been caustically critical of the pretensions of psychological science and of most claimants to the humanistic label.

In a very personal book commending encounter groups to the public as one of the exciting developments of our time, Rogers (1973) wrote that

> the encounter group or intensive group experience . . . is, I believe, one of our most successful modern inventions for dealing with the feeling of unreality, of impersonality, and of distance and separation that exists in so many people of our culture. (p. 127)

But then hear Koch (1973):

> It is my assessment that the group movement is the most extreme excursion thus far of man's talent for reducing, distorting, evading and vulgarizing his own reality. . . . It is adept at the image-making maneuver of evading human reality in the very process of seeking to discover and enhance it. It seeks to court spontaneity and authenticity by artifice; to combat instrumentalism instrumentality; to provide access to experience by reducing it to a packaged commodity; to engineer autonomy by group pressure; to liberate individuality by group shaping. Within the lexicon of its concepts and methods, openness becomes transparency; love, caring and sharing become a barter of "reinforcements" or perhaps mutual ego-titillation; aesthetic receptivity or immediacy becomes "sensory awareness." It can provide only a grotesque simulacrum of every

noble quality it courts. It provides, in effect, a convenient psychic whorehouse for the purchase of a gamut of well-advertised existential "goodies": authenticity, freedom, wholeness, flexibility, community, love, joy. One enters for such liberating consummations but settles for psychic strip-tease. (p. 639)

In the "encounter game," says Koch, "the essential complexity, indeed ambiguity, of the meanings of human actions and expressions, thus of personhood, is damped out" (p. 651).

The two quotations capture the main hopes and claims for encounter groups and similar intensive group experiences—and the main criticisms (strongly stated) from a standpoint that is humanistic in the traditional sense. They provide a frame for the evaluative consideration of encounter groups as a social movement. They anchor extremes of evaluation that run a gamut between hailing encounter groups as a solution to our current special vulnerability to loneliness and despair, through regarding them as mostly harmless and sometimes helpful substitutes for the grand-right-and-left mixers of an earlier day, to decrying them as shallow and meretricious eroders of personal and interpersonal integrity.

I do not think there is much argument about the general cultural situation to which the encounter group movement is responsive. Phrasings will differ, but Carl Rogers's way of putting it does very well: "the feeling of unreality, of impersonality, and of distance and separation that exists in so many people of our culture." It is our special version of the modern predicament initiated by the collapse of religiously based tradition and the erosion of *Gemeinschaft,* a predicament heightened for recent Americans by the decisive break with history in a nuclear and electronic age, by our national entanglement in a demoralizing war, by the assassination of our most hope-inspiring leaders, by the undermining of former bases for hope and commitment as the previously unchallenged doctrine of unending growth and progress becomes visibly untenable. As the practicing humanist Robert Penn Warren (1975) has written, "Any true self is not only the result of a vital relation with a community but is also a development in time, and if there is no past there can be no self" (p. 56). Since our ties to community in time have been strained and attenuated, our age has not been friendly to integral, well-rooted selfhood.

The Humanistic Psychology Movement

In order to be in a position to discuss the involvement of the encounter-group movement with humanistic psychology, I need first to review the background of the humanistic movement in American psychology, a revolt against the positivistic behaviorism that by midcentury had long dominated academic psychology and also a revolt against psychoanalysis, which provided a major theoretical basis for the rapid postwar growth of clinical psychology. There had long been a minor current of "abnormal and social psychology" that coexisted uncomfortably with the mainstream of positivistic experimental psychology. Out of this current emerged the psychology of personality in the late 1930s, under the leadership of such major figures as Allport (1937) and Murray (1938), soon to be joined by Murphy (1947), Maslow (1954), Kelly (1955), Rogers (1961), and May (1977).

All of the eminent psychologists just named, together with Charlotte Bühler (1933), who while still in Vienna had launched the study of lives in life-span perspective, met with various other psychologists and humanists in a conference at Old Saybrook, Connecticut, in 1964 that formally launched the humanistic psychology movement as a "Third Force" distinct from the then-regnant forces of behaviorism and psychoanalysis: a movement to bring psychology back to concern with human experience, values, and choices; to counteract the alienating stream of mechanism in psychology; to balance the concern wth pathology with a focus on positive human potentialities for love, creativity, and fulfillment (May, 1975). While apostles of the European philosophical currents of existentialism and phenomenology were among the group, it is important to recognize that it also included the entire academic leadership of personality theory, apart from strict Freudians, in what (in retrospect) now appears to have been its great period.

What began as a movement within psychology was soon swept away by forces characteristic of the 1960s into a trajectory that carried it out of contact with the academic science. The older academic leaders dropped out, and of the triumvirate—Rogers, Maslow, and May—to whom the movement looked for intellectual leadership, at least Maslow and May became profoundly ambivalent about the irrationality and kookiness perpetrated in the name of humanistic psychology. How did this happen? In effect, encounter groups and allied therapists captured the humanistic psychology movement.

Michael Murphy and Richard Price had started the Esalen Institute in 1962 (Tomkins, 1976), drawing on strands examined by Back (1972) from sensitivity training, Gestalt therapy (Perls, Hefferline, & Goodman, 1951), and the mystical disciplines. At about the same time, the two major modes of cultural alienation so attractive to youth in the 1960s both made their appearances in California: the counterculture (Roszak, 1968) of the flower children and drug-oriented hippies with its passive withdrawal, and the New Left of the Free Speech Movement at Berkeley and progressively more chaotic campus protest (Keniston, 1973)—respectively postures of copping out or lashing out in relation to the "square," conventional social order that to many no longer afforded a setting for hope and commitment.

The midsixties also witnessed a further flowering of the "sexual revolution," when for the first time since the 1920s major shifts apparently took place in patterns of sexual behavior away from the traditional double standard and toward an increasing acceptance of casual as well as relational sex by females as well as males (Chilman, 1983). Therapy fads proliferated, communes were established (Kanter, 1972), mystical cults spread, and the charismatic movement with its strange penchant for "speaking with tongues" penetrated the established churches (Bellah & Glock, 1976; Harrell, 1976).

So, even when encounter groups were at their height, they were hardly a separate movement, an isolatable phenomenon. They were, rather, as Rosabeth Kanter (1976) says of communes, part of "a more general culture of spiritual, therapeutic, and communal seekership in the United States, creating a demand for short-term personal growth experiences in temporary communities" (p. 148).

The "Culture of Seekership"

This "culture of seekership," which informed the encounter-group and human potential movements and engulfed humanistic psychology, can be described in terms of interrelated themes. I will tag them with the following labels: individualism, human perfectability, self-disclosure, emphasis on the "here and now," hedonism, and irrationalism.

Individualism

For all their emphasis on the intensive *group* experience, the encounter movement and humanistic psychology in general have been radically individualistic, a respect in which they resonate with a dominant theme in American culture at large. The group is put to service to save individual souls. The center of value is found in the fulfillment of the individual virtually stripped of interdependence and commitments to other lives. What has been called "the new narcissism" (Marin, 1975) has emerged. Thus Maslow's conception of self-actualization as the acme of personal growth (Smith, 1973a). Thus the hippie's careless tolerance of "doing one's own thing." Thus Fritz Perls's Gestalt prayer to feel responsible for one's *own* life, not to be one's brother's keeper. Thus the transitory character of intense relations in the weekend encounter group or in unstable "intentional communities."

The experience of self-dissolution in communion is indeed sought, but *as* an experience, a transcendental high, rather than as a confirmation of hard-earned and committing relations between real and complex people. The "transpersonal psychology" that has been widely touted as the creative front of the humanistic movement amounts to an eclectic mélange of the old mysticisms under psychological auspices (Tart, 1975): individual finite selfhood is taken as an inferior state to be transcended, but it is transcended in a mystical (and individual) experience of merging with the All, not in concrete and caring relations with finite others.

Human Perfectibility

A doctrine of human perfectibility runs through most writings in humanistic psychology, and distinguishes them from the somberness of Freud. Rollo May (1977), whose strong roots in European existentialism lead him to attend to the tragic aspects of life, is the major exception. For Rogers, Maslow, and many lesser figures, the prevailing doctrine is watered-down Rousseau: People are essentially good, and their good qualities will predictably unfold and blossom if only properly nurtured. It is a romantic or—better—a sentimental doctrine that predisposes those who hold it to neglect realistic considerations of politics and ethics, which are concerned with how to enhance actual life among imperfect creatures who are often at cross-purposes with themselves and others.

In the encounter and human potential movement as such, the assumption of perfectibility promotes seekership, and when it is combined with the equally American faith in instrumental gimmicks and prescriptions, the unattractive and superficial features, the manipulative features held up for scorn by Koch appear. Such an easy, such a delusory route to growth and perfection! Koch complains and I agree. But it is a route that has many precedents in our past, whether in the revivals, camp meetings, and faith healing of an earlier day or the Moral Rearmament sessions of *Susan and God* a generation ago. A further problem with the doctrine of perfectibility is that it breeds dissatisfaction with the imperfect relationships possible in the real world—with real marriages and families, for instance—and does not sustain the patient effort that is required to make them better or to make them last.

Self-Disclosure

Still another common theme is the high value set on self-disclosure—the "transparent self" (Jourard, 1971)—for its own sake and as a near-panacea for the troubles of the soul. Conventional reserve and the artificialities of politeness and civility are rejected as hypocritical; the thing is to "let it all hang out." Nakedness, both literal and symbolic, is idealized, and not just for sexual reasons. In a society that lacks the device of *tu-toyer* to distinguish intimate relationships, first-naming, symbolizing a readiness for intimacy, seems to be carried by the young to the point of serious inconvenience. The undoubted reassurance and healing that can come in a truly intimate relationship from sharing what is guiltily or troublesomely private is taken as a universal principle, leading to a general unconcern for the protection that privacy can give to vulnerable individuality. In loving personal relationships, intimate sharing is protected by the mutual attachment and care of the partners. In professional helping or therapeutic relationships, intimacy is shielded by the safeguards of professional ethics. Not so in encounter groups, or in the quick and easy self-disclosure of the culture being described. When intimacy is so readily claimed and granted, it gets cheapened. Supposed intimacy becomes less truly intimate. The promiscuously transparent self is at risk of becoming less a self.

The "Here and Now"

Emphasis on the "here and now" is shared by the encounter movement and Gestalt therapy; as a college teacher it seems to me to have characterized virtually a whole generation of youth and to pose very difficult obstacles to education. Deliberate narrowing of time perspecitve surely has its therapeutic uses, especially with people who are "hung up" on inhibitions and scruples carried over inappropriately from a different past. Zimbardo (1970) has illustrated the process involved: a narrowed time perspective releases impulsivity. There are obviously occasions when this is appropriate and desirable. And there are many when it is not.

Self-control and commitments to self and others only make sense in a longer time frame; self-respect, loving care, and planfulness can emerge only in lives that are linked to a past and a future. (We are reminded of what Robert Penn Warren [1975] had to say about the conditions of well-rooted selfhood.) Total immersion in the "here and now" strikes me as a tactic of the hopeless, akin to the fatalism of the culture of poverty. It is a stance that helps one tolerate bleak realities that one does not feel one can do anything about. Unfortunately, living in the moment may also exclude coping with realities that had better be faced.

Hedonism

The hedonism that runs through many byways of humanistic psychology, from sensual massage and sensory awareness training to "gut feel" as the criterion for ethical choice, is obviously related to life in the "here and now'' with minimal baggage of human or moral commitments, and thus with minimal sense of identity. "If it feels good, do it." Hendin (1975), a psychiatrist to youth, holds that the search for sensation follows from a basic estrangement from one's feelings, in which the desire to keep all options open reflects emptiness, not inner freedom; in which people out of touch with their feelings (and likeminded social scientists, I would add) come to think of life as wholly a matter of playing roles or even games. (Transactional Analysis—TA—with its game metaphors merges with Gestalt therapy as the most popular way of theorizing about encounter groups.)

Hendin, too, sees the root problem as one of hopelessness, and writes as follows:

> Increasingly what unites people in this culture is a sense of shared misfortune and depression, a feeling of impotence in the face of forces they feel they cannot shape or control. Erikson put it sensitively when he wrote that "any span of the [life] cycle lived without vigorous meaning, at the beginning, at the middle, or at the end, endangers the sense of life and the meaning of death in all whose life stages are involved." Erikson pulls back from confronting the forces today which endanger meaning. But we are a culture in which the elderly are treated as refuse, the middle-aged in their discontent turn to the young for salvation and in so doing undermine youth by expecting the impossible from them. (p. 334)

> The flight from emotion seems the only available way out in a culture where people are increasingly adrift in their discontent. (p. 339)

Irrationalism

Irrationalism completes the thematic package. Irrationalism is reflected in disrespect for intellectual content in the group process ("mind-fucking," Fritz Perls called it); in the affinity of humanistic psychology for the occult (belief in the firm factuality of ESP is taken for granted among humanistic psychologists); in reliance on intuition over evidence; in disparaging rational problem solving; and in the debased level of intellectual discourse in much that passes as theoretical writing in humanistic psychology and its associated therapies. Frankel (1973) has written eloquently about the inherently self-defeating aspect of irrationalism in the countercultural movement, saying, in effect, that the irrationalist inhabits a dream world in which reality imposes no obdurate limitations and people never have to resolve cross-purposes, for rationality is simply the hard-earned strategy and tactics of dealing with a difficult, limiting reality.

Instrumental rationality has obviously been abused, particularly in the linear, technological thinking, supposedly value-free, that has become especially identified with the defense establishment. It is true that attempted rationality has not been working very well for us. It is also true that the requirements of life and work in a bureaucratized, technological society have underplayed the life of feeling; have given, by an old metaphor, head one-sided priority over heart, or, by a newer one, left-brain thinking unbalanced predominance over right-brain thinking. Correctives and rebalancing are in order. But the pendulum swing against well-considered rational thought, as exhibited in the encounter-group movement and humanistic psychology, is destructive rather than corrective unless still further correction is applied to it.

Current Manifestations

The encounter-group movement has peaked and is in decline, but the culture of seekership as just sketched continues unabated. And the successors and competitors of encounter are no improvement. In particular, *est* (Erhard Seminars Training), last year's fad that may already be making its exit along with the more benign *TM* (transcendental meditation) as a general panacea, is an ominous phenomenon, the more so because it has received the enthusiastic endorsement of much of the leadership of the humanistic psychology movement including Michael Murphy, the cofounder of Esalen. Flagrantly individualistic, *est* claims to transform "Pawns" in De Charms's (1968) sense into "Origins" of personal causation. It is unabashedly commercial and drastically manipulative, drawing for its marathon sessions on strong techniques of self-reconstitution previously used in Synanon on hard-core addicts and by communist "brainwashers" on ordinary citizens. (Cf. Sarbin & Adler, 1970–1971.) It may well be effective, though its effects have not been measured. But what sort of "humanism" is it for a packaged venture in "human potential" to soften up its audience by browbeating its numbers as "ass-holes," by stretching their endurance of bladder tension, by fatiguing them to the edges of toleration? To the extent that this is clever applied psychology (and clever it appears to be [Fenwick, 1976]), it is a menacing development, and an insult to the idea of humanism.

It is surely a sign of the present disarray of the human potential movement that Robert Ornstein (1972, 1976), whose *Psychology of Consciousness* legitimized the esoteric psychologies of human potential for many, now feels compelled to inveigh against the false prophets with their profits. But he continues to hold forth the Sufi mysticism of Indries Shah as a truer gospel.

Where, then, are we? It is easy to decry the mindlessness of the encounter-group movement and its successors. In doing so, I come out sounding much like Sigmund Koch. But it is necessary to take the movement seriously for what it tells us about the serious lacks in our way of life that generated it. The movement did not solve our problems. All the same, attention to it may help us see more clearly what these problems are.

Underlying Social Lacks

Harking back for a closer look at themes touched on earlier, I see three interrelated lacks to which the encounter movement was responsive. These lacks, which can be thought of as different facets of the same complex problem, are deficits in community, in meaning, and in hope.

Deficit in Community

The encounter movement sought to meet the deficit in community by superficial communion, by *ersatz* "communitas" (Turner, 1969) among transparent selves. It sought to give quick gratification to lonely, rootless people's needs to feel accepted and loved. The lack that we suffer from is not so easily to be satisfied. Real steps toward solution, if they are possible for us at all, will come in the social and political realm, in the reconstruction of the world of work and school and family, of neighborhood and recreation. Our lack makes us vulnerable to pseudosolutions, which may be shoddy and mindless and could become fascistic. At least in our psychological theories we should be wary of giving further support to the predominant extremely individualistic values that undermine community. We need to bring human interdependence into better focus. The requirements of meeting our compounded ecological crises could help to foster such a fundamental reorientation.

Deficit in Meaning

The deficit in meaning is the familiar modern lack to which existential philosophy, Jungian psychology, and even modern psychoanalysis (Wheelis, 1958) is responsive, as is the proliferation of occult and mystical doctrine at the boundaries of the encounter movement. It is by no means firmly established that people as self-conscious creatures can live without the supernatural frame of meaning traditionally provided by myth, ritual, and religion: we have tried doing without it for so short a time, and not done well. It seems unlikely that people can live well without some frame of transcendent values. Perhaps the current popularity of cults and the occult foreshadows a new religious age, a dark age in terms of the Enlightenment values of science. Or perhaps we can work out a drama of significant purposes in more human terms. Whatever the outcome, I hope we can do better than the amalgam of psychology and mysticism that passes as "transpersonal psychology." Psychology can learn much from religious disciplines and symbolism, but when it tries to *be* religion, it is shoddy, superficial religion and bad psychology.

Deficit in Hope

The deficit in hope to which the encounter movement and humanistic psychology responded with hedonistic fixation on the "here-and-now" seems, as I have already suggested, the most plausible reason for the *timing* of the movement, and I therefore look on it as potentially the most remediable. Paradoxically, I am somewhat hopeful about our hopelessness, since the 1960s and 1970s were distinguished by such an unusual array of special events and circumstances that evoked hopelessness and cynicism. Given new national leadership that begins to face some of our difficult real problems, hope can regenerate, and with it the readiness of youth to make commitments, to reach back to the past and contemplate a desired future that is worth the effort. True, the problems of our country in the contemporary world may be beyond satisfactory solution. But hope, which to me is the primary human virtue and resource, is not the same as optimism. We can struggle hopefully with exceedingly difficult problems if we can select and maintain effective political and moral leadership.

Whither Humanistic Psychology?

So much for some lessons from the encounter movement concerning problems of our society and culture. What about the humanistic psychology that the movement captured and deflected? I think we need to start over again, more or less where its founders left off.

The need for a psychology respectful of human values is still inadequately met. But developments in scientific psychology in the meantime have reduced the gap between the assumptions of psychological science and the requirements of a humanistic psychology. The old dogmatic positivism that dictated the shape of a behavioristic science is largely discredited; contemporary mainstream psychology is far more open and tolerant of diversity in subject matter and method than the psychology against which the humanistic movement rebelled. At the center of the current mainstream is a cognitive psychology—a fact that would have astonished Watson and Hull, and still astonishes Skinner—which remains a kind of behaviorism but begins to deal with recognizably human processes of thinking, imaging, and remembering without the dogmatic exclusions of the old positivism. True, mainstream psychology has yet to deal adequately with the life of feeling. But a humanistic psychology no longer needs the same firm barriers against science that it once felt necessary to defend itself against the claims of scientism, which denied its right to exist (Chein, 1972). As mainstream science in psychology has become less monolithic and less antihumanistic in its claims, there is less occasion, or excuse, for humanistic psychology to be antiscientific.

We need a humanistic psychology that can talk coherently about feelings and about such matters as community, meaning, and hope; that can deal with the phenomena of selfhood and human interdependence in historical context. Such a psychology needs to take the emotional and irrational, the mystical, the transcendent into account. If in its own conceptual structure it can avoid the mistake of *being* emotional and irrational, mystical, or religious, there is no reason that it cannot join an open array of psychological sciences.

8

Can There Be A Human Science?

The symposium for which this essay was prepared raised the question: "After Maslow and Rogers, [do we now need] a new humanistic psychology?" For some time, we had accommodated to our status as "after Maslow." Over the years since his death in 1970, I noted, there had been a considerable effort to digest his ideas about the hierarchy of human motives and about self-actualization, to which I have contributed (Smith, 1973a, chapter 6 above.) We are just beginning to get used to the status of "after Rogers." So much of Rogers's substantial contribution has been woven into contemporary thought and practice far beyond the confines of Rogerian theory or humanistic psychology that there is a sense in which he will still be with us as a living contemporary for a long time to come. Happily, we are *not* "after" Rollo May, whose continued presence is a major force in the humanistic psychology of today. This symposium is an early attempt to accommodate to psychological life without Rogers. Do we need a "new humanistic psychology"?

My answer is a resounding yes, a yes that respects the contributions of the founders of humanistic psychology, and (in what I think is good humanistic spirit) accepts the developmental, dynamic nature of the humanistic enterprise. Since the 1960s, when humanistic psychology emerged as a "Third Force" (Smith, 1984), the context of mainstream psychology has changed radically from the domination of mechanistic versions of behaviorism and psychoanalysis. Now behaviorism has been succeeded by cognitive psychology, which admits consciousness as real but interprets it in terms of a vastly more sophisticated brand of mechanism, thanks to the metaphoric resources of the cybernetic and computer revolution. "Orthodox" psychoanalysis, on its part, has opened itself to radical internal dissent, among traditional drive-theoretic ego psychologists, object relations theorists, Lacanians, Kohutian self psychologists, and hermeneuticists. Psychoanalysis is now much more open both to participation in the scientific community of academic psychology and to genuine links with a humanistic perspective than ever before—ironic at a time when its status in the professional and academic pecking orders is unfortunately at nadir. The times are different! Another difference visible from my observation post in Santa Cruz is that the traffic back and forth to Esalen is far below its earlier flood, even though the irrationalism that captured the movement in the 1960s persists: New Age transpersonal psychology seems to play an ever-increasing role in humanistic psychology. It is indeed time to rethink the humanistic agenda in psychology.

A few years ago, in a plea for more attention to my own sector of humanistic psychology, which I identified as theoretically oriented secular humanism (chapter 5), I urged that we ought not to think of humanistic psychology as monolithic either in fact or in aspiration, any more than we should aspire to a unified scientific discipline of psychology as a whole. I still agree with Sigmund Koch (1976) that the dream of a unified science of psychology has been an attractive but destructive will-o'-the-wisp. *A fortiori,* I continue to think the same about humanistic psychology. There are aspects of humanistic psychology that merge comfortably with the humanities, traditionally considered. There are aspects that make good contact with academic psychological science. There are major parts of the field primarily concerned with professional practice in the human services. And there are others that overlap with the traditional concerns of religion. Tension among these competing directions of commitment is difficult, but it can be productive for everybody. The idea that we can or should "get it all together" seems to me at best fatuous and at worst destructive.

I therefore have no presumptuous intention to write a new charter for humanistic psychology as a whole. I am concerned rather with clarifying our options and setting some new goals in one aspect of humanistic psychology or perspective on it, which can be labeled as "human science." I hope to make clear that this label covers much ambiguity and may well disguise pseudoconsensus.

The collapse of logical positivism as received philosophy of science has left us in conceptual disorder. *Positivism,* as I understand the term, now refers to the inappropriate extension to the human area of an inaccurate interpretation of the nature of theory building in the physical-chemical sciences. (Mayr [1982] is eloquent on how the logical positivists ignored the methodological and conceptual basis of achievement in evolutionary biology.) The revolt against positivism often is part and parcel of a general rejection of science. Yet science remains an extraordinary cultural mutation that has changed the human world for better or worse in nonreversible ways. The revulsion against consequences of modern technology has led many humanists, in psychology and in general, to wishful thinking that would have science go away. It seems to be hard for humanistic intellectuals who are otherwise critically minded people to think clearly in this area. Yet if we are to aspire to "human science," we need some clarity as to what science is about.

For a start, we can look at how Rogers, Maslow, and May placed themselves on "human science" issues. In view of his career-long contributions, we should praise Carl Rogers for making the largest contribution of the three to mainstream science in psychology. He legitimized the recording of counseling/therapeutic interaction for research and training purposes (Rogers, 1942). He and his students essentially launched empirical research in therapeutic processes. Even in his later years when his attachments to academic science had frayed past repair, his theorizing about personal development and encounter groups focused on discovering and deploying the *causal* processes that lead to personal growth. Rogers was so fully invested in the actual, substantive problems of people that he paid little heed to metatheoretical arguments about positivism. Yet I think he retained from the positivist tradition its concern for evidence. We have to be concerned with evidence, even if debate has always been in order, and paradigms change, in regard to what we take evidence to be.

Abraham Maslow is a radically different case. In spite of his early training at the University of Wisconsin in hard-science research in primate behavior, he moved to a position that valued the auspices of science but, I think, really misunderstood what science is about. His *Psychology of Science* (1966) was wise about the essential identity of the creative phase in art and in science but utterly confused about the distinctive features of science as a human institution (Smith, 1966). He argued for a Taoist, concrete science of the *all* as *it is*, in contrast with the abstractive sciences that we know. How confused about science can you get? Of *course*, there is no common "scientific method" that embraces subatomic physics, cosmological astronomy, molecular and evolutionary biology, sociology, and psychology. Nevertheless, there is a common scientific agenda that has proved itself since the seventeenth century and is in no way discredited by the current critique of positivism. It has nothing whatsoever to do with the concreteness of the All.

That scientific agenda as I think I understand it—there are few things I feel so clear about!—is essentially a grand strategy to produce *progress* in our understanding of the world, and even in our understanding of ourselves in relation to the world if we can. *Progress* has come to look to us like a tricky concept that indeed has dubious meaning when we apply it to history. Its meaning in science is much less ambiguous. In the aftermath of Thomas Kuhn's loosely popularized ideas (Kuhn, 1970), it seems to me warranted to assert that science is one domain, perhaps unique if we expand it to include technology, in which progress can be talked about sensibly, in terms of the increased scope and power of the general formulations we create to understand phenomena that we observe or can produce.

Progress in science depends upon a historically based collective enterprise. It is the achievement of a scientific community whose members share in communication with one another a conception of problems and of the kinds of evidence that are regarded as relevant, so that they can challenge and therefore correct one another's proposals for their solution. They depend upon published and therefore vulnerable evidence. Underlying the entire endeavor is the commitment to *abstract* from the plentitude of "reality," to seek coherence, understanding, and predictability by throwing away much of the richness of experienced life and world. Science is thus a human project, an exceedingly ambitious yet explicitly limited one that is inherently abstractive, and cannot at all embrace the unrealistic aims of Maslow's Taoistic science. Maslow's concrete science of the All as it is is completely imaginary—or an oxymoron. Maslow was talking, though he did not know it, about the re-creative and evocative features of the arts, which are *not* progressive and make no claim to be so.

Where does Rollo May, who is still very much with us, fit into this intellectual tangle? As I understand Rollo, with whom I have felt stronger intellectual affinity than I do with Abe or even with Carl, he is not concerned with science at all, though he is certainly not opposed to it; he is even friendly to it. He is truly a humanist in the tradition that goes back to the dawn of the Renaissance, a humanist who has been looking for meaningful linkage between the insights of psychoanalysis and the lived experience of being human in the world cultural crisis from which we are all suffering, whether we know it or not. From his early work introducing the European existentialist tradition to American psychology, May (1977) has *not* been concerned with establishing his credentials in science. His realm is rather that of human meaning as he knows it in therapy and as it is unfolded. interpreted, and realized in literature and the arts—surely a source of "data" that has been scandalously neglected in mainstream psychology.

So: Among the three founders of humanistic psychology, Rogers *did* good human science, even though he ceased to care about science in the latter part of his career. Maslow started as a scientist but later had ideas about science that seem to me only misleading and confusing. May never was committed to science, and while he is friendly to science in psychology, his affinities and his contributions are to psychology in relation to the humanities as traditionally considered. That is, he helps us to understand the human condition in the context of values and meanings, which he interprets evocatively and persuasively. *Can* there be a human science?

With the background of this brief look at the positions of our founders, we need now to be more careful about our use of terms. What *do* we mean by *human science*? The easiest approach to this question, of course, is to ask, what *have* we meant?

For contemporaries, it is probably most useful to go back to Dilthey's turn-of-the-century distinction (Rickman, 1979) between the natural sciences *(Naturwissenschaften)* and the mental, human, or cultural sciences *(Geisteswissenschaften)*. Few of us have read Dilthey (I have not), but his distinction between the explanatory, causal realm of the *Naturwissenschaften* and the interpretive, meaningful, value-oriented realm of the *Geisteswissenshaften* is still with us. A recent good textbook on the history and systems of psychology that I have used in my own teaching (Kendler, 1987) translates *Geisteswissenschaft* as "human science," and goes on to compromise Kendler's own waning neobehaviorist positivism by giving "human science" in that sense equal status with natural science. *Wissenschaft* does translate roughly into science (but the boundaries of the concept differ in German and English). The *Geisteswissenschaften* as interpretative, often historical, cultural disciplines provide a major avenue to scholarly knowledge especially relevant to humanistic psychology, but they are not sciences in the sense of abstractive, would-be progressive enterprises.

Amadeo Giorgi (1970) has also used the term *human science* in this interpretative, hermeneutic sense, in his case drawing on the phenomeno-logical-existentialist philosophy of Merleau-Ponty (1962). I have no quarrel with the validity of his endeavor, but insofar as he aims at meaningful interpretation rather than causally lawful explanation, he is not engaged in science in the sense of a collective struggle toward better but never final approximations to truth. Of course, his essentially hermeneutic project is significant and valuable.

Is there a "human science" in a sense compatible with the "progressive" science that we have been talking about? Yes, there is, and it is active and productive at the interface between the causal, scientific formulations of the *Naturwissenshaften* and the interpretative, value-oriented, meaningful formulations of the *Geisteswissenschaften*. Over the past two decades, personality and social psychologists have shown in considerable detail how people's beliefs about themselves (especially internal control, competence, self-efficacy versus external control, powerlessness, and learned helplessness)—matters of reflexive self-interpretation and meaning—are embedded in causal networks of understandable antecedents and predictable consequences (chapter 15). In flagrant conflict with many previous philosophical dicta, psychology has indeed crossed an empirical bridge between the realms of cause and of meaning. If I regard myself as efficacious in a basically friendly world—matters of meaning—I am likely to take initiatives and find opportunities that would simply not come into my ken if I were trained in helplessness and mired in hopelessness. These are effects in the realm of causality. Psychology has been *doing* human science, in this important area, science in the good old sense, with impressive results that have considerable relevance to professional practice. I would like to keep the label of "human science" for this sort of inquiry, which aspires to augment our knowledge of ourselves progressively.

This is only a part of "humanistic psychology." I think there is a more purely humanistic part, too, which Rollo May has spoken for and of which my mentor Harry Murray, just deceased at ninety-five, was a rare exemplar (see Smith & Anderson, 1989; Smith, 1990), a psychology in close touch with the nonprogressive humanities. There ought to be free interchange between humanistic psychology in this sense and human science in the mode I have been advocating.

What of the transpersonal boundaries with religion? Since I am a hardcore secular humanist, I cannot talk supportively or probably even fairly about them. I admire the openness of William James (1985) to spiritual and religious perspectives at our beginnings, but I cannot be as open as he was to accepting beliefs that gain most of their standing from the strength of our need to believe in them. The psychology of our religious beliefs is surely a central topic for a humanistic psychology. I think it is a mistake for humanistic psychology to *be* a religion, however. I respect forthright religion more than religion that is sneaked in by the psychological back door.

A "new humanistic psychology?" Apart from what I have had to say about human science, I would also want to take issue with both Rogers and Maslow about self-actualization as a preeminent human goal. Of course the promulgation of this goal was not an "objective," value-free conclusion of scientific psychology. It was a historically given, blessedly temporary frame of valuing that justified much selfishness (a.k.a. narcissism). In the years since the flowering of humanistic psychology, we are becoming more critical of extreme individualism, and are rediscovering grounds for commitment to a *social* life, caring for one another. (See Bellah et al., 1985.) Our genes may be selfish, but we as biological and social phenotypes are *not* our genes, and in ever so many observable ways, we are not selfish entirely. The doctrines of self-actualization so central to the humanistic psychology movement should be set in a more caring context. (See also Gilligan, 1977.)

Where would I like to see humanistic psychology go? I would like to see it rejoin the "academic" psychology of personality, from which it originated in the 1960s, and reestablish connections with the empirical study of personality. The longitudinal approach in the spirit of Henry Murray's personology (Murray, 1981) brings the whole human person into focus, as contrasted with the fixation on variables and situational effects that has characterized so much of academic personality psychology in recent decades. Humanistic psychology needs an academic basis, if it is not to become one minor free-floating cult among many others. Humanistic psychology should not and cannot become monolithic, but its health as a movement depends upon its involvement with human science. I have sought here to give a clearer and firmer meaning to that term.

Note

Presented at the American Psychological Association, Atlanta, Georgia, August 1988, and not previously published in English. A German translation has been published (Smith, 1989).

9

Psychology and the Decline of Positivism: The Case for a Human Science

The series of lectures for which this chapter was prepared celebrated the first quarter century of the Institute of Behavioral Science at the University of Colorado, an instituion in which its participants and sponsors could take great pride. That was indeed an occasion for a stocktaking, for which there was ample precedent. In fact, most of the synoptic reviews of the social and behavioral sciences have been occasioned either by similar anniversaries, or by the ever-recurrent need to justify federal funding—or by both. The most recent review I had at hand when I was preparing the lecture (Smelser & Gerstein, 1986) reached back the furthest to commemorate the fiftieth anniversary of the so-called Ogburn Report (President's Research Committee on Recent Social Trends, 1933), but it was also the by-product of a need to justify federal funding, which led to the establishment of the Committee on Basic Research in the Behavioral and Social Sciences of the National Research Council that was responsible for the review (Adams, Smelser, & Treiman, 1982; Gerstein, Luce, Smelser, & Sperlich, 1988). Notable other anniversary volumes have come from the University of Chicago, which played a central role in the institutionalization of social science: reviews on the tenth, twenty-fifth, and fiftieth anniversaries of its Social Science Research Building (Wirth, 1940; White, 1956; Kruskal, 1982). The Boulder institute's anniversary celebration is in the grand tradition.

In developing the focus of my own review of psychology as behavioral science—from my perch in its tenderer branches of personality and social psychology—it is helpful to look back at least as far as the half century encompassed by the Smelser and Gerstein (1986) review. The Ogburn Report commissioned by President Hoover at the end of the 1920s reflected a simple, almost nineteenth-century positivism—faith in a natural-science approach to human affairs, prizing quantification and conceiving of science in Baconian terms, according to which the critical ingredient is the sheer accumulation of facts, joined with what now seems to us touching confidence that factually based understanding of social problems (themselves seen as factually given) would lead to social inventions to ameliorate them. As Smelser (1986) noted, even then there were dissenting voices.

The Emergence of Behavioral Science

As we know, the label *behavioral science* came into prominence after World War II, primarily through its embodiment in the behavioral science program of the new and feisty Ford Foundation, a program established in 1951 under the direction of Bernard Berelson and terminated in 1957 after a troubled career within the foundation (Sutton, 1985). Given the temper of the times, the term had intrinsic appeal, but the foundation's sponsorship surely facilitated its rapid acceptance. From then on, the big national surveys would refer collectively to "the behavioral and social sciences," without any attempt to sort out the behavioral from the social (see Behavioral and Social Sciences Survey Committee, 1969; Adams, Smelser, & Treiman, 1982; Gerstein, Luce, Smelser, & Sperlich, 1988.)

The temper of the times in the postwar United States did support behavioral studies enthusiastically, as I can attest nostalgically from my own experience during the war and after. Applied psychological and sociological research had flourished during the war. To mention only a few major ventures that had important consequences after the war, think of Flanagan's aviation psychology program; Likert's and Stouffer's major ventures in organized survey research; Hovland's work on the experimental study of the effects of mass communications; Lasswell's analyses of Axis propaganda; Murray's development of personality assessment techniques for the Office of Strategic Services. The many participants in these enterprises had good reason to feel that their work had been useful; they brought their enthusiasm back to the campuses at a time of rapid expansion and high academic morale.

Behind this burst of activity in which psychologists arguably played the central role lay considerable consensus on a version of positivism that was substantially different from the classical positivism of the Ogburn Report. Like the old version, the new also sought to apply the strategies of scientific inquiry that had proved so successful in the natural sciences, particularly physics, in the arena of human affairs. But there was a different, more sophisticated interpretation of these strategies, owing primarily to the so-called Vienna Circle of "logical positivists," who emphasized the deductive, logico-mathematical component of science as well as its empirical, observational aspect. Following their precepts, graduate students were now learning about the "hypothetico-deductive method" and about "operational definition" (P. W. Bridgeman [1927] had provided an independent channel for physicalistic methodology to reach the behavioral sciences). And in psychology neobehaviorists of the generation of Hull (1943), Spence (1948), and Tolman (1932) competed to sketch the outlines of general systems of behavioral learning theory developed on hypothetico-deductive lines modeled on Newtonian or post-Newtonian physics, and generated programs of research that sought but never quite managed to attain that philosopher's stone, the "crucial experiment" that could decide between competing systematic views.

The assimilative strength of this version of behavioral science, which dominated the immediate postwar scene without quite managing to monopolize it, is well illustrated by its relations with psychoanalysis, which was also at a peak of popularity academically and professionally. On the one hand, Frenkel-Brunswik (1954) earned gratitude all around by employing her strong Viennese credentials to argue that psychoanalytic theory, indigestible as it might seem, could be encompassed all the same in the logical positivists' "unity of science." And, on the other, Dollard and Miller (1950), participants in the heady interdisciplinary group at the Yale Institute of Human Relations in which Hullian and psychoanalytic ideas flourished, provided their own popular translation of psychoanalytic theory in terms of Hullian behavioral mechanisms. Behavioral science in the spirit of postwar logical positivism was not necessarily behavioristic in the narrow sense, but the pull was strongly in that direction.

The Waning of Logical Positivism

By 1960, when the Institute of Behavioral Science was founded, the crest of the wave had passed, and there were strong signs that the domination of physicalistic logical positivist methodology was on the wane. It is easier now to see the signs in retrospect than it was in 1960, but Jessor (1961), the present director of the institute, has a strong claim to having read them correctly. The particular omen that he cited was the massive and unique *Psychology: A Study of a Science* then appearing (Koch, 1959–1963), sponsored by the American Psychological Association and supported by the National Science Foundation. In his epilogue to Study I (the first three volumes, devoted to systematic presentations by all the principal contenders in this "Age of Theory"), Koch (1959) concluded (and Jessor quoted him in part):

> *It can in summary be said that the results of Study I set up a vast attrition against virtually all the elements of the Age of Theory code. . . . For the first*

time in its history, psychology seems ready—or almost ready—to assess its goals and instrumentalities with primary reference to its own indigenous problems. It seems ready to think contextually, freely, and creatively about its own refractory subject matter, and to work its way free from a dependence on simplistic theories of correct scientific conduct. (p. 783; Koch's italics)

Well, it turns out to have been only partly ready; many of the cohort who had been more committed to the behavioral enterprise conceived in logical positivist terms regarded Koch as a freak and a turncoat; there are diehards who still do.

Another sign had become available even earlier to suggest that attempts at grand hypothetico-deductive theory were about to collapse for internal reasons. In 1949, at the height of the behavioral boom, the Social Science Research Council sponsored a summer seminar of eminent younger behavioral psychologists to make a close analysis of the major contending learning theories. The book reporting their analyses (Estes, Koch, MacCorquodale, Meehl, Mueller, Schoenfeld, & Verplanck, 1954) was too technical to be a best-seller even to academics, but for those who could read it, it made a devastating case that none of the theories lived up to its pretentions to logical rigor and that the supposed contrasts between competing theories often seemed to turn more on semantic preference than on substantive difference. Indeed, the age of grand theory on the hypothetical-deductive model was soon over, and of the theorists treated by Estes and the others, only Skinner remains of more than historical interest. His experimental analysis of behavior represented an older variety of positivism in new guise, plus brilliant experimental ingenuity.

While these developments internal to psychology were going on, the prescriptive claims of logical positivist philosophy of science were being revised and then challenged radically. Early in the game, Popper (1968) had weakened the earlier insistence on the verifiability of scientific propositions to the more defensible claim that they be open to falsification but resistant to it. In this view, propositions are meaningful only if they are susceptible in principle to falsification. But the criterion turned out to be hard to apply. Any theoretical statement is very hard, maybe impossible, to falsify definitively—in general, not just in suspiciously troubled cases like that of psychoanalysis. You can't drive a stake through its heart! Gergen (1982) has reminded us that long ago, Quine (1953) had made it clear that the outcome of any empirical test of a hypothesis depends not only on its truth value but also on the validity of innumerable auxiliary hypotheses that must necessarily remain unstated for the most part—the assumptions about the "other things" that are supposed to be "equal" but seldom are. Negative results can always be attributed to failure in the realm of these auxiliary hypotheses rather than to the falsity of the hypothesis being tested, and we know that strong proponents of positions in scientific controversy are fond of making such attrributions.

From a still different angle, Kuhn's (1970) widely discussed analysis of "the structure of scientific revolutions" in physics called into question the degree to which the replacement of one scientific worldview by another, what he referred to as a paradigm shift, is governed by evidence. The loosely analogical application of Kuhnian conceptions in the social and behavioral sciences has been sufficiently scandalous that psychologists are indebted to Gholson and Barker (1985) for clarifying the issues in debate, incidentally retrieving grounds for our continuing to believe in the meaningfulness of progress in science.

In the years since 1950, the so-called cognitive revolution in psychology has evoked imagery of a paradigm shift, though in a preparadigmatic field the term was presumptuous. On the part of hard-nosed psychologists still committed to the positivist conception of psychological science, the widespread adoption of the computer-based metaphor of information processing was a liberating change from the strictures of behaviorism. Of course, the traditions of attitude measurement and survey research in social psychology had attended since their beginnings to people's beliefs—cognitions. The spread of the cognitive approach throughout psychology brought the mainstream closer to what social psychologists had been doing all along, as well as leading them to what might be regarded as hypertrophy in the subfield of social cognition.

My Own Engagement with Positivism and Its Demise

To bring this historical excursion to bear on contemporary issues, I need momentarily to become more autobiographical. Somewhat parallel to Jessor's (1961) example, one of my earliest theoretical ventures (Smith, 1950) within the logical positivist framework was a critical but basically supportive examination of the phenomenological perspective in personality theory. (I cherished a letter from Gustav Bergmann, one of the poohbahs of logical positivism, giving it his blessing!) In addition to my socialization to positivism, I had also incorporated in my psychological identity discordant themes that I had picked up from my teachers Gordon Allport (1937) and Henry Murray (1938), classic psychologists of personality; also from my mentors Jerome Bruner and Robert White (Smith, Bruner, & White, 1956), and from direct personal exposure to psychoanalysis. My practical involvement in applied research in the army with Hovland and Stouffer, as well as in the Flanagan program of aviation psychology, also contributed to my commitment to the softer areas of psychology in which the strictures of behaviorism had always seemed confining. I therefore welcomed the news from philosophers of science that it was becoming quite all right for us to back away from the sterner prescriptions of the positivist tradition.

I was also getting interested not only in the critique of hypothetico-deductive positivism in psychology but in alternatives that were being proposed to replace it. True, a good many of my colleagues continue even now to pursue theoretical constructions (small-scale, now, rather than grand theories) as if the challenge to positivism had never occurred; for example, the flow of publications in cognitive social psychology seems to be maintained on the old assumption that they will eventually add up as components of a universalistic, timeless science on the Newtonian model. Radically challenging this position, Gergen (1973) opened a long controversy by questioning, at first, not the causal nature of social psychological explanation but its transhistorical generality. (See also Gergen & Gergen, 1984.) He argued that social psychology ought to be construed as a historical discipline. What we think are fundamental social psychological principles—like exchange or equity theory—are specific to our particular location in history and culture. The argument was generalized by the advocates of contextualism as a root metaphor (Overton & Reese, 1973; Reese & Overton, 1973; Reese & Overton, 1970; Sarbin, 1977; Rosnow & Georgoudi, 1986.) In Sarbin's (1977) version, contextualism goes beyond the reasonable claim that we should be cautious in our search for universal generalizations since historical and cultural context matters, to assert an almost Heraclitian view of the flux of events that seems radically incompatible with a generalizing scientific enterprise.

An equally radical rejection of the usual framework of causal explanation in personality and social psychology is embraced by advocates of a descriptive account of human action in terms of intentions, meanings, rules, roles, and narratives, within a socially constructed moral order (Harré & Secord, 1972; Shotter, 1984; Harré, 1984; Sarbin, 1986.) Their enterprise has affinities with Dilthey's turn-of-the-century conception of the *Geisteswissenschaften* (Rickman, 1979)—the mental or cultural sciences conceived in contrast with the natural sciences—as reprocessed by the philosophers of ordinary language from Wittgenstein (1953) to Ryle (1949). Gergen (1982) now makes common cause with this group in his social constructivism, joining what has become a "postmodernist" movement that cuts across the humanities, philosophy, and social science, with affinities to major currents of feminism. As I read him, he questions the role of evidence so radically that social or behavioral theory becomes more a matter of political negotiation than of disciplined inquiry, a view that is also maintained by "critical theorists" in the Marxist tradition (e.g.,

Sampson, 1981) about theoretical perspectives other than their own. I think Gergen's critical axe chops through the limb that supports his arguments. He can hardly expect his own arguments to be taken more seriously than those he attacks.

The chaotic variety of assumptive frames within which leading contemporary social and behavioral scientist are operating, and the sense of unease or crisis that many of them share, are nicely displayed in Fiske and Shweder's (1986) *Metatheory in Social Science*. They subtitle their volume "Pluralisms and Subjectivities," which indeed evokes the multiplicity of ways in which many participants challenge or reject the postivist tradition of "objective" inquiry.

My personal agenda in the present stocktaking should now be apparent. I take the criticisms of positivism in its various guises seriously, but I am unready to accept the extreme pluralism or contextualism or relativism that seems to me to lead to the nihilism of "anything goes." I feel constrained to play the unpopular and uncreative role of "reasonable man" in an attempt to save valuable aspects of the positivistic tradition from the brilliant iconoclasts. I want to grant much of the criticism, while strongly asserting my conviction that there *is* a future for behavioral science!

I take heart in finding myself in essential agreement with Edelstein (1983), whose perspective on issues of relativism is a helpful corrective to that of the contextualists. Edelstein starts by quoting comments by Campbell (unpublished) in his 1977 William James Lectures at Harvard, in which Campbell distinguished two contrasting roles for relativism in the scientific enterprise:

> On the one hand, [relativism] can serve an important critical function in improving our knowledge, in removing false reifications, etc. On the other hand, [it] can motivate the relinquishment of the goal of knowledge in favor of a view that each person or tribe or historical period creates its own so-called 'reality' which is as valid as any other and that there is no real reality to which to compare any one of them.

Psychology, in Edelstein's view, may be more vulnerable than his own field of sociology to being demoralized by the radically relativist critique, since psychologists have not had the benefit of prior immunization by exposure to long-standing emphases of their field. A total relativization not only is incompatible with the aspirations for a cumulative, generalizing science but, as Edelstein points out, also undercuts any justification for basing recommendations for applied social practice on scientific results: science then can have no special privilege. As a sociologist, Edelstein looks to universals of modernization as a partial framework that escapes relativization. In the territory of psychology other quasi universals are available.

Issues in Personality/Social Psychology

I will now address some problems in personality-social psychology, my own area of special interest, in relation to the confusion of perspectives that we have been exploring. In recent years, I have been particularly concerned with attaining a coherent formulation of selfhood—the term I use to refer to the crucial features of being a human person, especially those that hinge on language and self-awareness—drawing on what can be gleaned from human prehistory, from cross-cultural and transhistorical studies, and from developmental research on the individual. (See chapter 2.) The venture as I conceive it goes much beyond concern with the self-concept, and indeed tries to establish a critical vantage point on personality theory as it has developed in psychology.

Cultural and Historical Context

From this standpoint, two central metatheoretical problems emerge from the themes that we have just reviewed, and as we will see, they cannot be kept separate from each other. The first relates to the role of cultural and historical context. As I noted earlier, Gergen (1973) made a strong case for the historical nature of social psychology, setting in motion a debate as to whether social psychology should be regarded as history or as science. It has seemed to me from the start (Smith, 1976) that the polarity was wrongly stated: If many of the regularities in our social relations are specific to our time and culture, perhaps the best chance social psychology has to be a good *science* is to regard itself as a historical one!

Theories of personality have not been scrutinized systematically from a contextual standpoint (but see Sarbin & McKechnie, 1986; Veroff, 1986). All the same, the evidence is emerging that good scientific formulations about personality structure and development will also have to be specified contextually in regard to history and culture. In this connection, it strikes me as paradoxical that in the vigorous new field of life-span developmental psychology (Baltes, 1979) central methodological tenets of the approach *require* human development to be placed squarely in its historical and sociocultural context—thus the now-familiar concern with teasing out so-called cohort and period effects from true age trends. No debate there about history versus science! I will return to issues concerned with cultural context after we look at the second metatheoretical problem.

Alternatives to Linear Causation

The second metatheoretical problem concerns what to do about the clash and apparent incompatibility between the explanatory, causal approach consonant with that of the natural sciences that is characteristic of behavioral science in the positivist, empiricist tradition, on the one hand, and the interpretative approach in terms of human intentions, meanings, and values characteristic of theorists like Harré, Shotter, and Gergen, on the other—an approach that sometimes gets tagged with the humanistic label of "hermeneutics." Before I try to clarify the special features that this clash presents for the formulation of selfhood, I need to clear aside some ambiguities in the application of causal analysis to human behavior.

The older positivism that is built into much behavioral science methodology assumed a mechanical view of linear causation, on the folk model of impacting billard balls. Behavioral and social scientists mostly realize that the linear model is a poor fit to complex human affairs, but all the same it is deeply embedded in our customary ways of thinking and in our ways of doing research in terms of independent and dependent variables—causes and effects linearly arranged. It was not long ago that I heard a prominent social psychologist express his readiness to tackle almost any applied problem: "Have ANOVA [analysis of variance], will travel." The way of thinking learned with analysis of variance and experimental design is intrinsically linear.

The critical attack on the linear causal model may lead in either two directions. It may stay within the framework of explanatory, causal analysis but shift to a more sophisticated causal model in terms of interdependent, system relations among variables, with reciprocal and recursive effects, feedback loops. This is the "transactionalist" solution (see Altman & Rogoff, 1987). Thanks to cybernetics and information science, we now know how to conceive of causal relations in such terms, though it is a major challenge to bring our research techniques into line. The other alternative is to reject the causal model entirely for a hermeneutic one, as do Harré, Gergen, and others. A good deal of confusion in the critical literature results from ambiguities in what different theorists mean by cause, and in not seeing clearly the very different ways in which simple linear causation may be rejected.

In the realm of selfhood, there is another reason for confusion in these matters: the phenomena with which we are concerned simply do not allow a clean separation of causal and interpretative perspectives. This point requires elaboration.

The key consideration is human reflexiveness. Thanks to our human symbolic capacities that are surely very dependent on language (if not so absolutely dependent, as G. H. Mead [1934] thought), we are objects to ourselves—or become so by the end of our second year of life (Kagan, 1981). We can look ahead to the future and back to the past, seeing ourselves in time perspective; we can evaluate our own performances and show concern for how they are evaluated by others; we can make commitments and hold ourselves and others responsible. We can feel guilty or ashamed. Indeed, we can exhibit the whole array of distinctively human characteristics that make the interpretative, hermeneutic perspective attractive. But our reflexive awareness, our "intentionality," can also be examined from a causal perspective, and an exciting aspect of present research involves just such an enterprise. A consensual insight supported by several independent lines of research holds that our self-understanding—how, in Kelly's (1955) terminology, we construe ourselves—makes a difference empirically (see chapter 15). Attribution theory in social psychology (Fiske & Taylor, 1984) and labeling theory in sociology (e.g., Murphy, 1976) converge in offering research-based *causal* analyses of the conditions and consequences of making evaluative attributions of one's successes or failures, and of being labeled evaluatively by others for one's deviant behavior.

Consider, for example, how attribution theory was used by Seligman and his colleagues (Abramson, Seligman, & Teasdale, 1978) in extending and enriching his theory of learned helplessness (Seligman, 1975) as a dynamic of depression and other self-defeating reaction patterns. According to this analysis, the depressive posture involves a vicious circle of self-defeat sustained by the learned tendency to attribute failures to the self, in terms of global rather than specific characteristics of the self, and stable rather than temporary ones. (That is, "I failed the test not because it was too hard but because of my own inadequacies, and it's not just a matter of my poor math ability or my lack of sleep—I'm just stupid, so there's no point in trying.") Whether or not Seligman's formulation requires revision or correction is beside the point, which is that a productive research program has applied causal analysis to matters of self-interpretation that are clearly hermeneutic. With the proscriptions of logical positivism out of the way, we need no further philosophical rule making to keep us from interleaving interpretative and causal/explanatory modes of analysis. There is a strong empirical case that what we come to believe and expect about ourselves is likely to become the basis for self-fulfilling prophecy (see Jones, 1977), a critically causal matter. Can we mix causal and hermeneutic approaches? My reaction is like that of the rural respondent questioned as to whether he believed in baptism: "Hell, I seen it done!"

The Ethnopsychology of Selfhood

We can now return to my first methatheoretical theme, the role of cultural and historical context in our formulations of selfhood. The last few years have seen a spate of important publications that begin to give us the basis for comparative ethnopsychology: how indigenous peoples around the world conceive what it is to be a person (which, by the logic we have just explored, should influence how they relate to one another and themselves, and thus partly constitute the persons that they actually are). (See for example Heelas & Lock, 1981; Shweder & LeVine, 1984.) A cursory acquaintance with this literature supports a conclusion with strong implications for personality theory: amid the great variety of indigenous psychologies displayed, the individualism embodied in much of our current personality theory indeed fits the ethnopsychology of our Western tradition, but it is dramatically out of alignment with most other ethnopsychologies that have been described. We are an outlier, the exceptional case. We may have been elaborating on our own peculiar ethnopsychology when we thought we were producing universalistic science; that is the great risk of culture-boundness in the human sciences.

The recent literature also is suggestive in regard to processes by which culturally transmitted semantic systems may play a radically constitutive role in the shaping of selfhood. I was particularly taken by Lakoff and Johnson's (1980) now-classic analysis, *Metaphors We Live By,* in which they illustrated in detail how the metaphorical structure that we acquire with our mother tongue provides warp and woof for our implicit conceptualization of matters in everyday life. In more recent work, Kövesces (1986) applies Lakoff and Johnson's approach to display the cognitive models of anger, pride, and love inherent in American English, squarely a contribution to enthnopsychology. I believe we are on the verge of getting a purchase on ways in which the special character of our version of selfhood gets culturally transmitted (see chapter 4).

Systematic evidence about the relevance of historical context is harder to come by, but it is easy to speculate, for example, that some of the features of Freud's psychology of women that contemporary feminists find especially objectionable (such as penis envy) can be understood as not altogether inappropriate metaphorical expressions of late Victorian relations between the sexes, realities that have since undergone radical change. How much rarer it is to withhold moral condemnation on grounds of historical relativism than it is on grounds of cultural relativism! At least, my students are much more ready to forgive the Ik or the Alorese than they are to make allowances for the benightedness of their forebears. For another example, the evident shift from Freud's time to ours in the forms of psychopathology of most interest to therapists, from hysteria and the obsessions and phobias to borderline and narcissistic conditions and existential complaints, also suggests contextual effects on both the etiology and the social definition of psychological disorders that theory in psychopathology has yet to assimilate.

The Prospects for Human Science

Let us pull together the strands that run through my previous discussion. What implications can we draw about the prospects of human science in psychology at a time when the external strictures of positivism no longer carry the weight they had when the concept of behavioral science was being launched? How ought we to revise our conception of behavioral science, as it appears from the perspective of my sector of psychology?

We can rejoice that psychological researchers are no longer so likely to internalize dogmatic prescriptions and proscriptions that tell them what is proper science and what is not. My quotation from Koch (1959) has finally become essentially true: *"For the first time in its history, psychology seems ready . . . to assess its goals and instrumentalities with primary reference to its own indigenous problems"* (p. 783;. Koch's italics). We can now follow our own sense of problem as researchers, which need not be consensual. A good many more flowers can bloom, but the accompanying sense of liberation does not free us from concern with evidence and disciplined inquiry.

Concern with evidence and disciplined inquiry are at the essential core of science, other criterial features at which are its collaborative/competitive social process, with publication and criticism, the whole point of which is to produce cumulatively more adequate understanding of its topic. What becomes consensually regarded as good evidence in a particular line of inquiry, what are regarded as good methods, what as adequate concepts are, or ought to be, a matter of pragmatic opportunism in this social process. We set the criteria for one another, and the proof of the pudding is in the results. During the heyday of positivism in behavioral science, we made unduly restrictive rules for one another in the mistaken notion that what turned out to be a faulty model of procedures in physical science should guide our strategies of inquiry in human psychology. Now we know better. We are less grandiose in our expectations, but we should be able to take greater satisfaction in our necessarily modest results.

Koch (1985) has argued, I think convincingly, that the dream of a unified science of psychology combined with our fetishism of method to distract psychologists from productive scientific work. Some areas of psychology obviously are embedded in the biological sciences; others just as obviously require humanistic interpretative methods. There should be room in the world and even in psychology departments for both; it is hard to envision a Procrustean bed for them that could yield an integrated marriage. For the area of my special concern, I have been arguing that we need to use the causal explanatory and the interpretative/hermeneutic approaches in tandem if we are to deal at all adequately with selfhood. Without external rule givers, we can find ample justification in the fact that productive researchers have been doing it.

Our serious neglect of the historical and sociocultural context in personality and social psychology poses an urgent agenda for us. One direction in which we might turn is toward better-specified contextual understanding that befits our own time and place; this I understand is the caution urged by Cronbach (1982, 1986), whose warranted skepticism of "generalizations that reach beyond time, place, and population" (1982, p. 71) leads him to advocate what amounts to analytically documented description of our own lives and times—a kind of disciplined current history. I have no objection to this reasonable recommendation, except if it were to exclude the complementary direction that I have been urging as most needed in the psychology of personality: to marshal our resources to reach outside our special niche in space and time. Because we necessarily start from our own historically given assumptions and categories, and because of horrendous data problems, we can only partly succeed. The effort should be rewarding, however. Whatever understanding we gain from cross-cultural and transhistorical investigation of the processes involved in the development and formation of selfhood should have a securer standing as "universals" of human nature than what we project from our own limited and partly culture-bound perspective.

I have not talked about the dichotomy of "basic" versus "applied" psychological research, though success in application during World War II clearly had much to do with the enthusiasm with which the idea of behavioral science was launched, and problem-focused research conceived in generic and generalizable terms (which is what "basic" amounts to) has always been prominent in the Institute of Behavioral Science. In the tradition of Kurt Lewin, I have never wanted the distinction itself to be taken as "basic." I would recur, rather, to the conception that all the strategies and tactics of science are measures developed collectively to make it *progressive,* to make the endeavor *advance* our understanding cumulatively. That requires a sense of direction: Which way is forward? Without a clear sense of direction, fields get dominated by successive fads and fashions. In parts of psychology, and at times, direction is no problem; the front of advance is clearly in view. But at least in social psychology, doubts have often arisen. A great merit of problem-focused research is that the problem *defines* what is progress. I believe that the most promising aspects of contemporary social psychology are problem-focused: for example, health psychology; gender psychology; the emerging psychology of conflict resolution, war and peace. I recognize, of course, that no single discipline can embrace any real-world problem adequately. We need institutions like the Institute of Behavioral Science to orchestrate interdisciplinary collaboration in the all-too-disciplinary world of academia.

To conclude, psychology as a behavioral science has changed substantially since the institute was launched a quarter century ago. The decline of positivism has left us in a position to follow the problems that interest us with methods that seem to fit them best. Substantively, the replacement of narrow behaviorism by the cognitive, information-processing perspective is a real gain, though the affective, motivational aspects of being human (which the computer metaphor gives us little help with) remain to be integrated—agenda for the coming decades. I have focused especially on problems that seem to require joining the interpretative approach familiar in the humanities with that of causal explanation characteristics of the natural sciences and of the positivist tradition in psychology. If the metatheoretical disagreements that currently flourish are frustrating, they are also liberating. My attempt to navigate them leaves me convinced that psychological behavioral science as human science has a promising future if not a secure one. Can more be said for any of us?

10

Beyond Aristotle and Galileo: Toward a Contextualized Psychology of Persons

Psychologists of my generation will recognize the implicit reference in my title immediately: to Kurt Lewin's (1931) classic paper that introduced most of us to the excitement of his ideas when we read it as the initial chapter of *A Dynamic Theory of Personality* (Lewin, 1935). When Lewin wrote "The Conflict Between Aristotelian and Galilean Modes of Thought in Contemporary Psychology" over a half a century ago, it was indeed a breath of fresh air. Along with a very few other books and papers, it stands out in my memory as having had a large part in forming my enduring perspective in psychology. It surely played a similar role for many others, by no means just Lewinians. We cannot readily recall its content since we have absorbed it and built it into the very fabric of our thought.

I turn back to Lewin's essay because it represents the physicalist tradition in psychological theory at its best, free of many faults that tainted the behavioristic expressions of positivism. All the same, the hermeneutic and contextualist critique of positivism should leave us dissatisfied with Lewin's version of a Galilean strategy for psychology. In one respect, thus, I am using this occasion for my own "me-too" endorsement of postpositivist theorizing, joining with Harré and Secord (1972), Harré (1984), Gergen (1973, 1982), and Shotter (1984) among others.

My second concern here is to focus attention on the need for a culturally and historically contextualized approach in personality theory. For accidental reasons (if it is fair to call Gergen's [1973] intervention accidental), the case for a historically contextual approach in the human-oriented, personality/social sector of psychology was made first in the especially hostile territory of experimental social psychology. Personality psychology was then in the doldrums symbolized and promoted by Mischel's (1971) antipersonality text, and personality theory was most aptly represented by the competing chapter-versions of timeless human nature presented in the successive editions of Hall and Lindzey (1957). The task of reformulating personality theory in the postpositivist mode remains largely to be done, though we are seeing some encouraging new developments in the current renaissance of personology.

Finally, I want to talk some sense about postpositivist perspectives in psychology. As usual, the conceptual innovators have not been very reasonable. *If* a contextualized psychology of persons is to be advanced, we need a more plausible version of contextualism than is being argued by the leading polemicists. This is also an effort, therefore, to domesticate a contextualized approach, to accommodate it to its prospective role of defining a new mainstream of theorizing at the softer, more human end of the psychological spectrum.

Lewin's Formulation Revisited

To begin with, then, let us turn back to Lewin's attack on what he saw as Aristotelian features of the psychology of a half century ago. Lewin made it clear, by the way, that the target of his objections was not the writings of the historical Aristotle but rather the styles of conceptualization generally favored in medieval natural science, in contrast with those of modern physical science as heralded by Galileo. He was also explicit in disavowing any stand on physicalist reductionism, while arguing that conceptual approaches effective in physics should also be appropriate for psychology.

Many features of his argument are still pertinent and persuasive today. Thus his objection to *essentialist* modes of explanation—to instinct or trait or factor theories, for example, in which causes are sought in the properties of the individual taken in isolation—as contrasted with his Galilean strategy: *"The dynamics of the processes is always to be derived from the relation of the concrete individual to the concrete situation,* and, so far as internal forces are concerned, from the mutual relations of the various systems that make up the individual"* (p. 41; Lewin's italics). In social and personality psychology, we are still struggling to regain and substantiate in research the interactionist approach that Lewin formulated so clearly, which for long was misinterpreted in social psychology as a mere situationism.

Lewin's sophisticated treatment of the role of the situation is well illustrated in his incisive disposal of the heredity-environment issue, in a passage that follows from his criticism of the concept of an "optimal" situation as developed in the psychology of mental test performance:

[The] question at the center of discussion of the situation is, quite in the Aristotelian sense, how far can the situation hinder (or facilitate). The situation is even considered as a constant object and the question is discussed: which is more important, heredity or environment? Thus again, on the basis of a concept of situation gotten by abstraction, a dynamic problem is treated in a form which has none but a statistical historical meaning. (p. 39)

That is, the question usually put about the relative influence of heredity and environment admits no general answer, only a particular historical one limited to a particular population under particular environmental conditions. Much of the heat dissipated in disputes about heredity versus environment in the intervening years could have been conserved had Lewin's analysis been grasped more widely.

Another central point, still valuable, was Lewin's insistence on the lawfulness of the individual case and the potential misleadingness of statistical generalization, especially when tied to essentialist conceptualization. Merely actuarial prediction in psychology falls short of understanding as it ducks the challenge to analyze the underlying processes.

In his own day, Lewin had to face considerable debate about his insistence on contemporaneous as versus historical causation. The issues in that debate are not those that concern us now. Looking back, I think it is fair to say that in an imaginary state of ideally complete knowledge, the historical lines of explanation favored then by followers of Freud, Hull, and Skinner converge with Lewin's preferred version of contemporaneous causation. If you know everything, you could use the past to construct the present situation. The trouble is, we do not have and will not have complete historical knowledge about the lifelong sequence of anybody's person-situation interactions, nor do we or will we ever have valid X-ray vision to detect the momentary array of personal and situational determinants of behavior, to fill in the data required in principle by Lewin's analysis. In regard to *this* argument, it is only fair to say that historical and contemporaneous strategies are both required, neither is self-sufficient, and using them together, we still have a hard enough time.

Having paid our respects to the continuing relevance of Lewin's critique of conceptualization in psychology, we must now note some fundamental ways in which his vision seems dated. Lewin saw his efforts as contributing to the emergence of a theoretically systematized psychology modeled on the physics of Newton and Einstein. His version of "field theory" was less naively mechanical than the associationist behaviorism of Hull and Spence, but his conception of the goal of scientific endeavor in psychology was essentially the same as theirs: a fully articulated and mathematicized, deterministic, timeless system of axioms and postulates, theorems, and coordinating definitions. Many of us cannot believe in that goal any more, not just because we have been chastened by the failure to make discernible progress toward achieving it but more fundamentally because our conception of the scientific enterprise, in general and especially as it bears upon the science of people, has changed. The hegemony of logical positivism is over, though the news of this state of affairs has not yet spread to all quarters.

As I see it, at least two distinct lines of challenge have been successful in ending logical positivism's unquestioned hegemony in psychology. On the one hand, the timeless validity of psychological explanation has been called into question, especially by Gergen (1973) in his assertion that social psychology is an essentially historical discipline. (He has since [1982] come forward with still more radical challenges to the positivistic interpretation of the human sciences.) On the other hand, the very nature of explanation in the human sciences has been challenged, questioning not only the models of linear causation traditional in psychology (and built into the usual design of experiments) but also the interactive "field" determination characteristic of Lewin and the Gestalt theorists, and the recursive feedback loops of more recent cybernetics and general systems theory, from a point of view that stresses meanings, intentions, and rules instead. (Harré and Secord [1972], Harré [1984], and Shotter [1984] are recent exponents of this line of attack, under the banner of rule-role or ethogenic theory, or interpretative or "hermeneutic" approaches.) The two lines of attack readily merge, since meanings, intentions, and rules are formulated and constituted in terms of symbol systems that are culturally and historically provided. If we are to take these two lines of criticism as seriously as they demand, we perforce must go beyond Lewin's vision of a Galilean psychology, though we can retain most of his insights into the limitations of Aristotelian strategies that still persist in psychology a half century later.

Even in the latter respect, some of Lewin's strictures against Aristotelian features of psychological analysis need reconsideration, in light of post-Galilean developments in the formulation of human action. Lewin objected to the intrusion of anthropomorphic concepts, of value concepts, and of dichotomous formulations into psychological theory. But if our meanings are constructed within culturally provided symbol systems, and if our conduct is governed by how we construe ourselves and our world, then to the extent that our conceptions of one another and of the social world are riddled with anthropomorphic concepts and value concepts and (if George Kelly [1955] was right) also with dichotomous ones, there is a prima facie case that we ought not to exclude concepts of these kinds arbitrarily from our more formal psychological theories. At least, our theories must make a place for accounts of how such concepts participate in constituting our human nature as it has emerged in culture and history. Developments in cybernetics and information science since Lewin's time also legitimize new interpretations of the Aristotelian principle of teleology, another item on Lewin's hit list.

Cultural and Historical Context in Personality Theory

As I have already noted, it seems surprising that the challenge to ahistorical systematic science on the softer end of psychology has been debated primarily in the ultrapositivist context of experimental social psychology rather than in personality psychology, where, on the face of it, the case would seem to have been more obvious and potential receptivity greater. Traditional theories of personality, the sort presented in Hall and Lindzey (1957), have characteristically been put forward in universalistic, ahistorical terms. Even such an influential theorist as Allport (1937), who was explicitly critical of the dominant positivist tradition and open to European phenomenological and existential trends, remained blithely history- and culture-bound (and in Lewin's terms, also Aristotelian in his emphasis on the psychophysical systems of the abstracted individual).

Perhaps one reason that personality psychology was slow to respond to the vulnerability of mainstream positivism was the ill fate of the culture-and-personality movement of the 1930s and 1940s. In the work of Mead (1939), Benedict (1934), Kardiner (1939), Hallowell (1955), Du Bois (1944), and others, interesting and important problems were addressed concerning the linkage of economy, child rearing, modal personality, and the coherence of cultural beliefs and institutions. As a collaboration between anthropology, psychoanalysis, and to a small extent psychology, the movement was a major step toward focusing awareness on the cultural context of personality. But writers in this tradition mostly assumed the universal validity of some version of neo-Freudian psychoanalysis or of neobehaviorism rather than remaining open to more radical ways in which the organization and dynamics of personality might vary across cultures. And the soon-recognized excesses of wartime interpretations of national character sped a decline of interest in the field, more rapid and complete than the similar decline in the status of psychoanalysis. Only a few contemporary writers in psychological anthropology continue the older culture-and-personality tradition (e.g., Le Vine, 1973; Spiro, 1967). I am encouraged, now, by the resurgence of interest in essentially the same area, under the more cognitively framed aegis of "culture and self" (see Heelas & Lock, 1981; Marsella, De Vos, & Hsu, 1984). Elsewhere (chapter 4), I have tried to contribute to these developments in ways complementary to this chapter.

In principle, cross-cultural variation and historical change should have essentially the same conceptual implications for a science of personality. Each brings in contextual considerations that our traditional theories have ignored. In fact, the historical perspective on personality is even more underdeveloped than the cross-cultural. Most of the salvos charging "history-boundedness" that get fired in the theoretical disputes of psychology are themselves likely to be history-bound. That is, the critic challenges the universalist claims of the theory being criticized, on grounds of its unwitting determination by its historical context—while assuming the universal validity of his or her *own* preferred theoretical position. Much of the feminist criticism of Freud seems vulnerable in this respect. Freudian theory is charged with reflecting the prejudices and pathologies of patriarchal bourgeois society in turn-of-the-century Vienna. Indeed, it does reflect them, but one's judgmental tone is different if one sees the Freudian accounts, say, of penis envy, castration anxiety, and the super-ego merely as false projections of male prejudice, or whether one rather sees them as not-so-bad metaphors for the fate of the sexes in *that* society at that time. Along these lines, I am continually impressed by the difficulty my students seem to have in attaining any degree of *historical* relativism of perspective, students who are enthusiastically imbued with the spirit of *cultural* relativism. It takes confrontation with cultures that sanction infanticide or clitoridectomy to shake their nonjudgmental stance. Unlike us Americans, the Buga-Buga can do no wrong, but our parents and grandparents can never be forgiven their benightedness.

If we look for a treatment of personality that is truly contextual historically, the tradition of Marxist scholarship, particularly in the Frankfurt school, comes especially to the fore. Horkheimer (1936), Marcuse (1955), and Fromm (1941) drew jointly on Marxism and psychoanalysis to give substance to a line of theorizing linking personality to social structure in historical perspective, a research tradition that paralleled the culture-and-personality collaboration of psychoanalysis and anthropology but had little contact with it. Fromm in particular laid out in *Escape from Freedom* (1941) a sophisticated neo-Freudian, revisionist Marxian account of the interplay of social history and "social character" in accounting for modern vulnerability, especially in Germany, to fascism and nazism. As he further developed his ideas about a historically grounded characterology (1947), they provided the basis for Riesman's (1950) popular and still provocative analysis of tradition-directed, inner-directed, and other-directed character types in recent history and the contemporary United States.

And Riesman's analysis gave me, in turn, a convenient framework to put competing theories of selfhood in historical context (see chapter 2). It seemed to me that the Freudian super-ego and the integral Allportian ego or "proprium" both represent conceptions of personality congruent with the historical predominance of Riesman's inner-directed type (metaphorically "gyroscopic"), whereas the unintegrated—or disintegrated—ideas of selfhood linked to Laing (1959) (*The Divided Self*), Lifton (1976) (the protean self), Gergen (1971), and the dramaturgical approaches (Goffman, 1959; Sarbin, 1977) could occur only to authors who take for granted the personality orientations that Riesman labeled as other-directed (metaphorically, governed by radar). If these theories are seen as addressed to salient features of the character structure of their time, they need not be forced into confrontation as mutually exclusive versions of universal human nature. We have recently been reminded by Shweder and Bourne (1982) that tradition-directed conceptions of the person are still much alive in the contemporary world. By their analysis, such conceptions of concretely situated behavior may correspond more closely to Lewin's process-oriented Galilean ideals than do our Aristotelian folk habits of trait attribution.

The most articulate call for an explicit historically contextual approach to personality has come not from the central territory of the field but from its borders, in the interdisciplinary area of life-span or life-course human development, a still-recent movement that got its start as an orientation to gerontology but has become a mainstream orientation of human development and developmental psychology. If we consider the metatheoretical hemming and hawing about history and science in social psychology, and my own hemming and hawing here about historical aspects of the psychology of personality, it is remarkable how little metatheoretical fuss has been made about the role of history in formulations of human development: the concern there has been primarily *methodological,* and it seems to be taken for granted by developmentalists that history can contribute to good science. It would never occur to them to pose the issue as it came to be framed in social psychology: social psychology as history *versus* science.

A central methodological feature of the life-span approach was drawn from the highly technical but essentially atheoretical discipline of demography: the concept of birth *cohorts* (cf. Ryder, 1965), sets of people who enter the course of history at about the same time. The life-span approach stresses the importance of distinguishing between the effects of aging as such from cohort effects—consequences of a particular intersection with history that were commonly confounded with age effects in the earlier literature on aging, which depended on cross-sectional rather than longitudinal research. Making this clear distinction led initially to a radical revision of our understanding of the fate of intellectual abilities (since the older people in any U.S. cross-section were also less well educated, more likely to be immigrants). More recently, attention to cohort differences is turning out to be just as fruitful in throwing light on the impact of historically structured life events on personality development (Elder, 1974). Current empirical research on personality development not only is open to historically contextual contributions but is actively seeking them out.

In considering the need to bring cultural and historical context into the study of personality, and the efforts that have been made to do so, I have passed over an issue of conceptual strategy that needs to be looked at explicitly. How radical should we be in our contextualism? Do we envisage the cultural and historical context primarily as providing *content*—values of variables and parameters, so to speak—within structures and relationships that are humanly universal? Lewin would have had no difficulty with this sort of contextual formulation, so it becomes understandable why Sarbin (1977) could classify him as a contextualist. The culture-and-personality theorists with their commitment to neo-Freudian or neobehavioristic principles fall at the same universalistic pole of contextualism, which is implied by the old anthropological postulate of the "psychic unity of mankind." At the other pole is a radical contextualism that amounts to a thoroughgoing relativism. Should we be open to the possibility that the rules of the game change with contextual effects: that a few? some? most? structures of personality and principles of personality development and interpersonal relations differ with the historical and cultural context?

In chapter 9, I noted in passing Edelstein's (1983) criticism of the extreme relativism that radical contextualism implies, which undercuts any justification for basing recommendations for applied social practice on scientific results. Edelstein finds such a demoralizing, even nihilistic view, exemplified in Kessen's (1979) essay, "The American Child and Other Cultural Inventions"; social psychologists will recognize it in Gergen's (1982) recent writings, and in aspects of the current treatments of selfhood by Harré (1984) and by Shotter (1984). The intellectual challenge is drastic, and it has to be taken seriously. Edelstein's way of taking it seriously is so well formulated that I will quote him at length:

> Neo-universalist programs [that challenge extreme relativism], obviously, run into difficulties. Their proof systems rest on plausibilities that differ from the validational conventions of the accepted probabilistic methodologies. They have to reach beyond relativistic and particularistic knowledge and to construct, both from synchronic and diachronic dimensions of child development, an overarching yet dynamic structure of the whole, which encompasses both the contexts of child development and the dynamics of transformation affecting childhood and its organization. . . . [The] immediate impression from child studies is that contextual embeddedness and societal change deeply affect child development.

Two consequences emerge from this observation: first, the study of child development, if it is to be adequate to its object, both represents and, to some extent, presupposes the study of the developmentally relevant structures and parameters of the society itself; second, the culturally relative data that such studies yield need to be ordered in view of a criterion or theory that transcends them. (p. 53)

Edelstein's own life experience in Iceland with the extraordinary sudden transition after World War II from the age-old traditional world of subsistence farming and fishing to a modern stratified society gives especial authority to his sociologically framed attempt to escape from the nihilistic implications of extreme relativism. On the social-historical side, he draws on the traditions of Marx and Weber for an analysis of the major worldwide dimensions of "modernization"—a process that features the newly universal institution of formal schooling and a novel social definition of childhood and youth in relation to this impacting institution. In the modern world, affluent or poor, bureaucratic schooling replaces the transparently valid ways in which the child used to become a participating member of the family enterprise *through* participation, with an abstract and rational age-graded system for inducting new members to the roles that society requires of them—one that tends to be opaque in its justification for participants. In his view,

the interaction between development and the social structures—which both generate and constrain development—contains contradictions that appear to limit its course towards cognitive and moral autonomy and functionally adequate self-identity. Such contradictions appear to channel socializing forces towards the production of the orally dependent, alienated, angry, or depressive type that Lasch (1979) has described. (p. 54)

At the same time, the requirements imposed by modernity result in the emergence of Piagetian sequences of cognitive development, not as biological givens but as nonarbitrary historical emergents. Such a contextualized view indeed presupposes frames of interpretation that transcend the culturally and historically relative; there is no royal road to their attainment, validation, or correction. I will return to the broad issue contrasting radical and limited contextualism later.

Contextualism Reconsidered

So far, I have been discussing historically and culturally contextualized approaches in psychology from what seems to me a fairly-down-to-earth perspective, in terms of their motivation, their variants, and some of the conceptual problems to which they give rise. I have not given any explicit attention to "contextualism" as a distinctive metatheoretical or philosophical model. But such a model is exactly what Sarbin (1977) and Reese and Overton (Reese & Overton, 1970; Overton & Reese, 1973) have been promoting, in espousing the classic formulation by the Berkeley philosopher Pepper (1942) as the basis for metatheoretical criticism and prescription in social, developmental, and personality psychology. We need to look more closely at Pepper's conception of contextualism since it has recently informed so much provocative discussion. I will assert that while Pepper's treatment may have served his original purposes very well in the analysis of historically given metaphysical systems—"world hypotheses" in his terminology—it is not as ready for export to meet the needs of psychological theorizing as Sarbin or Reese and Overton seem to believe. After this excursion, I will return to the more commonsensical view of contextualized analysis that we have been pursuing.

Contextualism for Pepper is one of four relatively successful "root metaphors" underlying the various metaphysical systems that thoughtful people have developed. He explains the idea of root metaphor as follows:

A man [he wrote before we were self-conscious about sexist style] desiring to understand the world looks about for a clue to its comprehension. He pitches upon some area of common sense fact and tries to understand other areas in terms of this one. This original area becomes his basic analogy or root metaphor. He describes as best he can the characteristics of this area, or, if you will, discriminates its structure. A list of its structural characteristics [categories] becomes his basic concepts of explanation and description. . . . In terms of these categories he proceeds to study all other areas of fact. . . . As a result of the impact of these other facts upon his categories, he may qualify and readjust . . . so that a set of categories commonly changes and develops. (p. 91)

Pepper's four major root metaphors include formism, mechanism, contextualism, and organicism. The root metaphor of formism hinges on similarity and leads to classificatory systems like those of Plato, Aristotle, and the Scholastics. That of mechanism hinges on the machine, be it a clock, a dynamo, or a computer, and, as our currently dominant worldview, it deals in terms of cause and effect. Contextualism is harder to grasp.

When we come to contextualism, we pass from an analytical to a synthetic type of theory. It is characteristic of the synthetic theories that their root metaphors cannot satisfactorily be denoted even to a first approximation by well-known common-sense concepts such as similarity, the artifact, or the machine. . . . [Could it be that his metaphor of root metaphor is breaking down?] The best term out of common sense to suggest the point of origin of contextualism is probably the historic event. And this we shall accordingly call the root metaphor of this theory. (p. 232)

Pepper has in mind the "dynamic dramatic active event," the act-in-context, and it turns out that the family of philosophical systems that he is thinking of is the American pragmatism of Peirce, James, Dewey, and Mead in which he himself was raised.

> There are similar problems with organicism: As with contextualism, so with organicism, no ordinary common-sense term offers a safe reference to the root metaphor of the theory. The common term "organism" is too much loaded with biological connotations . . . and "integration" is only a little better. Yet there are no preferable terms. . . .
>
> Actually, the historical event which is the root metaphor of contextualism is a nearer approximation to the refined root metaphor of organicism than any common-sense term. This is so true that it is tempting to regard these two theories as species of the same theory, one being dispersive and the other integrative. It has occasionally been said that pragmatism is simply idealism with the absolute left out, which in our terms would be to say that contextualism is simply dispersive organicism. (p. 280)

It is clear that Pepper's concern here is with the underlying category system of absolute idealism in the style of Hegel, Bradley, and Royce. He is definitely not considering the holistic biological conceptions of organism so prominent in the history of psychological theorizing.

This is of course not an appropriate occasion for detailed criticism of Pepper's classic analysis, nor do I have the philosophical capability for it. The little I have already said, however, may suffice to make the point to those who take their Pepper at second hand by way of his contextualist advocates in psychology: that his typology constructed for the analysis of philosophic systems need not necessarily suit our different purposes as psychologists. The lines of cleavage that he finds between the major philosophical outlooks are inherently arbitrary to a degree. Why should we expect them to draw the distinctions that are most relevant to psychological theorizing? Formism and mechanism, yes: we can readily apply these root metaphors to the clarification of our theoretical assumptions. Recent psychologists have had little truck with absolute idealism, so Pepper's version of organicism does not meet our needs. When we move from old-fashioned machines and dynamos as models to general systems theory, to computers, cybernetics, and information science, the meaning and boundaries of mechanism get obscured in ways that Pepper gives us no help with. Why should we expect such help from what he published in 1942? His detailed treatment of the categories of contextualism in terms of change and novelty in the quality and texture of events does not seem to me to make fruitful contact with our real problems of conceptual strategy in dealing with context in psychological theorizing. In no way does he tackle the phenomenological, hermeneutic, and dialectical traditions, which now seem very relevant to psychology. Have we perhaps been drawing on Pepper's terminology for polemical purposes, without finding his actual analysis of much real use?

I am challenging the authority of Pepper in our domain not only because he does not highlight the distinctions that may be most important for us but also because I am not ready to accept for psychological theorizing his strong argument against eclecticism: that one cannot legitimately criticize one "world hypothesis" or philosophical system in terms of another; that we should not compromise or combine them; that our root metaphors should not be mixed. In specific regard to the tasks of psychology, I remain convinced that the phenomena of selfhood can be grasped only by some kind of deliberate mixing or alternation of causal-explanatory (mechanistic) and interpretative (contextual and hermeneutic) points of view, root metaphors if you like.

As I have argued elsewhere (chapters 2, 3, 8, 9), our reflexive self-awareness and all that goes with it in our existence as embodied persons indeed thrusts us into two worlds: the world of the natural sciences in which we look for causal explanation following strategies that are no longer readily sorted into Lewin's Aristotelian versus Galilean dichotomy, and a human symbolic, historical, and cultural world of meaning and value that requires of us an interpretative approach. These worlds empirically intersect in us as persons, as human actors. We psychologists who wish to give an account of personhood—or as applied practitioners who want to use our psychology to advance human ends—cannot avoid dealing with our topic in both the causal and the interpretative mode. Indeed, some of the most fruitful foci of our research in recent years involve concepts like locus of control or self-efficacy or learned helplessness in which self-attributed meanings—aspects of the interpretative world—have been subjected to causal analysis of their conditions and consequences. From a perspective influenced by existentialism, we seem indeed to be creatures intrinsically linked to mixed metaphors. To constrain our psychological accounts to one "root metaphor" is humanly wrong.

Toward a Contextualized Psychology of Persons

Though I think it is wrong, it may nevertheless be provocative and useful to push a self-consistent point of view as far as it will go. That is how I interpret the recent ventures of Gergen (1982), Harré (1984), Shotter (1984) and Sarbin (1977), all in one way or another "contextualist," all creatively unreasonable, all making major forays into the territory of personality study.

In his radical reaction against positivism, Gergen seems to me to have cast off anchor from the evidential, empirical base that is essential to any enterprise that has a call upon the label "science." Our theories indeed have an ideological aspect, and he is right that we partly negotiate our generative conceptions of social theory among disputants, just as, according to Goffman (1959), we negotiate a socially validated conception of ourselves. But this is a partial truth, part of the truth, not the whole truth. Even though what we take as evidence, as *data,* is subject to debate, the never-finished business of the scientific enterprise requires a critical if never fully conclusive concern with evidence. I am not ready to dismiss the concept of human science, as it seems to me Gergen virtually proposes.

In recent ambitious works, Harré (1984) and Shotter (1984) follow the British tradition of Wittgenstein (1953) and Ryle (1949), which takes its philosophic stance in the clarification of everyday language. They set an agenda for psychology unconnected with natural science. Harré, whose treatment is the more systematic, spells out many implications of a view that takes the radical option between the contextualist alternatives as I posed them earlier. Both authors make major claims toward the radical reconstruction of personality theory. Psychologists of personality have not hitherto been part of their audience. They should be. Yet I think Harré and Shotter have proposed a valuable elaboration of only one side, a partial view, of what is needed for an adequate psychology of persons.

In the course of a long and productive career, Sarbin, on his part, has advanced the dramaturgical metaphor of personhood as a major spokesman for "role theory." He has also been one of Pepper's prominent advocates. In various passages I read him as adopting a radical version of contextualism that places the historic event in a broader context of virtually Heraclitian flux. Yet at the same time he is able to call both Lewin and Piaget contextualists in psychology. The concept of contextualism does get slippery! I have to classify Sarbin, too, among the creatively unreasonable, since he persists in pushing the valuable dramaturgical metaphor or model well beyond the territory that it can handle comfortably—thus, on the empirical side, in his recent treatment of schizophrenia (Sarbin & Mancuso, 1980).

For my part, I want to put Pepper aside, and simply to insist on the importance of much closer attention to historical and cultural *context* in personality psychology than has been characteristic of the field. I welcome the contribution of the contextualist radicals, as opening important new perspectives on being a person, perspectives that also provide useful linkage to the symbolic interactionist tradition in sociology. But I want also to keep open the issue highlighted by Edelstein. In placing personality theory in its cultural and historical context, must we give up aspirations for transcendent, universalistic formulations? Not without trying as hard as we can to attain them, I would urge. But as a matter of strategy, I agree with the symbolic anthropologist Clifford Geertz (1973: p. 53): "In this area [of human studies], the road to the general, to the revelatory simplicities of science, lies through a concern with the particular, the circumstantial, the concrete . . . ," a concern organized, he urges, by analyses at multiple levels from the biological to the cultural, with especial concern for the interplay between levels. A strongly contextual approach, in the weaker sense, but with no commitment at all to a single root metaphor!

A contextualized version of personality theory need not deny universals or be embarrassed by them. Surely some follow from our common biological makeup, the results of our evolutionary history genetically encoded. Others must be entailed by common social and cultural consequences of the life cycle of individuals and families, everywhere. Still others would be expected from the universal human existential predicament of self-aware mortality. A different type of universalist consideration might come from uniformities of social history, of the sort emphasized by Edelstein. Our formulations in context should capture such transhistorical, transcultural features, and we should be delighted when we find them.

Our attempts at general theories of personality have been severely history- and culture-bound, so we need to do better. In psychoanalysis, which has been so central in the course of personality study, the move toward a more hermeneutic formulation is a step in the right direction. (See, for example, Ricoeur, 1970; Schafer, 1976.) But the present challenges in personology, at least as I see them, can be more fully specified in terms of a set of orienting questions. In offering them as my shopping list, I partly summarize points that I have been trying to make; partly I introduce an even larger agenda schematically.

1. How can we formulate a psychology of personality that recognizes adequately the culturally and historically contextual nature of personality, and deals adequately with the sources of individuality in particular settings, in terms that *transcend* culture and history and particular settings? This has emerged as the central question in this chapter.

2. How can we give an account of personality that allows for degrees of unity or disunity or conflict, and degrees of self-determination or external control—without *postulating* absolutes of unity or protean dispersion, or of free will or external programming? Such openness seems to be required by the range of cultural and historical variation. The challenge, thus, is to create a "morphogenic" theory in Allport's (1961) sense, a theory that does not assume or prescribe any single potential to be actualized, any predetermined goal.

3. How can we regain a *biosocial* conception of personality? Murphy

(1947) was working along the essential lines, but his influence faded because he was so reasonable!

4. How can we reconstruct a *dynamic* theory of personality, without the metaphor of libido energy or its equivalent, which has been made obsolete by the revolution of information science?

5. How can we integrate an intentional, phenomenological psychology of meaning with a causal, explanatory psychology? As I have been urging, an adequate psychology of personality has to deal with both facets.

Perhaps a relatively abstract formulation like Silvan Tomkins's (1979, 1987) script theory, one in close touch with the general psychology of affect and cognition, may provide the framework within which these issues can be dealt with productively; perhaps the growing edge may turn out to lie in life-span developmental psychology.

These issues indeed involve considerations of metatheoretical strategy that carry us beyond the Aristotelian and Galilean alternatives that Kurt Lewin had in mind when he wrote *A Dynamic Theory of Personality*. The reigning positivism of his day has fallen in a scientific revolution. For the area of personality study, I have urged that we scrutinize our present theories critically to question aspects in which they are history- and culture-bound; that we accept more limited objectives with explicitly restricted historical and cultural reference as entirely legitimate; but that we remain responsive to the big challenge to find theoretical footholds that transcend history and culture. In this endeavor, moreover, I would carefully distinguish rejection of dogmatic positivism or scientism (Chein, 1972)—I am all for that—from complete skepticism about the role of evidence in psychological inquiry. I want to retain, though critically, the indispensable element of empiricism that lets us hold onto the ideal of a human science, a science of persons that is corrigible and partly cumulative, the more so because it is attentive to the historical and cultural context of personhood.

III

Humanism and Social Issues

11

Psychology in the Public Interest: What Have We Done? What Can We Do?

This is an interesting time for psychologists because all the critical problems of our time (including the remaining threat of nuclear war, political injustice, the increasing gap between the affluent and the impoverished, and environmental disasters) have their psychological aspects, experiential and behavioral. Of course, none of these problems is *essentially* psychological; the problems and the possible ways of coping with them (I don't say "solutions") transcend professions and disciplines. We should be applying ourselves to developing and promoting psychological contributions toward ways of coping. This is surely the most fundamental context in which to consider the public interest.

Any attempt to advance the public interest is inherently political. In the politics of the American Psychological Association (APA), we are experiencing the head-on clash between the two major interest groups, both pursuing their legitimate guild interests: the clinical practitioners, who now hold the majority, and the scientist-academics, now in the minority. My strongest commitments are to the "third force" in APA, the groups self-identified with the public interest. That is a much weaker force than the guild interests generate, but it *requires* an APA with both scientists and practitioners to sustain it.

My aspiration here is to take a sounding as to what APA has accomplished in the name of the public interest, what has *not* been accomplished, and what challenges are before us. Although we can find valid reasons for satisfaction in our record, we have no grounds for complacency. Our public interest activities have been most successful when they have also advanced the individual and group interests of socially disadvantaged categories of our membership. Our other attempts to promote psychology in the public interest have been more controversial, and *in toto* they have been less effective. In order to understand this pattern of differential success and perhaps get beyond it, we must give serious thought to what we mean and *can* mean by *the public interest*. Identifying the public interest in general and in psychology is no simple matter, and in a serious sense it is intrinsically political. Like all political issues, it involves a continuing, ongoing process and is never finally resolved. So I will end by defending a prominent place for *advocacy*—specifically, advocacy for public interest issues—in APA politics.

Accomplishments in the Public Interest

As a major association in the social and behavioral sciences, APA has been a leader in advocacy for the rights of the disadvantaged, and a role model in action on their behalf. The concerns of disadvantaged categories of our own membership have mobilized the APA to take the lead in aligning psychological competence with justice. This enterprise has a long history, but for most purposes we can go back to Kenneth B. Clark, whose legacy to APA from his 1971 presidency was the Board of Social and Ethical Responsibility for Psychology (BSERP). BSERP nurtured APA's advocacy and modeling roles in regard to ethnic minorities, women, disabled and handicapped persons, and gays and lesbians. BSERP spun off committees and boards, each of which (with one exception that I will discuss later: the Committee on Children, Youth, and Families) represents the call for justice from a particular disadvantaged category of APA members.

Advance in justice comes in small packages, and it is very much to the credit of APA that in advancing justice toward its own disadvantaged members, it has played a visibly useful role in national affairs. In 1952 we refused to hold our convention in racially segregated locales. In 1977 we refused to meet in states that had not ratified the Equal Rights Amendment (ERA), taking a financial risk by abrogating standing contracts. (This was a more divisive issue among APA members than our stand against racial segregation, but in referendum a majority supported the board's action.) As a major sponsor of large national meetings, APA was very effective in getting convention hotels to make their facilities available to physically handicapped persons. More recently, APA has been a national leader in pressing for government support of the counterattack on AIDS and in marshaling the competence of psychologists to help cope with the crucial behavioral aspects of prevention and treatment.

In all of these public interests concerns, justice as most of us would conceive of it is congruent with the self-interest of major segments of our own membership. Black, Hispanic, female, gay and lesbian, and physically handicapped psychologists have had to suffer unfair deprivations within their own discipline and profession and association; thus, the actions that they have mobilized APA to take in its own affairs and in the world outside are energized substantially by their own group interests (and other members' empathy with them). It should be no surprise that the public interest activities of APA have worked best when group self-interests converge with justice. Again, with the exception of the Committee on Children, Youth, and Families, these *are* the public interest concerns that have become built into the board and committee and even the divisional structure of APA.

The boards and committees that represent these interests make an immense difference to their constituencies and play an important role in putting psychology in the service of justice. When the APA was recently in tight financial straits and board and committee meetings were being rationed severely, this aspect of public interest psychology suffered badly. The conventional wail that board and committees drain APA dollars made no sense. The cost was a minuscule fraction of the APA budget; the gain from these board and committee activities has been large in sustaining APA's humane role, in making APA worth belonging to.

Troublesome Topics and Difficulties

It is the other set of topics, social issues not specifically linked with justice to ourselves as APA members, that have been most troublesome for APA governance. These include our involvement with protest against the Vietnam War, our endorsement of the nuclear freeze, our stand against corporal punishment in the schools and against aversive interventions in behavioral modification, and our positions on international human rights, among others. *Should* APA take stands on social issues beyond the promotion of psychology as a science and as a profession? Does our concern with human welfare, legitimated by the preamble to our bylaws, warrant our intrusion into affairs outside the small world of APA? There never has been agreement about it. Our perennial debates about "advocacy" have cleaved us along rather traditional lines of liberal versus conservative, radical versus reactionary. The controversy about APA's advocacy role never goes away and it is never settled. I think there are intrinsic reasons that it never *can* be settled, and it might improve the quality of our political discourse if we could share more common understanding as to *why*.

Behind the many different concrete ways in which the issue continually arises in APA are two underlying difficulties. One is a general feature of modern American culture in which American psychologists participate: our extreme individualism (accentuated during the Reagan years) in which the pursuit of self-interest or group interests is taken for granted and altruistic concerns are discounted cynically as naive or self-deceptive. Self-interested activity seems almost always to be unquestionably legitimate, in the APA as elsewhere; it is activity supposedly in the public interest that has trouble justifying itself. With the popular doctrines that psychology has exported concerning reinforcement and exchange theory, which seem to give scientific authority to self-interestedness, psychology has even been part of the problem.

The prevailing suspicion regarding public interest advocacy is also grounded in sound reasons for skepticism, which constitute the second, more fundamental difficulty. Who is to decide what is the public interest? On the one hand, we are all subject to the self-serving bias that warps our perception of our private self-interests so that we see them as also being in the public interest. From Charlie Wilson's "What's good for General Motors is good for the country," it is not very far to "What's good for advancing psychological science is good for humanity," or "What's good for the practice of psychology is good for mental health." And, apart from the self-serving bias, we hold divergent views of what is right and proper, so each of us defines the public interest implicitly or explicitly according to our own lights in a different way. People who are absolutely sure that they know what the public interest is, the "true-believer" types, do a lot of damage, as we know all too well. The damage does not necessarily come just from the religious fundamentalists who claim a pipeline to God's truth, though they have indeed become very difficult.

Individualism as a Problem

Let me go back to the problem of individualism, which was accentuated in the "me" epoch with considerable help from both my humanistic and my behavioristic colleagues. In cross-cultural perspective, American culture is really over the edge in its individualistic ethos, and the costs to people that this extreme orientation entails are increasingly visible. Enthusiastically promoted from on high in the Reagan years, our accentuated individualism has given rise to a degree of corruption in American public life that has little precedent, even in the rotten splendors of the gilded age. (Reagan's appointees have been wrung out through the courts; the Pentagon procurement scandal, the Wall Street inside trading scandal, and the savings and loan scandal, which cost billions of dollars, were being followed as I wrote this by the scandal in the Chicago futures market and by charges of bribery in the previously lily-pure Federal Drug Administration about generic drugs. The scandals continue!) Unashamed predatory self-interest is becoming visible to the victimized public, and I hope that perpetrators will be held to account—and that an overdue pendulum swing is occurring.

More than just a pendulum swing is needed for humane values to prevail. It is good that psychologists and other social sientists are beginning to provide a thoughtful critical base, in touch with our science though hardly derived from it, that supports a view of what is possible for people in society that is different from the hedonistic individualism with which psychologists have mainly been identified hitherto. I am thinking, of course, of Robert Bellah and his colleagues in sociology and philosophy (Bellah, Madsen, Sullivan, Swidler, & Tipton, 1985), whose book, *Habits of the Heart,* reached a large audience, taking the contemporary United States to task for giving precedence to individualism over community in the explicit values in terms of which Americans justify themselves. (The self-accounts of the psychotherapeutic subculture were treated roughly in the book.) I am thinking of the early essay by Ed Sampson (1977) that pointed out the degree to which unrecognized individualistic assumptions pervade American psychology and of his recent manifesto relating his analysis to the current world situation (Sampson, 1989); of Paul Wachtel's (1983) powerful criticism of the individualist tradition in psychology and psychoanalysis; of Barry Schwartz's (1986) reexamination of "human nature"; and of the important critique provided by Michael and Lise Wallach (1983) in *Psychology's Sanctions for Selfishness,* now followed by their courageous new attempt to break through the bad choice between liberal relativism and authoritarian absolutism in *Rethinking Goodness* (1990). I also have Seymour Sarason's numerous contributions (e.g., 1986, 1988) in mind. In the past, our influential social critics have come from the humanities, the other social sciences, and psychoanalysis—not from psychology. Cheers for the emergence of strong and clear critical voices from our own ranks!

As I understand and resonate to the message being put forth by these colleagues, they are telling us that we psychologists have given the sanction of science uncritically to implicit individualistic values that are, of course, preempirical, not legitimately accessible to "scientific" support on such lines. The pursuit of self-interest, of self-development and self-actualization as the primary ends of existence, has not been dictated by firm psychological knowledge but arises from our having been shaped by particular features of our culture in their historical vicissitudes. To the extent that the psychology we "give away" (Miller, 1969) has supported the basically selfish trend in our times (the word *narcissistic* is too fancy and entails too much bad theory!), I hope that we may now be getting into a position in which we psychologists are not a major part of the problem.

What Is the Public Interest?

Granted, then, that the individualistic orientation that psychology has shared with its environing culture has made us complacent about letting guild intersts and special group interests dominate APA politics and that psychologists are now beginning to pose a fundamental challenge to this feature of our culture, there remains the second difficulty: How are we ever going to discover or define the public interest? Like the rest of you, I have strong intuitions as to what the public interest is, in psychology and in the world at large, and I act on them in my political participation in the APA and in local and national politics. Like everybody else, especially members of the Public Interest Coalition in APA, I *know* what is in the public interest! Because I also know, however, that my conviction that I know is not to be trusted (it will not be trusted by others, so I shouldn't trust it myself), I have to back away from my commitments in order to consider the broader issue of how to discover and define the public interest.

Of course, there is no simple solution: I will have to wind up favoring an open politics that gives voice to competitive claims, and expects only temporary resolutions of them. Whatever *can* we mean by the public interest? In trying to come to an answer that could satisfy others besides myself, I looked back to a respected commentator, Walter Lippmann, from a generation before mine, who wrote very persuasively about the public philosophy. As a political commentator and social theorist, Lippmann (1955) began his discussion of the public interest with "We are examining the question of how, and by whom, the interest of an invisible community over a long span of time is represented in the practical work of governing a modern state" (p. 41). Let me extract from what Lippmann (1955) wrote three decades ago, which is not irrelevant to issues in contemporary psychology:

> In ordinary circumstances voters cannot be expected to transcend their partic-
> ular, localized and self-regarding opinions. . . . In their circumstances, which as
> private persons they cannot readily surmount, the voters are most likely to
> suppose that whatever seems obviously good to them must be good for the
> country, and good in the sight of God.
>
> I am far from implying that the voters are not entitled to the representation of
> their particular opinions and interests. But their opinions and interests should
> be taken for what they are and for no more. They are not—as such—proposi-
> tions in the public interest. . . .
>
> Let us ask ourselves, How is the public interest discerned and judged? . . . [W]e
> cannot answer the question by attempting to forecast what the invisible com-
> munity, with all its unborn constituents, will, would, or might say if and when it

ever had a chance to vote. There is no point in toying with any notion of an imaginary plebiscite to discover the public interest. We cannot know what we ourselves will be thinking five years hence, much less what infants now in the cradle will be thinking when they go to the polling booth.

Yet their interests, as we observe them today, are within the public interest. Living adults share, we must believe, the same public interest. For them, however, the public interest is mixed with, and is often at odds with, their private and special interests. Put this way, we can say, I suggest, that the public interest may be presumed to be what men [we would now say *people*] would choose if they saw clearly, thought rationally, acted disinterestedly and benevolently. (pp. 41–42)

In modern mass democracies, Lippmann thought, the challenge to political leadership is to promote the public interest so conceived in dialogue with the many voices of private and special group interests. He saw the modern record as poor and attributed the crisis in twentieth-century democracies to attrition of what he called the "public philosophy" as a shared underlying political ideology, his phrasing for the Natural Law doctrine of the Enlightenment. In his words, it amounts to

the postulate that there is a rational order of things in which it is possible, by sincere inquiry and rational debate, to distinguish the true and the false, the right and the wrong, the good which leads to the realization of human ends and the evil which leads to dstruction and to the death of civility. The free political institutions of the Western world were conceived and established by men who believed that honest reflection on the common experience of mankind would always cause men to come to the same ultimate conclusions. (P. 134)

Do you perceive Lippmann, as I read him, anticipating recent intellectually fashionable writers on the conservative side, such as Alasdair MacIntyre (1981) and Alan Bloom (1987)? In *After virtue,* MacIntyre traced the present plight of moral philosophy, with its cacophony of voices and loss of moral meaning to the collapse of the Aristotelian tradition as sustaining and sustained by a moral community—the collapse of the public philosophy in Lippman's sense. Bloom's best-selling jeremiad against the liberal relativism of the world of American colleges and universities, *The Closing of the American Mind,* explicitly sought to restore the reign of natural law as a frame for personal philosophy. For that matter, Bellah and associates (1985) in *Habits of the Heart* introduced their critique of contemporary American culture, according to which commitment and community as intrinsic sources of human value suffer in our excesses of what they term *utilitarian* and *expressive individualism,* by reminding us how the Biblical and Republican traditions moderated our individualistic tendencies in public life at the nation's origins. They too are nostalgic for the "public philosophy."

As you may have guessed, so am I! I share their yearning for community and their discontent with anomic relativism (though I may weigh more heavily than they the favorable shift in the balance of human values that came about for most of us when so many people left the arduous and spiritually destructive poverty of traditional rural life and the narrow constraints of Main Street for the broadened vistas and healthier prospects of the modern world.) All the same, I do not think we can retrieve the old Enlightenment faith, at least as Lippman phrased it, by any fiat of Jamesian "will to believe." Our faith in the two pillars of modern thought since Descartes, reason and empiricism, has been too deeply shaken. In fact, we do live in a multicultural nation in a multicultural world, in which the older certainties are moot. There are liberating advantages to our intellectual and moral situation, just as there are heavy human costs. But we cannot wish our situation away. Future generations, if they survive the life-threatening world problems of which we are already aware, might reemerge into community in the old style after a new dark age, which some of our true believers are promoting, but the community of traditional consensus is beyond our deliberate reach. A good many modern psychologists, I among them, would be among the last people to believe that, by reason and evidence, we could or should all arrive at the same conclusions.

In other words, I cannot defend as tenable for our time the public philosophy that Lippmann called on to justify the public interest. For better or worse, we are stuck in a pluralistic society and world in which there is little prospect of our agreeing on first premises about abortion, the meaning of gender, or any of the things that people seem still to be ready to fight about, including religion and nationhood. Nevertheless, I want to endorse the essence of his conception of the public interest and to argue that even without consensus on fundamentals, we can do much better than is usual for us by trying, in our leadership and individually, to emphasize informed, rational, disinterested, benevolent decision making. Just as in our scientific roles we should and most do act *as if* there were truth "out there" that we only have to be clever enough to discover (whether or not the constructivists are right, that is surely the only pragmatically justified stance for scientists to take), so in our personal, political, and psychologist roles we also do well to act *as if* there are objective right and wrong, better and worse choices and policies. We are surely mistaken if we have the presumption to believe we are *absolutely* right about our own choices, just as we are mistaken if we are sure about the absolute truth of our factual beliefs. But we are adrift as persons and useless as citizens if we do not try to find and pursue the right and if we do not take our own convictions—

and those of our opponents—seriously as attempts to advance the right and give it reality. We become literally "de-moralized."

As I see it, the least common denominator of politics is the negotiation of competing self- and group interests. At its best, politics is the arena in which different conceptions of the right—of justice and the public interest—get threshed out, modified, mutually accommodated, and negotiated with the various special interests. Politics so conceived never settles issues, but it contributes centrally to the quality of human life at least as it has been experienced in the Western tradition. Psychologists generally are not used to thinking along these lines. (For access to the intellectual sources on which this way of thinking is based, I am most indebted to Hannah Arendt [1958] and Isaiah Berlin [1978].) I hope we can come to "give away" a psychology that is more concordant with this way of thinking. And I hope we can apply it to thinking about the public interest, as APA policy and action bear on it.

The Politics of Public Interest in APA

I will now leave these underlying issues of philosophical perspective, which are hard to discuss persuasively despite their importance, and return to the public interest politics of APA. First, I will continue my consideration of APA advocacy on public interest issues. Then I will discuss the public interest aspect of psychologists' major guild commitments as scientists and as professionals.

Conservatives in academic science have time and again parted company with members typical of the Society for the Psychological Study of Social Issues (SPSSI) to insist that APA respect a sharp separation between psychologists' and citizens' roles in regard to advocacy on issues other than the promotion of guild and (sometimes) member-category interests. They have argued that APA, and its members when they speak as psychologists, should present only the conclusions of our scientific research, only on the basis of *data*. Only when we have solid data have we a right to speak as psychologists, they insist, and our advocacy should be restricted to summarzing and interpreting the data "objectively." I cannot agree. "Data" are seldom conclusive, and data are not our only or even necessarily our most important contribution to the public interest—though it is great when we have conclusive data. Kiesler (Kiesler & Sibulkin, 1987) has some very important data that help redefine the public interest in hospitalizing mentally ill pesons. But the role of data is mostly different. In the area of international conflict and peace, our major contributors— Urie Bronfenbrenner (1961), Ralph White (1970), and Morton Deutsch (1983)—have had their largest impact through the use of their research to *reframe* the problem of international conflict. They do not prove a policy position; they employ research to illustrate or dramatize a view of the conflict process that focuses on the symmetrical, mirrorlike enemy images that develop, which tend to exacerbate and escalate the conflict, rather than focus exclusively on the evil of the adversary as is common even in national councils of policy. Such contributions open important options for policy discussion, although they do not involve definitive conclusions that are firmly based upon data. They have been influential in the past, and appropriately so (see chapter 13).

There is also much misunderstanding about the actual role of APA in "advocacy." In the Council of Representatives, much heat has been generated over the years by resolutions proposing that APA endorse one or another policy position. Rarely do such resolutions have real-life effects that justify their cost in organizational strain. They may be worth the cost, however, when they instruct the activity of APA staff specifically, or when there are organizations and constituencies outside APA that are in place to use them (as, for example, with APA's position, taken in 1975, against corporal punishment in the schools). APA can usually advocate more effectively for public interest matters along lines similar to its support for guild issues: providing relevant information and testimony in close liaison with the government's legislative and executive branches and disseminating public information skillfully. This is not at all in the same realm as passing resolutions!

APA *has* gone substantially beyond our guild interests and the special interests of our own disadvantaged categories of members in ways that do not strain our internal politics, in spite of the contrary broad characterization I have made of our public interest activity. A prime example is the relatively recent BSERP Committee on Children, Youth, and Families that I have already mentioned (but its establishment *was* a motherhood issue that was hardly debatable!) APA might still do much more by way of research and advocacy on behalf of children, so many of whom are poor. Among the divisions of APA, there is especially the Society for the Psychological Study of Social Issues, which had a prior independent existence before the reorganization of APA after World War II, and has consistently advocated broadly conceived public interest concerns in APA and at large. Members should also know that APA's policy staff, well equipped to represent APA in the national political process, regularly address public interest issues as well as guild issues. When I was preparing this essay, I read in the newsletter of the Division of Population and Environmental Psychology the following statement from its president, Ralph Taylor (1989), after his participation in the 1989 Division Leadership Conference: "As a member of APA who has felt in the past that the organization was not applying research to policymakers as much as it should, I find recent developments in the PID [Public Interest Directorate] *extremely* heartening. These activities also point up the substantial clout that APA is capable of having'' (p. 3). Taylor was particularly impressed by the careful, scrupulous, and effective representation that APA made to Surgeon General Koop concerning the inconclusive research evidence about the psychological effects of abortion on women, although there was a trend suggesting that abortion causes minimal trauma.

Our Guild Issues: Professional and Scientific

Public interest issues have received much attention in APA politics, but I have no doubt that it is how APA handles its guild issues—of psychology as a science and profession—that has the greatest impact on the public interest, however we may interpret it. What we do as a science, what we do as a profession, makes a difference to the public weal. It can even be harmful; it is often neutral; we all hope that it makes a positive contribution. I have long argued that our guild concerns, whether scientific or human-service-oriented, ought to be compatible with promoting the public interest. At a minimum, they should be at least orthogonal, though because of our self-serving bias, a degree of skepticism about such assertions is always in order. APA's advocacy roles are so heavily focused on guild interests that scrutiny of their compatibility with the public interest is highly desirable and inherently political.

Because my own affilations are closer to the scientific than to the professional wing of psychology, I tend to give psychological science a relatively clean bill of health in terms of its involvement with the public interest. I do believe that the development of psychological science is mostly in the public interest. As a long-term SPSSI member, I am delighted when competent science-oriented psychologists devote themselves to attacking problems to which contributions should be humanly important. I worry that insufficient scientific attention is being paid to the psychological aspects of the world-shaking issues of war and peace and environmental pollution and depletion, the essential life-and-death issues that I mentioned at the outset, and to the causes and consequences of poverty, which underlies so many human problems. But I am just as delighted when others are so captured by their intrinsic sense of direction in basic research that such an applied focus would seem immoral to them. I am worried about the ethics of experimentation with humans and with animals, especially when dubious practices of deception became normative for a whole subfield, as they did for a while in social psychology, but I think our record is mostly good. Under current regulative pressure, it seems to me that the risk of losing important knowledge that may ultimately help people (and other animals!) probably exceeds the risk of damaging ethical violations. Our ethics of research is becoming too bureaucratic, at the cost, perhaps, of becoming less internalized.

On the professional side, I also believe that a strong and responsible profession of psychology is in the public interest. But continued warfare with psychiatry over issues of turf—essential guild interests—may be to the disadvantage of the troubled people whom we say we serve, who suffer from the heavy cutting of government funds that have supported both psychiatry and psychology. I think our reflex rejection of anything labeled as a "medical model" is self-serving and wrong. Many problems of "mental health" that properly concern us also have their medical aspects. And I do not like our recent single-minded focus on the financial aspects of practice—third-party payments, health insurance, Medicare, and the rest. It is all justifiable and understandable, but it somehow blocks out the *service* values that may have been a little more prominent earlier on, though not so prominent as in social work, which seems to have undergone a similar value transition.

Can Psychologists Give *Pro Bono* Service?

Psychologists got into professional human service too late to emulate the earlier *pro bono* traditions of medicine, now in attrition in the era of Medicaid and Medicare. Unlike earlier medicine and even contemporary law, psychology has *no* tradition of *pro bono* practice, even though the concept is endorsed in our formal ethical code. On the science side, which includes scientist-practitioners, there is normative pressure to contribute to peer reviewing of papers and research proposals. On the clinical side, I see no equivalent.

I am not suggesting that clinical practitioners take on charity cases paternalistically—we have outgrown that era. Rather, psychologists might take initiative to provide consultation, *not* guidance and control, to the burgeoning realm of self-help and volunteer organizations (see Jacobs & Goodman, 1989). It has seemed to me for a long time that self-help and volunteer programs are *the* most constructive development imaginable in the field of mental health. For people with problems in living, there simply cannot be enough professionals or even paraprofessionals to treat patients on a one-to-one basis (Smith & Hobbs, 1966). The widespread replication of these mutual support systems clearly is based on real merit. They will not necessarily or perhaps often want the help of psychologists even if we proffer it, but with genuine concern and respectful tact, professional psychologists can surely make a valuable contribution to them—on a *pro bono* basis. Psychologists might also find ways of involving themselves more actively, for example, in evaluating the effectiveness of differently organized programs and in stimulating the trial of new models. In my limited range of direct acquaintance, I know of a community suicide-prevention hotline that benefited greatly from the volunteered aid of a psychologist who developed training materials and contributed largely to the recurrent training of new cohorts of telephone volunteers. There are surely many examples of such contributions, but they have not become a normative component of professional careers in psychology.

Conclusions

In closing, let me draw together the complex issues that we have been considering. However we may conceive of the public interest, the ways in which scientists and professionals in psychology pursue their guild interests have more effect on the public interest than any activities that they carry out explicitly in its name. Let us be sure that our guild activities at least do not harm the public interest, and let us hope that we do better. Understandably, APA has met with most success in its public interest activities when they converge with the special interests of justice to particular disadvantaged segments of our membership. Our record in other areas of advocacy is more mixed, but we have used our strong presence with the executive and legislative branches of the federal government effectively on matters not tied to our guild concerns. May these efforts continue!

When we ask ourselves, what *is* the public interest, our attempts to generate informed, reasonable, disinterested, and benevolent answers will not automatically produce consensus. Open political debate about divergent interpretations of the public interest is good for the APA. Because there can be no valid claims to absolute truth about the public interest, it is the best we can do. However, as we debate these issues, I hope we can bear in mind the urgent problems of human survival and social justice that I noted at the outset. The Reagan years, which I despise, have made us too accustomed to acquiescing in human (and biological) disaster. Psychologists have much to contribute in recreating a more humane and sustainable world. APA can do much more to facilitate it. I hope that APA will continue its involvement in public interest issues in our national politics and that psychologists, as members of APA and the American Psychological Society and individually, will keep in touch with public issues that affect the lives of people and become politically active on the side of justice and human welfare.

12

McCarthyism: A Personal Account

I have used this occasion[1] to pull together my memories of the wretched episode called McCarthyism and to document them. I was amazed to discover their state of disarray, considering how central the issues had been in my life. It *is* hard to keep the past straight! Maybe the review that was useful to me can also help my contemporaries and juniors get that period in perspective. I will draw especially on my own minor part in the events, as my best way of giving them the immediacy that may make them relevant to our situation today. These were events and issues in which SPSSI (the Society for the Psychological Study of Social Issues) and SPSSI members were deeply involved—issues that tore lives and careers apart, and that are still with us.

What Was McCarthyism?

The phenomenon of McCarthyism is much broader than the meteoric career of Senator Joseph McCarthy, from his first publicized charges, in 1950, of Communists in the State Department to his downfall, in 1954, with the Army-McCarthy hearings—which the new medium of television allowed many of us to watch with fascination. It has often been observed that McCarthy was basically nihilistic, a destroying angel who fortunately built no party and left no antidemocratic organization behind him. Whereas his personal style was spectacular, McCarthyism as a historical phenomenon began before McCarthy and lasted long after his collapse.

We can begin with the spring of 1947. President Harry Truman heralded the cold war with his Truman Doctrine calling for aid to the anticommunist forces in Greece and Turkey; on the domestic front, he instituted the infamous attorney general's list of dubious organizations implicated in communist, fascist, totalitarian, or otherwise "subversive" activities. Ini-

195

tially developed for internal governmental use in screening prospective government employees for more intensive investigation, the list soon was made public and became a multipurpose instrument of intimidation.

In the new cold war climate, the House Un-American Activities Committee (HUAC), which as the "Dies committee" had had a long history of harassing New Deal liberals and leftists, rolled into high gear. With young Congressman Nixon playing a prominent role, the committee's first big quarry was Alger Hiss, who was indicted for perjury at the end of 1948 and convicted after a second trial in the beginning of 1950. In 1949, the regents of the University of California voted to impose a special anti-Communist oath on all faculty, initiating the loyalty oath controversy that lasted into 1952. (Edward Tolman, a SPSSI president, led the nonsigners, who immediately forfeited their jobs; Nevitt Sanford, also a SPSSI president, was a nonsigner too, along with Hugh Coffey.) In 1950, as we have noted, McCarthy made his initial charges; in 1953, he acquired the chairmanship of the Senate Permanent Investigating Committee, which gave him large resources. In 1951, Julius and Ethel Rosenberg were condemned to death for espionage. By 1953, J. Robert Oppenheimer was suspended by the Atomic Energy Commission as a security risk. And on March 2, in the same year (on a ridiculously different scale, though it hardly seemed so to me at the time), I testified under subpoena before the Senate Internal Security Subcommittee—the so-called "Jenner committee" that was the Senate's counterpart to HUAC.

The immediately significant context for this crescendo of domestic preoccupation with loyalty and internal security, of course, was the inability of the United States, the great victor of World War II, to have its way in the postwar world, in which the Soviet Union had already established control over Eastern Europe. (Our wartime alliance with the Soviet Union seemed by then a brief aberration from our usual distrustful antagonism.) The forces of Chairman Mao, then a Soviet ally, conquered China in 1949, and when the Soviets exploded a fission bomb of their own in 1949 our atomic monoploy was ended. The Korean War began in June 1950. In spite of Oppenheimer's opposition, we tried out our first hydrogen bomb in 1952, and were taken aback when the Soviet Union came forth with its first fusion bomb the following year; treachery was suspected. Given this rapid set of developments, it is also hard to remember that the court fight against legally enforced racial segregation in the schools, another matter in which SPSSI was deeply involved, was coming to a climax at about the same time.

My Encounter with the Jenner Committee

My 1953 appearance before the Jenner committee was neither heroic nor really dastardly. It felt unique to me, but I now suspect my experience was more typical than I could recognize at the time. It left me feeling very bad about myself, so I have almost never talked about it since. With the stimulus of this occasion, and the help of the Freedom of Information Act, I recently obtained the transcript of my testimony. When it arrived, I hardly dared look at it—not only from general repugnance, I now realize, but because I had actually revised my memory of the events in a self-serving way and was afraid of the truth.

I need to give a little background first. Fifty years ago, as a student at Reed College, I had become first a "fellow traveler" in the large chapter of the American Student Union (ASU), a Popular Front organization including major old-Socialist components, and had later become a pretty good Stalinist in the much smaller covert chapter of the Young Communist League (YCL) that provided the ASU leadership. With most of my friends I soon came to see things very differently, after the Moscow trials that purged the Old Bolsheviks and after the Nazi-Soviet pact. But by the time of McCarthyism, I felt—and I still feel—very much as Lillian Hellman (1976) expressed it in *Scoundrel Time,* the account of her encounter with HUAC. As a former "fellow traveler" but not a Communist party member, Hellman wrote,

> I am still angry that the anti-Communist writers' and intellectuals' reason for disagreeing with McCarthy was too often his crude methods. . . . Such people would have a right to say that I, and many like me, took too long to see what was going on in the Soviet Union. But whatever our mistakes, I do not believe we did our country any harm. And I think they did. They went to too many respectable conferences that turned out not to be under respectable auspices, contributed to and published too many CIA magazines. The step from such capers was straight into the Vietnam War and the days of Nixon. (pp. 154–55)

I did not want to join the anti-Communist hue and cry, and particularly, I did not want to "name names," the crucial symbolic act demanded of those subpoenaed to testify.

When I received the subpoena, I had just joined the staff of the Social Science Research Council (SSRC) after having chaired the Psychology Department at Vassar. Self-analyses of motives are always dubious, but I think my motives as I planned my testimony included principled opposition to the committee's witch-hunt (then focused on "Reds" in education), together with selfish reluctance to jeopardize my career and family. The top foundation lawyer whom the SSRC made available to me agreed with my strategy to cooperate with the committee to the extent of naming the publicly identified members who were our organizer-leaders, letting my memory for events fifteen years earlier stop at that point. Here are some extracts from my testimony:

MR. MORRIS [counsel to the committee]: Were you ever invited to join the Young Communist League?

MR. SMITH: I belonged to it.

MR. MORRIS: Would you be willing to tell this committee the names of the people who were members of that union [*sic*]?

MR. SMITH: I would be very reluctant to do it.

MR. MORRIS: You are talking here in Executive Session.

THE CHAIRMAN [Senator Jenner]: This is not for publication.

MR. SMITH: I would still be very reluctant, but I know that the law is the law. I would prefer to answer in general terms first and then leave it to your discretion whether to put further questions to me, because, for myself, I have no feeling of particular regret or shame at having belonged at that point way back in my student career, and I think it was, if anything, a healthy sign rather than a bad one. It certainly didn't make an adult Communist out of me. . . . I would say this, however: that of the people that I knew in connection with the Young Communists' League there at Reed, none of them are important people today, and we had no official tie with any faculty group. So I have no guilty knowledge in that respect, and the persons that I have been in touch with since have all completely changed their point of view, as I have. . . . So I will answer your questions if you insist on putting it to me, but I very much hope you won't feel the need to.

MR. MORRIS: Mr. Chairman, we would like, for purposes of investigation, just to determine whether or not the reasons given by the former professor are true, namely, whether or not those people who were once active in the Communist organization are any longer active, to have the names.

THE CHAIRMAN: It would be a big help to the committee if you would do it. We have to find out the facts and have information. This is an executive session. The record will not be divulged. It will not be made public. Even the fact that you are testifying will not be made public. It will give us a basis of facts to go on.

MR. SMITH: I understand, and it is really my conscience that I am struggling with, not merely a point of law. [*Why* did I feel the need to share that scruple with *them?*]

MR. CHARIMAN: We would appreciate it if you would give us the names. (Subcommittee, 1953, pp. 49–52)

And I gave names—the ones I had originally planned who were public in their recruiting role, but to my shame—and as I had really managed to "forget," also a couple of others, people I knew well and would swear were no longer at all sympathetic to communism. I had not intended to but I did, and that still leaves me deeply ashamed.

There were some ridiculous aspects to the transcript:

SENATOR WELKER: . . . In these little meetings in the lounge that you had, you had some literature furnished to you?

MR. SMITH: Often we bought it ourselves, at whatever the Communist bookstore was called, downtown. . . .

SENATOR WELKER: You mean that in Portland they had a Communist bookstore?

MR. SMITH: Certainly, sir. (pp. 57–58)

The committee was interested in things I had signed:

> MR. MORRIS: Do you know an organization called the Bill of Rights Conference, in New York, in 1949?
> MR. SMITH: I have some dim memories of it. It doesn't mean anything very concrete to me.
> MR. MORRIS: Were you active in that organization?
> MR. SMITH: No, I wasn't active.
> MR. MORRIS: Did you sign a statement on behalf of that organization?
> MR. SMITH: I may have done that, sir. What happened, if I can just expand a little bit, is that during the course of a year about a dozen pieces of mail would come in and ask for me to sign this, that, or the other thing. I tossed ten or eleven of them into the wastebasket because I feel that these groups for the most part are Communist inspired. By the time I have tossed the tenth one in, when the thing that is on paper in front of me is a thing I deeply believe in, regardless of whether it is Communist supported or not, I get feeling sufficiently badly about the thing that I sign it.
>
> I think the things I have signed are a somewhat random selection of the things that come in my mail and don't have anything significant of themselves, except in the case of the Civil Rights Congress or whatever it was. I am very firmly in favor of civil rights. (pp. 54–55)

In retrospect, I was addressing the wrong audience with my talk about scruples and my rationale for signing statements. The committee members could not have cared less. By politely letting me go on talking like a professor, they probably lured me into going beyond my original uncourageous but defensible intention. That I did so left me feeling demeaned and wretched. I had violated my basic values, though as I look back on it, I do not believe I actually hurt anybody else. But what I said *could* have hurt them. I remember slinking back to my small room in the old Willard Hotel feeling physically sick. Maybe people felt better who took the Fifth Amendment or who, like my former colleague Lloyd Barenblatt, went to federal prison for taking the First Amendment. But Lillian Hellman, who made her refusal to give names to HUAC stick on her own terms, writes about how wretched she felt. Such an inquisition is a chilling experience.

My Security Problems at the National Institute of Mental Health

My other encounter testifies to the long-lasting effects of the acute episode of McCarthyism. It became known in the early 1960s that the National Institute of Mental Health (NIMH) and, indeed, the Department of Health, Education and Welfare (HEW) to which it belonged screened prospective members of scientific advisory ("peer-review") panels for suitability on security grounds. People who were turned down mostly never heard about it, and were never given the chance to learn what derogatory information was involved or to respond to it. I had learned through the grapevine that I was on such a blacklist, though I had been a consultant to the Veterans Administration (VA) beginning in 1957 and to the National Science Foundation (NSF) in 1962, having listed my YCL membership on the government personnel form in both cases.

Recently, I obtained from the Department of Health and Human Services a copy of a report dated June 26, 1957, concerning a security check made on me in connection with my proposed appointment to the "Mental Health Study Section of the National Institute of Health [sic]." (I had not known until now that I had been considered at that early date.) The report quotes my account of ASU and YCL membership on the personnel forms in connection with my VA appointment. It mentions my presence at the head table of a fund-raising dinner for the Spanish Refugee Appeal in Boston in 1948 (I remember being proud of sitting next to the then-famous music critic Olin Downs), and signing a protest in the Harvard *Crimson* against the Mundt-Nixon anti-Communist bill, also in 1948.[2] I was also noted to have joined a Communist-front protest against the discharge of three professors from the University of Washington for alleged Communist involvement. (One of them was Ralph Gundlach, who was active in SPSSI.) To my amazement, the report also said,

> The records of the Civil Service Commission contain information indicating that the Department of the Army advised the Civil Service Commission that it had a file . . . indicating that one M. B. Smith, Room 82, Perkins Hall, Oxford Street, Cambridge, Massachusetts [yes, me as a beginning graduate student at Harvard before the war], was an alleged Nazi [sic]. Military records were checked during the course of the investigation and no information regarding the information allegedly furnished by the Army to the Civil Service Commission was found. It is not believed that this material is of any significance.[3] (Department of Health and Human Services, 1986, p. 3)

The substantive part of the report ended,

> In general, the Subject's associates, neighbors, and co-workers commented most favorably regarding his loyalty to this country. [Good!]

In its conclusions, the report stated:

> If the Subject is believed, his interest in Communism was the result of youthful immaturity and was shortlived. If such was the case, it is not felt that his membership in the American Student Union or the Young Communist League would be a bar to his appointment to the Mental Health Study Section. However,

some information has been developed indicating that possibly the Subject in the late 1940's was connected in some fashion with Communist organizations. [Here the items quoted above are summarized. There is a funny reference to my appearing at the Spanish Refugee Appeal Dinner.] . . . It is not known whether the Subject is identical with the M. Brewster Smith who reportedly attended the meeting in question. However, the Subject is rather generally referred to as M. Brewster Smith rather than as Mahlon Brewster Smith. It is felt that this fact increases the likelihood that the M. Brewster Smith who reportedly attended a meeting of the Spanish Refugee Appeal of the Joint Anti-Fascist Refugee Committee is identical with the Subject. . . .

While it cannot be stated that the activities of the subject previously mentioned are necessarily reflective of pro-Communist sympathy on his part, it is certainly obvious that these activities in view of his previous Communist connections raises [sic] a very grave doubt as to the Subject's present attitude regarding Communism. In order to reach a security determination in this case, it is believed the comments of the Subject regarding his reported activities in the late 1940's would be essential. (Department of Health, 1986, p. 4)

The document was initialed with the date 6/28/57, with a handwritten addition similarly initialed:

Advise PHS [Public Health Service] that it would be necessary to obtain further information including a possible confrontation of derogatory information to Dr. Smith, before we can reach a security decision. . . .

Of course, I was not so confronted—nobody was in those days.

It was only on my rereading the full account in *Science* of the HEW blacklisting, still persisting in 1969, that I was reminded how I got off the blacklist in the mid-1960s: "by the somewhat accidental intervention of a senator important to the welfare of HEW" (Nelson, 1969, pp. 1501–2). (It must have been Senator Morse of Oregon, since one of his senior staff was an old friend of mine.) I was immediately appointed to the Psychology Training Committee of NIMH as soon as I became available—in 1967, ten years, as I now learn, after I was initially proposed by NIMH staff.

The same article lists other psychologists turned down by HEW on security grounds: Theodore Newcomb and Stuart Cook, both SPSSI presidents, and Stephan Chorover of the Massachusetts Institute of Technology. According to *Science*:

One university professor interviewed by *Science,* who said that he knew that he had been refused clearance for participation on an NIMH panel, said that he had surreptitiously been given a list of people who also were not eligible for NIMH advising. This list, a copy of which is now in the possession of *Science,* has 37 names marked "Currently ineligible" and 11 additional names marked "not nominated recently but ineligible in the past." The professor noted that many of the names on the list were older, established psychologists who are active in the Society for the Psychological Study of Social Issues (SPSSI). An NIMH official also speculated that activity in SPSSI might have been a factor in keeping some people from being cleared. There are, however, some SPSSI leaders who are members of HEW panels. Many of the nation's leading social psychologists are active in SPSSI, a group founded to facilitate application of the findings of the social sciences to the solution of social problems. (Nelson, 1969, p. 1501)

This was written in 1969, almost two decades after the height of the McCarthy blight.

The *Science* article describes how in July 1968, under the leadership of the American Orthopsychiatric Association [AOA], representatives of eight scientific and professional associations (including the American Psychological Association) addressed a letter to then-HEW Secretary Wilbur Cohen and met with him, asking for abolition of security checks for nonsensitive advisory positions or, at the least, an opportunity for scientists to know and challenge the information being used against them. To quote *Science:*

Participants in the meeting said that Cohen appeared sympathetic to their requests but worried that a lapse in HEW investigating rigor might lead congressmen to try to cut HEW funds. . . . After receiving Cohen's reply, Dane G. Prugh [president of AOA] wrote the interested organizations that Cohen's "answer must be read as a rejection of the position taken in our letter. . . . Individuals denied clearance still have no opportunity to confront the 'record' against them. There are still no stated standards for determining whether an appointee is clearable." (Nelson, 1969, p. 1500)

Of course, Secretary Cohen, the "father of Social Security," was a strong New Deal liberal. His pragmatic justification of the security clearance system in terms of HEW funding illustrates, as did my Jenner committee testimony, the inadequacy of good liberal intentions.

SPSSI's Involvement with McCarthyism

In the fiftieth anniversary number of the *Journal of Social Issues,* Sargent and Harris (1986) provide us with a fuller account of the involvement of SPSSI in civil liberties and academic freedom, especially in the cases of prominent psychologists like Ralph Gundlach and Bernard Riess, who lost their jobs because of Red-baiting. Neither SPSSI nor APA, which was also involved, could be really effective in dealing with such cases. Understandably, Gundlach and Riess (1954) were not happy with the quite academic treatment of academic freedom in the special issue of the *Journal of Social Issues,* "Academic Freedom in a Climate of Insecurity" (Melby

& Smith, 1953), for which I was partly responsible. They wanted a more resounding statement of position, and they objected with real justification to gestures toward anti-Communism in the introductory essay by Melby, then dean of education at New York University, which had an institutional record that was by no means unblemished.

Psychologists and SPSSI were involved with McCarthyism by being victimized, and by resisting victimization or accommodating to it. Another characteristic SPSSI response is to do research on the problem so as to gain a better understanding of it. Here our record is rather slim. Nevitt Sanford (1953) gave us a sophisticated participant-observer account of the University of California oath controversy (see also Gardner, 1967; Stewart, 1950). But the most substantial work was that undertaken by Marie Jahoda and Stuart Cook, both former SPSSI presidents and Lewin Award winners, on the impact of the loyalty-security program on federal employees and of the effect of blacklisting in radio and television (Jahoda, 1956a, 1956b; Jahoda & Cook, 1952, 1954). Cook (1986) has recently summarized the outcome of these qualitative studies:

> In spite of being familiar with . . . group mechanisms [such as pressures toward conformity under conditions of external threat], the investigators were still not prepared for the extent to which people were adjusting their behavior to avoid *exposure* to pressure to conform. Individuals did not wait for their behavior to be questioned. Their knowledge that certain categories of behavior were under surveillance was sufficient to lead them to make anticipatory behavioral changes. (p. 70)

At an institutional level, we saw Secretary Cohen anticipating sanctions from Congress in much the same way, in maintaining security procedures that he did not personally like, without, one gathers, any overt pressure from Congress.

And Now—

As far as I am aware, the conservative atmosphere of the Reagan administration with its strong anticommunist rhetoric has still not produced anything like the constraint against free consideration of policy alternatives that was felt in the McCarthy era. We cannot take this state of affairs smugly for granted, as we are reminded by the existence of neoconservative campus groups that have set themselves up to spy on the teaching of liberal or radical professors. In human terms, I have recently been involved with a more serious case in which the Immigration and Naturalization Service, under instruction from the State Department, incarcerated on what appear political grounds an advanced graduate student in psychology—a foreign student—on his return from an international psychological meeting. On the morning of the occasion on which this account was presented, the *New York Times* (August 21, 1986) carried the account of Choichiro Yatani's release from detention after six weeks—a victory for justice and I hope a precedent for the future. But six weeks in jail after nine years of responsible conduct in the United States is wrong. The *Times* later cited his case in its lead editorial of November 13, 1986, under the headline, "Why Fear Foreigners' Free Speech?"[4]

McCarthyism is a piece of history, but American history in a larger perspective includes repeated episodes of Know-Nothingism. The experience of the 1950s will not be our last, granting that our history *has* a long continuation.

Notes

1. The Celebration for SPSSI at Fifty, Washington, D.C., August 21, 1986.
2. I was then a junior assistant professor.
3. Much later it occurred to me that (in 1939–1941) I was on the mailing list of the German embassy—also the Italian, British, and French embassies—to build up my collection of "propaganda." That is the only basis I can think of for the charge.
4. There is a happy ending to that story. Early in 1990 the provision of the McCarran Act under which Yatani and others were denied admission (or readmission) to the United States was repealed.

13

War, Peace, and Psychology

Often recipients of the Kurt Lewin Memorial Award have honored Lewin's memory by drawing on their own contributions of socially relevant research, research that was a primary reason for their having been chosen. I did not receive the award because of my research, so I address in his memory the topic on the long-term agenda of the Society for the Psychological Study of Social Issues (SPSSI) that now most urgently needs our attention: war and peace.

Some Preliminaries

I do not need to argue for the preemptive importance of avoiding war and preserving peace. Informed people agree that, if it occurred, all-out nuclear war would be so destructive as to make all other issues irrelevant. The world's military potential for destructiveness is continually growing, and our knowledge of the potentially conclusive consequences of nuclear war is growing too. (I wonder if our fascination with the recently discovered iridium layer at the boundary of the Cretaceous and the Tertiary, associated with the demise of the dinosaurs, may not reflect our unwanted awareness that there may be no people—no future geologists—to detect the stratum of radioisotopes deposited in a global nuclear winter. We have good reason to identify with the dinosaurs!) In spite of over three decades in which mutual deterrence between the United States and the Soviet Union has almost miraculously saved humankind from the consequences of our inventiveness and folly, we have reason to believe the risks of nuclear holocaust are now probably greater than ever, with the inexorable proliferation of nuclear technology and competence. The destabilizing potential of contemporary technical developments in the accuracy of missiles, and in antisatellite and antimissile defenses, is also lending new plausibility to first-strike options and to quick automatic nuclear response to the first unreliable indications of nuclear attack.

The fiftieth anniversary of the founding of SPSSI makes it especially appropriate for me to use this occasion to attempt to gain historical perspective on how psychology has dealt with matters of war and peace. SPSSI's anniversary actually coincides with the fiftieth anniversary of my first course in psychology as a sophomore at Reed College. (Psychology then was not thought to be appropriate for first-year students.) The next year brought my first contact with Kurt Lewin's ideas, in J. F. Brown's (1936) radical text, *Psychology and the Social Order*, which combined orthodox Lewinian, Freudian, and Marxist perspectives.

My agenda today is to share perspectives on our role as psychologists in trying to prevent nuclear holocaust, not to present data. I assume—and it is important to make the assumption explicit—that virtually everyone here and abroad wants to avoid nuclear war: doves, hawks, and "owls," President Reagan, Secretary Gorbachev, almost all of us. (Here I use "us" in the fully inclusive sense that I wish were more prevalent.) I also assume, and take this assumption as equally important, that psychological knowledge and expertise touch only a small part of the big problem. If we are to contribute what we can and maintain our sanity, it behooves us to avoid hubris and chutzpah. The world's peril is neither primarily our fault nor our responsibility, except to the limited extent that responsibility follows from our meager resources and power. We should avoid grandiosity in both our pretensions and our guilt. But we have to live and die in our endangered world, which we hope our children also will enjoy, so we surely ought to do all that we can. From this perspective, we could be doing a lot more.

Psychology in the Wars

It is a stock complaint that psychology and psychologists are readily mobilized to contribute to their nations' wars but are slow to accept social responsibility for the preservation of peace and the promotion of social justice and human welfare in peacetime (Reiff, 1970). But this is only to be expected (Smith, 1970). World War I "put psychology on the map," and as O'Donnell (1985) reminds us in his fine history, *The Origins of Behaviorism*,

> one cannot read the reminiscences of participating psychologists without sensing that their military experiences represented the high points of their professional careers. . . . Not even "pacifist principles" and "doubts about the war" could keep Quaker-bred Edward Tolman from seeking a commission in the

psychological testing service. . . . Incredibly, Yerkes regretted that the war did not last longer. . . . The newly discovered ability . . . to see their research rapidly translated into practical action provided many psychologists with a sense of satisfaction and accomplishment that their university experiences could not have furnished. (P. 239)

World War II, in which my generation participated, mobilized a maturer psychology on a much larger scale, leaving in its wake the new professions of human factors and clinical psychology, and a greatly expanded and inspirited subdiscipline of social psychology. Psychologists again felt the euphoria of constructive involvement, which, if I am correct in my historical perceptions, has left American psychologists with a considerably better aftertaste than after psychology's participation in World War I—just as to many of us the war against Hitler still seems to have had a grim historical necessity that we can no longer quite find in the war against the kaiser.

Each of these wars created a strong national consensus in which most psychologists participated. And it was not just American psychologists who rose to their country's call: psychologists of each belligerent nation were called to duty. (Of course, Jewish psychologists in Germany were not asked, and were fortunate if they had managed to flee.) The prepotency of national identity over international science during these wars should remind us of the extraordinary continuing power of nationalism (or of ethnocentrism or tribalism—they amount to the same thing) as a disastrous feature of our century, a feature that has played a much more salient role in international affairs in the years since World War II than psychologists or other social scientists ever anticipated.

National consensus and the effective mobilization of psychology have been at their peak in our participation in the two world wars, but our wars do not automatically produce either consensus or psychological mobilization. Psychologists cannot claim any discernible credit for our ultimate withdrawal from Vietnam, but at least they were not united behind its prosecution, and several of them prepared *The Dove's Guide* (Rosenberg, Verba, & Converse, 1970), which is still an exemplary distillation of research findings for the guidance of peace activists. As the United States moves ever closer to overt belligerency in Central America, seeming to yield a grimly negative answer to Lloyd Etheredge's (1985) pertinent *Can Governments Learn?*, at least there is no indication that American psychologists are rushing to bring their talents to the support of the Contras.

The role of socially concerned psychologists must certainly be different in periods of *dis*sensus than it is in those rare times when they are in agreement with one another and with almost everyone else about national priorities. Political conflict on the national scale is inevitably mirrored within the American Psychological Association (APA). Even when it is possible to pass resolutions on public policy through the APA council, as was the case with the 1982 resolution supporting a freeze on nuclear weapon tests, the more usual situation in which substantial disagreement remains presents radically different challenges to American psychology than it faced in the two world wars. The challenge to those of us who set a very high priority on moving toward peace is to induce more of our colleagues and our fellow citizens to agree with us—and to bring our skills and resources to bear as psychologists and citizens without any invitation from the government and without the support of a national consensus.

Fear Appeals or Empowerment?

My part in trying to meet the challenge involves initiatives like this chapter that I hope advance the peace agenda. An approach that is tempting is to dramatize the horrors of nuclear holocaust to gain people's attention and mobilize them into action. In pursuing this strategy, Helen Caldicott (1980) and Jonathan Schell (1982) have surely made real contributions, and it was important to dramatize the futility of civil defense when the government was still pushing it as a prominent component of national policy. But such authors have made their point by now. On *psychological* grounds, I do not think it is helpful to raise people's level of overt anxiety about nuclear holocaust, except when they are provided with very specific things to do about it (Leventhal, 1970).

Correspondingly, I have serious reservations about Robert Lifton's (1967) often-cited concept of "psychic numbing" as a metaphor for our dangerous inattention to the nuclear threat. The term indeed fits the adaptation of Hiroshima survivors to the inconceivably extreme emotional stress to which they had been subjected. But to use it for our own avoidant reactions seems inappropriate and cheapens the concept as originally applied—as if we were to equate our own careless disregard of the Nazi death camps with the emotional devastation of their surviving inmates. The kind of denial that is involved when we push the prospects of nuclear holocaust away from our central consciousness is much more like the way that we usually disregard our human mortality in the course of everyday life.

We are all mortal, but most of us, most of the time, do not dwell on the prospect of our death. Nor should we—there is no point in it, and the morbid concern would not only spoil our current enjoyment of life, it might even get in the way of our coping effectively with those stresses and dangers that we *can* manage. Richard Lazarus (1983) has rightly begun to rehabilitate the mechanism of denial, which psychoanalysis proposed as the most primitive of defenses. Even though we pretend to be immortal, many of us *have* stopped smoking. Some of us *are* using our seat belts. Our everyday denial of death need not stop us from adopting measures that are likely to prolong our lives (though the seat-belt example indicates that overcoming "normal" denial is no simple matter; many of us still fail to "buckle up").

A diagnosis of psychic numbing leads to the prescription that we should escalate the stimulus so as to break through the affective barrier.[1] But what *is* the barrier, if we are dealing with normal denial? It is not affective numbing, I think, but helplessness, lack of a sense of efficacy. We cannot avoid dying—so why worry about it?—*except* when there are concrete things to do that might postpone it. Individually and collectively, we feel powerless in the face of the ever-escalating arms race. So why dwell on the horrors ahead?

Of course, there is a rich psychological literature in which essentially the same point emerges from diverse theoretical perspectives that tell us how feelings of low competence (White, 1959) or low self-efficacy (Bandura, 1977) or learned helplessness with its accompanying attributional style (Abramson, Seligman, & Teasdale, 1978) impede effective coping in what can become a vicious circle. I think that the empirical findings underlying this area of substantial agreement are among the most humanly important in recent psychology. (See chapter 15.) But there is nothing new in seeing the relevance of helplessness to our avoidance of issues of nuclear war. Morawski and Goldstein (1985) remind us that in an early number of the *Journal of Social Issues* devoted to nuclear matters, Woodward (1948) commented on the seeming contradiction between the high level of awareness of the dangers of the bomb and the surprisingly small numbers expressing fear or worry. He wrote: "It seems unlikely that many people will feel active concern about a problem before which they feel helpless" (p. 11). Morawski and Goldstein cite several other psychologists who, as researchers and commentators in the early 1950s, attributed people's sense of impotence to their readiness to leave matters to expert authorities. From this diagnosis of the problem, it follows that what is needed most in order to get people involved in the attempt to prevent nuclear war is to increase their sense of potential effectiveness. People need to be empowered by precept and example, and by political organization.

Without paths for constructive action clearly in view, raising people's level of anxiety may actually defeat its purpose. For that reason, the kind of campaign mounted by the public-health authority Victor Sidel (1983) makes more sense to me than continuing to stress "the last epidemic." Sidel has been telling all the audiences he can reach about the heavy costs in health and social welfare entailed by our current investments in the arms race. The costs that he dramatizes are within the grasp of reason, and do not immediately evoke self-protective denial. His strategy, of course, involves head-on challenge to the main thrust of policy in the Reagan administration. As I emphasize later on, the central issues *are* political and have to be faced in political terms.

Our prescription for the general public must also apply to ourselves as psychologists. Our failure to rise to the challenge of nuclear war to a degree commensurate with its importance can plausibly be attributed to our own bafflement in the face of its enormity. We also need to be empowered. With ourselves as with the general public, however, a slick public relations job will not do. We need a convincingly realistic basis for our involvement. We have to take our experience of relative ineffectiveness into account, and must learn from it.

A Prospectus for What Follows

In Paul Boyer's (1985) valuable review of "American thought and culture at the dawn of the atomic age," *By the Bomb's Early Light*, repetitive cycles of involvement and withdrawal with respect to nuclear issues are documented, which Morawski and Goldstein (1985) spell out for our own narrower field. I agree with these authors that historical perspective may help us get off this wheel of fate, as we must if we are to deal effectively with the world's peril and our own. To contribute toward this end, and in the spirit of SPSSI's semicentennial celebration, I will look selectively at SPSSI's relations to war and peace in its early days (before the bomb), then again at the period in the early 1960s when psychologists were most active (and I think effective), as background for an appraisal of present priorities.

Some Historical Perspective

The 1930s

The views of the world that were prevalent among American psychologists and their students in the mid-1930s when SPSSI was founded are so remote from ours today that it requires a strong imaginative act to evoke them. Although Hitler's recent rise to power presented a new threat, it is hard for us to remember the extent to which liberal psychologists and social scientists remained in the shadow of World War I and postwar disillusionment about the dismal outcome of its supposed ideals. I remember being much impressed as an undergraduate by Lasswell's (1927) classic study of wartime propaganda. Along with the munitions makers, propaganda became the popular villain of the 1930s, a social-psychological villain, so much a matter of public attention that my favorite humorist James Thurber even wrote a fable about the Very Proper Gander (Thurber, 1940). The Institute for Propaganda Analysis (Institute for Propaganda Analysis, Inc., 1937–1941; Lee & Lee, 1939) was established for research in methods used by propagandists in influencing public opinion. (Not surprisingly, it folded in 1941.) The focus on propagandists and munitions makers (who were seen as insidiously linked) was mostly tied to pacifism and isolationism, related but not identical positions endorsed by a variety of political types, including radicals of Norman Thomas's socialist persuasion.

The enormous social and economic dislocations of the Great Depression and the rise of Hitler had led, of course, to a different sort of radical politics centering on the Communist party, its various fellow-traveling affiliates, and the handful of "deviationist" radical cliques, all visible in the country at large but especially salient among intellectuals and around New York City. This was the time of the Spanish Civil War and the volunteer Abraham Lincoln Brigade from the United States, and of the Popular Front in which Communists and democratic Socialists made temporary and unstable common cause. It was a time when Franklin D. Roosevelt held the United States together in ways that are impressive retrospectively. Yet it was also a time of extreme dissensus, with Liberty League Republicans viewing FDR's New Deal as treacherous socialism, and the radical left seeing him as a reactionary "social fascist"; in which Stalinists and Trotskyites hated each other more intensely than they did the capitalist oppressors, and Stalinists could hardly distinguish between Trotskyites and Socialists.

For the Left, it became a time of enormous confusion, when suddenly the Soviet Union, previously the bastion of antifascism, entered into the pact that gave Hitler the fateful green light for his final steps toward war. As a student, I had become a pretty good Stalinist—a "fellow traveler" within the American Student Union at first, then a member of the Young Communist League. I have vivid memories of the soul-searchings, recriminations, and strenuous cognitive reorganization and reinterpretation that ensued for me and those I was close to, continuing well beyond the entry into the war by the United States (and my getting drafted into the army).

As Finison (e.g., 1986) and Stagner (1986) have told us in their recent accounts of SPSSI's early years, these crosscurrents of radical politics essentially immobilized SPSSI in regard to matters of peace and war. Stagner tells how the plans of a SPSSI committee that he chaired for a yearbook on that topic were stymied by the impasse, until after Hitler had invaded the Soviet Union, between the ideological positions of the Second and Third Internationals. If we need an antidote to our nostalgic semicentennial romanticism about SPSSI's radical past, we may find one in noting that irreconcilable disagreement about what brand of radicalism to espouse produced results as defeating to radical ends as no radicalism at all.

Looking Toward Peace in the War Years

In 1944, near the end of the war, thirteen eminent psychologists (including Hilgard and Klineberg, who are among us today, and Allport, Likert, Murphy, and Tolman, other early SPSSI presidents) circulated a statement on human nature and the peace for signature by psychologists at large. One can read most of this "psychologists' manifesto" today with assent and respect. The "motherhood" principles that it announced and commented upon could *not* be taken for granted in wartime, and their prominent expression was a good proactive step attempting to influence policies about peace treaties, the occupation, and the launching of the United Nations. Note, for instance, the following principles.

1. War can be avoided: War is not born in men; it is built into men.
4. Condescension toward "inferior" groups destroys our chances for a lasting peace. . . . The great dark-skinned populations of Asia and Africa, which are already moving toward a greater independence in their own affairs, hold the ultimate key to a stable peace. . . .
5. Liberated and enemy peoples must participate in planning their own destiny.
7. If properly administered, relief and rehabilitation can lead to self-reliance and cooperation; if improperly, to resentment and hatred.
10. Commitment now may prevent post-war apathy and reaction.

A few other principles, unexceptionable as ideals, strike me as less realistic, given the tragedies of the intervening decades:

3. Racial, national, and group hatreds can, to a considerable degree, be controlled. Through education and experience people . . . can learn that members of one racial, national or cultural group are basically similar to those of other groups. . . . Prejudice is a matter of attitudes, and attitudes are to a considerable extent a matter of training and information.
8. The root-desires of the common people of all lands are the safest guide to framing a peace. . . . The man in the street does not claim to understand the complexities of economics and politics, but he is clear

as to the general directions in which he wishes to progress. His will can be studied [by adaptations of the public opinion poll]. . . .
9. The trend of human relationships is toward ever wider units of collective security. [Would that it were!] (Murphy, 1945, pp. 454–57)

Then no more than now could psychologists count on being listened to. They were nevertheless acting responsibly when they publicized their psychological perspective at a crucial human choice point.

At about the same time that the manifesto was being promulgated, and with a fresh start, Gardner Murphy finally produced the desired yearbook for SPSSI, under the title *Human Nature and Enduring Peace* (Murphy, 1945). Although he reprinted the manifesto in his concluding chapter, the rest of the book, composed of framing essays by Murphy and interrogatories put to over fifty collaborating "authorities," does not fare so well from our point of vantage. The perspective is pervasively individualistic, with emphasis on frustration as the primary cause of war (the "frustration-aggression hypothesis"), and the proposed remedies mainly wishful and naive: among them, changing our fundamental attitudes toward ourselves and the world, and developing an international social psychology, with great research centers that would use modern polling techniques. As if he were taking the sort of doubts we would now have about this formulation into account, however, Murphy prominently inserted a penultimate "note on insecurity" by Ralph White—one that Ralph could well have written today. Ralph mentioned two implications of "the fear motive in international relations":

1. The element of realism in the fear of aggression, and in the nationalist's reliance upon military power to achieve security, should be taken fully into account in any organization for peace or education for peace. . . .
2. At the same time, the element of unrealistic, undiscriminating fear and suspicion of foreigners as such, which is characteristic of nationalist psychology everywhere today, is the central obstacle [to be] overcome if "peace-loving nations" are to remain firmly allied, or give up some aspects of sovereignty to a world organization. (Murphy, 1945, pp. 451–52).

In developing the second point, he turned explicitly to the prospect of U.S.-Soviet conflict, which elsewhere in the book received only the smallest passing attention, as compared with extensive treatment of our relations with former enemies: "If, for instance, an Anglo-American bloc fails to work harmoniously with a Soviet bloc throughout the coming decades, the chief disruptive factor seems likely to be an unrealistic, exaggerated fear and suspicion on one side or on both'' (p. 452). White ought to receive a prize for prescience, as well as for his continued wisdom and dedication to peaceful international relations.

Prescience, however, has not generally distinguished the future-oriented prescriptions of psychologists in this area, and despite White's example, we cannot usually count on it—a fact that we might bear in mind as qualifying our assurance when we take strong stands that depend upon predictive assumptions. Of course, we have little basis for prescience. In particular, psychologists cannot be blamed for not anticipating the atom bomb, which as we now know has changed everything.

The 1960s

Let us jump to the 1960s, which were a major turning point in recent American culture. In regard to Soviet-U.S. relations and the threat of war, they included brinks and détente. They also included our deepening involvement in the disaster of Vietnam, the hippies' summer of love, the assassinations. As Morawski and Goldstein (1985) tell us, "The early 1960s witnessed a shift from psychological studies on civilian and military attitudes to investigations of the psychological dimensions of international relations in the nuclear age" (p. 280). For my purposes, the work of Urie Bronfenbrenner, Ralph White, and Charles Osgood is exemplary.

Bronfenbrenner (1961) and White (1970) especially highlighted the reciprocal processes of misperception illustrated in the cold war (Bronfenbrenner) and in the Vietnam conflict (White). To employ White's terms, in both conflicts each party held a diabolical image of the enemy and a moral image of the self. The descriptions and analyses of this "mirror image" phenomenon provided by Bronfenbrenner and White can be lastingly persuasive to people who encounter them; by now they have entered into social psychological common sense, though hardly into the common sense of the general public.

Bronfenbrenner and White sharpened our diagnostic acumen concerning a major psychological feature of international conflict; Osgood (1962) proposed psychologically sophisticated therapy in GRIT—graduated and reciprocated initiatives in tension-reduction—based on the same view of the preponderance of security considerations that Ralph White had advocated seventeen years earlier (in Murphy, 1945). Osgood's scheme involved modest unilateral iniatives toward deescalating the conflict, always within limits that protect national security, and within a publicized framework of commitment to further deescalating steps if the adversary reciprocates.

Morawski and Goldstein (1985, n. 4) tell us that not only was the GRIT plan well received among psychologists but it was also taken seriously by policymakers. They cite documentation that it was examined by President Kennedy and his staff. Certainly, Kennedy's unilateral initiative in his American University speech on June 10, 1963, announcing "a strategy of peace" is a clear example of the GRIT approach in action (Etzioni, 1967). It led to the atmospheric nuclear test ban treaty, one of the few clear successes in U.S.-Soviet negotiations to limit the arms race. His assassination shortly thereafter deprived us of further examples until just recently, when the Reagan administration has twice failed to respond to Gorbachev's parallel initiative for a general moratorium on nuclear testing. I cannot talk about this "disconfirmation" of GRIT without bitterness.

The Present

Psychological contributions to the understanding of international relations as of the mid-1960s were summarized and assessed effectively in the classic volume *International Behavior* edited by Herbert Kelman (1965), still a uniquely valuable resource. No such single source is yet available to pull together the much richer array of research and theory becoming available today from the resurgence of interest in nuclear conflict, provoked in the 1980s by unease about the policies of the Reagan administration. All the same, there are four excellent sources to which newcomers to these concerns may profitably turn to get their initial bearings—works that old hands can also savor with admiration, and learn from too. I want to use this occasion to advertise them.

One is the excellent *American Psychologist* article by Philip Tetlock (1986), under the title "Psychological Advice on Foreign Policy: What Do We Have to Contribute?" In a compact exposition and analysis, Tetlock provides a wise and comprehensive review of recent psychological research and theory that bears upon improving the policy-making process or generates knowledge to inform the content of foreign policy decisions. Two other sources were both produced by Ralph White, whose earlier major contributions to our topic I have already praised. In a comprehensive edited book of interdisciplinary readings, *Psychology and the Prevention of Nuclear War*, sponsored by SPSSI, White (1986) offers thirty-five selections, previously published or specially written for the volume, that illustrate all of the major facets of the topic and exhibit most of the major contributors to it. His own recent volume, *Fearful Warriors: A Psychological Profile of U.S.-Soviet Relations* (White, 1984), also belongs on this "must list," as the fullest and best-grounded treatment of *its* topic. It also provides a unique example of the extent to which a psychologist can make himself master of the international relations trade as well as his own.

My fourth suggested source was provided by Morton Deutsch (1983) in his International Society for Political Psychology presidential address, which I think is the best current brief theoretical analysis of war-threatening international conflict. Drawing on his own earlier research on modes of conflict resolution (Deutsch, 1973) and integrating ideas developed by Bronfenbrenner (1961), White (1970), Osgood (1962), and others in the 1960s, he depicts conflicts like those between the United States and the Soviet Union as involving a spiraling, malignant social process that arises in anarchic social situations in which "rational" behavior is impossible so long as the conditions for social order or mutual trust do not exist. In such situations, Deutsch notes, for either party to pursue its interests in its own welfare or security without regard for the other is self-defeating. The earmarks of the malignant process, the escalating vicious spiral, are a win-lose orientation, inner conflicts (within each of the parties) that get expressed in the external conflict and magnify it, cognitive rigidity, misjudgments and misperceptions, unwitting commitments that develop in the course of the conflict and make it hard to reverse, self-fulfilling prophecies (security-seeking responses to anticipated threat being themselves perceived as threatening, and evoking in turn behavior that is realistically threatening), and a gamesmanship orientation that loses sight of realistic substantive issues in an abstract conflict over power as such. Deutsch has a number of suggestions for undoing the malignant process, establishing fair rules for competition, and developing a cooperative framework, which like his analysis are congruent with Osgood's and White's suggestions.

It was easy for me to select these excellent points of entry to the current psychological literature on the prevention of nuclear war, but it is virtually impossible to make a justified selection of particular projects or programs to illustrate the major themes in that literature. I will not even try, except to mention Kelman's (1979, 1982) field trials of direct communication between Palestinians and Israelis, and Janis's (1985) work on crisis management, the subject of last year's Lewin Award address.

Implications for Psychologists' Roles

With this selective bird's-eye view of psychological contributions to the cause of peace, what precepts can we draw to guide and perhaps to encourage us in our own efforts?

I take a rather more charitable view of the part psychologists have played than do Morawski and Goldstein (1985), who lament how psychologists have followed the times in spite of their claim to scientific objectivity, how they have mainly served the establishment with "benign counseling" that can have little impact on events. I take it for granted that, as the record shows, psychologists have little prescience and that most do not get too far out of step with the dominant assumptions and ideology of their times. I do not expect psychologists to save the world; nor do I blame them much when they share all-too-human failings with their fellow citizens.

Since the times of SPSSI's founding and the end of World War II, all the same, I think psychology has gained in mature realism as it has become better qualified to make a distinctive contribution. In *By the Bomb's Early Light*, Boyer (1985) tells us that

> in the early post-Hiroshima period, spokesmen for a quite amazing diversity of professions and ideological persuasions argued passionately that their particular expertise or ideology had suddenly become crucial to mankind's survival. . . . Social scientists seem to have felt their new responsibility especially keenly. . . . (p. 151)

Psychologists were among the foremost in reiterating the need to base policy decisions on social science knowledge. Morawski and Goldstein (1985, p. 278) quote E. R. Hilgard as arguing (in a 1945 manuscript in the SPSSI archives), "Millions of dollars invested in social science research in the immediate future would be a small price to pay if the costs of war could be avoided." We would still like those dollars, but I think we are now more modest in our expectations.

As a spokesman for the social science establishment, the sociologist Neil Smelser has recently discussed the "kind of paradox" that emerged when he compared the pretensions and competences of the social sciences a half century ago and today. The old positivistic assumptions included

> faith in the capacity of objective knowledge to identify social problems, faith in the capacity of cumulative social knowledge to result in social inventions, and faith in the capacity of those inventions to solve social problems. That particular set of faiths permitted [policy recommendations that were] simultaneously naive and pretentious—at least as judged by our contemporary understanding—about the role of the behavioral and social sciences in social policy. . . . I believe we have become, paradoxically, both more sophisticated in our research design and measures and less pretentious in our aspirations than we were 50 years ago. (Smelser, 1986, pp. 33–34)

The common understanding today in mainstream social science holds that the social sciences are embedded in the social and political processes of the society in a much more complex fashion than had previously been assumed. This is not to say that they do not have the potentiality for consequential influence. Indeed, they do.

In the record that we have reviewed, the strongest case for actual influence on national policy concerns Bronfenbrenner's (1961) treatment of mirror-image perceptions and Osgood's (1962) GRIT proposal. Even if the Kennedy administration had arrived at its own version independently, at the very least the psychological analysis lent support to a way of thinking about Soviet-U.S. relations that pointed toward a substantial change in policy, a change that by our current lights still makes sense. Even one such case in our record seems to me occasion for considerable satisfaction.

Note that the psychologists' contribution was not a direct conclusion from research data, though it was informed by research. The contribution was in the realm of *ideas*—a new way of looking at Soviet-U.S. relations, from which new considerations of policy followed. This kind of contribution is *not* usually recognized in current discussions in APA. Time and again in the recurring debate about APA's proper role in regard to controversial social issues, the point is made that APA should get involved, and psychologists should get involved *as psychologists* (rather than just as citizens), *only when our contribution is based on research data.* With such issues it is more often than not the case that our greatest contribution is the conceptual one of framing the issues differently from what has become conventional, one of asking different questions more than of drawing different conclusions. Thus, Deutsch's (1983) formulation of the arms race as part of a malignant social process includes the mutual diabolical images of "evil empires" as part of its symptomatology. People, whether voters or policymakers, who have grasped this way of looking at things will be more likely to focus on what can be done about the process, less locked into tunnel vision of the reprehensible characteristics of their adversary. This kind of contribution is scientifically legitimate, and it is by no means trivial.

A rich tradition of research underlies the formulation of good ideas such as these. Research can also play its usual role of *legitimizing* ideas and proposals—to our own internal constituency of psychologists and fellow social scientists, who need to be enlisted in the cause, and to policymakers when we can gain access to them. When he reports it in full,[2] Janis's (1985) research on the quality of U.S. decision making in crisis management is bound to attract the attention of the intellectually minded stratum of the foreign affairs establishment, which has more influence in some presidential administrations than in others. The scrupulousness with which Janis designed his study is critical for its scientific legitimacy; under favorable circumstances, it should contribute to its political legitimacy too.

I have no objection in principle to the role of the psychologist or social scientist as technical adviser—I only wish government *would* seek our advice—but in fact social and psychological research has had very little influence along these lines on policies affecting war and peace, even in administrations far more favorable to the social sciences than the present one. In a more favorable political climate, psychology could certainly make useful technical contributions from research on the variety of topics illustrated in White's (1986) edited volume. Even in such happier times, however, I think our role in conceptual reformulation would be more important.

"In a more favorable climate?" I end with politics, because the whole topic of national and collective security, the arms race, and steps toward war or peace is intrinsically and intensely political. Psychologists who involve themselves with it, as I hope many more of us do, cannot avoid political involvement and commitment. There are political challenges within the APA to direct more of its organizational resources toward peace issues. There is local and national politics, where participation in SPSSI and in specialized organizations like Psychologists for Social Responsibility offers channels that should be expanded, but where the traditional routes of grass-roots organization and political pressure remain crucial.

Psychological and other social research on all the interconnected topics bearing on war and peace should be encouraged and supported to improve our general understanding of the complexities that policy must deal with— this in the long run for the guidance of members of the policy elite, if they will listen, and for the enlightenment of the attentive and voting public, which requires concerted effort to be reached. But a first, most urgent priority in the short run is to assure that there *is* a long run, an eventuality that cannot be taken for granted.

Preserving the long run means lending our personal support to political efforts to restrain the Reagan administration from acting on its primitive and romantic conceptions of peacekeeping in the mode of a John Wayne fantasy about the western frontier. It means exerting concerted pressure by phone calls, telegrams, and letters when each concrete issue is before Congress: "Star Wars," the MX missile, the nuclear test ban, whatever. It means supporting political efforts to build a Democratic Senate as well as a Democratic House of Representatives to hem the administration in. It means supporting political efforts to replace the Reagan administration with one more likely to give priority to deescalating the life-threatening global conflict. Of course, the APA cannot engage in this activity, nor SPSSI, but concerned psychologists can. To be a concerned psychologist implies becoming an active citizen in these respects.

Near the beginning of this chapter, I noted our own need for empowerment, our need for a hopeful sense of efficacy if we are to be ready to open our eyes to the threatening dangers and do our utmost to avert them. I think the perspective that I have tried to share with you *is* potentially empowering. True enough, we have no grounds for the fantasies of omnipotence that erstwhile accompanied the positivistic view of social science. As Freud well knew, however, omnipotence and impotence turn out to be identical. There are many modest things we can do that collectively can make a difference.

I take heart especially from the conclusion that psychologists have already made a substantial contribution to *thought* about nuclear war, international conflict, and the arms race—to reframing the issues so that current preoccupations with the diabolical mirror-image that go with continuing escalation drop from the central focus, and new questions come to the fore promising more hope for mutual security and goal attainment. Simply to communicate something of this emerging perspective far and wide would improve the political climate in which conflicts are managed for better or worse. To communicate it effectively, we ourselves must understand it in depth. In the course of this chapter, I have made a number of suggestions about how those of us who have held off from involvement with the issue may inform ourselves.

Understanding and communicating with a view toward political influence is a role that we all can play. (Well-focused financial contributions toward political influence are also important, such as supporting the Council for a Livable World.) Those of us who have the inspiration and the opportunity to conduct relevant research should by all means do so, since in the long run, even if it cannot be expected to yield pat technical answers to inherently political problems, it is the basis from which our understanding gets corrected and enriched. There is no royal road by which psychologists can best contribute to peace. There are many paths, which should suit the different resources and opportunities of all of us.

Notes

1. Sandman and Valenti (1986) reject the Caldicott strategy (and say that Physicians for Social Responsibility now also rejects it) for essentially the same reasons as mine. They support the idea of psychic numbing by interpreting it as denial: "working at not caring." We are in substantial agreement on essentials, though not about terminology.
2. The report has now been available for some time (Janis, 1989). I am not so optimistic about its influence on the Bush administration.

14

Value Dilemmas and Public Health

Andie Knutson, whose contribution to public health this memorial address honored, was a few years older than I, but our lives shared many links. We both had had Social Science Research Council Demobilization Awards following World War II experience, and we had both been involved in the early days of public opinion research. After the war, Andie took his Ph.D. at Princeton with Hadley Cantril, whose holistic and phenomenological orientation in psychology was much influenced by his own doctoral mentor, Gordon Allport, who was also mine. (Our common intellectual heritage made me find Andie's research concerns especially congenial.) After directing research and evaluation and behavioral studies in the U.S. Public Health Service with distinction, Andie came to the University of California at Berkeley in 1957 (just two years before me) to initiate the program in behavioral sciences in the School of Public Health. He joined the Institute of Human Development as research associate at the same time that I did. In 1970, a couple of years after I had left Berkeley, he served the institute as acting director.

Andie Knutson's Contribution

Andie represented the behavioral sciences in public health along a broad front (see Knutson, 1965), but I think he will be remembered most enduringly for his pathbreaking studies carried out in the mid-1960s: studies of the beliefs and values of public health professionals concerning the beginning of a human life, its nature, its value, and the human or spiritual agencies that properly exercise control over it. This was essentially a venture to explore the "assumptive worlds" of public health professionals—a felicitous term introduced by Hadley Cantril (1950) and elaborated upon by Jerome Frank (1973). Each of us takes our own assumptive world for granted: that *is* our reality. So when we find ourselves in irreconcilable disagreement about matters like euthanasia or abortion or capital punishment, we get exasperated, sometimes to the point of violence, by our opponents' inability to listen to reason. Of course, they *do* reason, even if they don't listen, but they reason from unarguably different premises.

Knutson found that people's present religious orientations and those of their childhood homes, not their professional identities or other demographic characteristics, made the big difference as to whether they held a spiritual or a psychosocial conception of human life, and this in turn mainly sorted out the positions that they took on the five test issues about which he inquired: euthanasia, suicide, human experimentation, uses of the body after death, and capital punishment or shooting in self-defense. Of course, the details are more complicated. But it captures a crucial aspect of the abortion controversy to know that Catholics are likely to say that a human life begins with conception or in the first trimester, in contrast with secularly oriented professionals. His findings about when a human life begins, about its definition and value, and about organ transplants were reported in a series of important articles in the late 1960s (Knutson, 1967a, 1967b, 1968). The full report on his research is available in the manuscript of a book (Knutson, 1979) that remains unpublished, perhaps because Andie's doggedly scrupulous, carefully qualified style that so well suited his high standards of science and scholarship did not quite fit publishers' concepts of what is salable.

I said this was pathbreaking research. We have been subjected to such a continuing barrage of debate between "right to life" versus "freedom of choice," and we are so continually bombarded by new developments in medical technology that pose ethical problems for which there are no established consensual guidelines that it is hard for us to realize how very original Andie's research was at the time he conceived it. The problems that his work highlighted are of course still with us, multiplied. It is difficult to cope with the lack of consensus on issues of health care in the public served by medicine; it is disturbing to see the extent that members of the health community are themselves at odds about fundamental conceptions. But that is news that should be brought back home.

The Agenda of This Chapter

In what follows, I begin with Andie Knutson's concern with values and existential beliefs that bear on human health and medical practice. I want to consider the frameworks of thought within which we deal with these issues. For a long time I have been actively perplexed about this boundary region that links empirical behavioral science and practical philosophy. Almost a decade ago, I devoted a memorial lecture in honor of Gordon Allport (chapter 1) to worrying about the ways in which psychology bears upon value issues, so it feels right for me to return to the difficult problems at this time.

In the interim, the discipline of applied bioethics has become increasingly professionalized and institutionalized. Although I had a hand in developing the human-subjects code for the American Psychological Association (American Psychological Association, 1973), I have remained an incorrigible amateur. I am not an "ethicist"! I want, at this point, to make an advantage of my amateur standing, to share concerns and perplexities that involve us all *as* amateurs. We may be professionals as scientists, teachers, and practitioners; the difficult value issues are those that concern us as interconnected persons. In that capacity we are all amateurs, even the ethicists.

Assumptive Worlds in Collision

A first point that needs to be made explicit can be made very briefly. Since the time of Andie Knutson's research, all the issues that he dealt with remain actively controversial, and new ones continually press for attention: "Baby Doe" cases about surgical intervention with defective infants; "pulling-the-plug" cases involving the concept of "brain death"; issues of compulsory drug testing or AIDS screening; issues of resource allocation for dialysis and other expensive heroic treatments; China's one-child family policy with its implications for abortion and even female infanticide, its coerciveness, but maybe its social necessity; problems of genetic counseling and decision making, now much complicated by the increasing power of high-tech presymptomatic screening of fetuses and adults. Our increasing technical competence complicates our ethical choices rather than simplifying them.

It is also the case that people are in sincere, intense, and often shrill conflict about these and other value issues. Just a week or so ago, I read in my local newspaper an essay by a civil libertarian calling the roll of many issues about which different groups are embattled in righteous mutual intolerance (the health-related issues were only a couple among many others), ending with a statement of his gratitude for the First Amendment guarantees of a free press and the right of peaceful assembly. As he wrote, "If all of these 'good, sincere people' had their way, we would have nothing left of books, magazines, speeches, films and theatrical presentations but Bambi and Bugs Bunny" (Joelson, 1986). That caught my attention since I had just noted how Neil Smelser, speaking for the

Academic Senate of the University of California to the regents of the university at their meeting September 19, 1986, defended the regents' policy against the awarding of honorary degrees by saying wry words to the effect that given the vehement value dissensus on the campuses, who besides Jacques Cousteau would be generally acceptable to receive our honorary doctorate? I guess he didn't consider Bambi and Bugs Bunny.

We are indeed living in a time of value conflicts that seem in principle to be unresolvable. I think it is an appropriate metaphor to speak of *assumptive worlds in collision*. In regard to a great many matters of central human importance, of which Andie Knutson sampled a few, the citizenry, the intellectual and cultural leaders, the political leaders, the health professionals are divided among themselves, starting from different premises and coming to different conclusions; they cannot argue with each other persuasively.

The Collapse of Moral Community

The moral philosopher Alasdair MacIntyre gives essentially the right diagnosis of this situation, I think, in his contribution to a Hastings Center symposium volume (MacIntyre, 1980) and in his modern classic, *After Virtue* (MacIntyre, 1981). His view of our contemporary crisis is a grim one, which I take seriously without following him to the same conclusions. In his analysis from the history of philosophy, he contends that the terms and claims that pass one another by in our ethical arguments are relics of coherent ethical worldviews that have lost their meaning for us, so that our ethical controversies become incoherent and close to nonsensical. Linked with his critique from the history of ideas is an essentially Durkheimian sociological assertion: that such coherent worldviews are the expression of the society as a moral community, something that we have lost. Lacking moral community, the best we can do is *negotiate*.

Thus, to pick an example from an area apart from health, MacIntyre sees the Supreme Court as keeping

> the peace between rival social groups adhering to rival and incompatible principles of justice by displaying a fairness which consists in evenhandedness in its adjudications. So the Supreme Court in *Bakke* both forbade precise ethnic quotas for admission to colleges and universities, but allowed discrimination in favor of previously deprived minority groups. . . . [It] played the role of a peacemaking or trucekeeping body by negotiating its way through an impasse of conflict, not by invoking our shared moral first principles. For our society as a whole has none. (1981, pp. 235–36)

Will the emerging Reagan Supreme Court define its role in the same fashion, or will it attempt to adjudicate in terms of first principles—as *it* conceives of them? To pose that question is both to accept the cogency of McIntyre's analysis and to raise some glimmerings of doubt about the warrant for his evident regret at our present state of affairs. The tradition of liberal individualism that MacIntyre deplores still has its advantages.

Our contemporary American society does not provide us with the comforts of moral community, but neither does it impose its severer constraints upon us. The modern world that we inhabit has lost the coherence that was universal in the local parochial cultures that were once the common human lot. Increasingly, we live in a flux of worldwide communication and confrontation, in which youth crazes spread around the globe little hindered by political or ideological boundaries and barriers. We live in a world in which, for the worldwide cultural elite, we have physical and psychological access to the entire historical and cultural range of art styles that André Malraux evoked for us in his elaborate image of the "museum without walls" (Malraux, 1953)—yet also a world in which we find it hard to settle on our own styles, or to enjoy our contemporary artists as much as we still enjoy their predecessors in the museums. Our world is one in which the sacred meanings of traditional religion have substantially eroded, yet also one in which new fundamental-isms, Christian and Moslem, are militantly asserting themselves against the pervasive secularism. From the standpoint of any one of the contend-ing new absolutist views, religious or ideological, the cacaphony of con-tending voices is evil because it denies the Truth. The trouble is, the different versions of the Truth—the different assumptive worlds—contend and collide with one another. Who can be *sure* of having the Truth—or rather, given the dissension, who *ought* to be sure? History is replete with examples of how sincere representatives of contending assumptive worlds have successfully sought to slay each other.

It was the great virtue of modern liberalism, from the time of Voltaire and the Enlightenment until just yesterday, to recognize and deplore the *damage* done in the name of moral consensus. From the nineteenth century until quite recently, participant observers seemed confident that in pluralistic modern societies, democratic institutions would enable peo-ple to modulate their claims against one another and to accommodate them for the most part to the good of all. Perhaps it is our loss of faith in Progress, whether in the metaphysical realms of the Hegelian or Marxist dialectic or in the crasser materialism of technological advance and eco-nomic growth, that makes us more strident, less willing to accommodate, when our basic assumptions come in conflict. Or am I neglecting the extent of strident conflict in a past that is too easy to idealize?

MacIntyre is nostalgic for the dream of moral community that he identifies with the Aristotelian tradition. Since he cannot expect to turn the clock or the calendar back, he ends his book by evoking the situation of citizens of the incipient Dark Ages in the late Roman Empire when the challenge, as he reconstructs it, was to withdraw from the ruined shell of the empire to sow the germs of moral community anew. Thus with us, too, he says:

> What matters at this stage is the construction of local forms of community within which civility and the intellectual and moral life can be sustained through the new dark ages which are already upon us. . . . This time, however, the barbarians are not waiting beyond the frontiers; they have already been governing us for quite some time. And it is our lack of consciousness of this that constitutes part of our predicament. We are waiting not for a Godot, but for another—doubtless very different—St. Benedict. (1981, p. 245)

I keep quoting MacIntyre because I agree with much of his vision of our current predicament and find the rest of it tempting. I am quite capable of being nostalgic too! I doubt, all the same, whether nostalgia is an adequate response to our situation. In retrospect, the Utopian communes of the 1960s were more a symptom of our plight than a solution to it.

Nostalgia for Moral Community

Important recent social critics from the social and behavioral sciences share MacIntyre's nostalgia. Seymour Sarason (1981, 1986), for example, has been an eloquent critic of the ways in which psychology contributes to what he sees as the pathological individualism of American society. Since, as he says,

> one of the laws governing human behavior is that "you always pay a price; there is no free lunch," . . . one must ask what price has been paid in the substitution of the concepts of morals and values for that of sin as a transgression of divine law? I would suggest, as have many others, that the price we paid was in the weakening of the sense of interconnections among the individual, the collectivity, and ultimate purpose and meaning of human existence. (1986, p. 899)

Sarason discusses in these terms the case of Baby Jane Doe in which the parents did not wish to permit a life-sustaining operation for their severely defective daughter:

> If *my* seriously defective offspring is *my* responsibility, about whom I make life and death decisions according to *my* morality, it is quite consistent with the increasingly dominant ideology of individual rights, responsibility, choice, and freedom. If I experience the issue as *mine*, it is because there is nothing in my existence to make it *ours*. And by ours I mean a social-cultural network and traditions that engender in members an obligation to be a part of the problem

and possible solution. It is *my* offspring, but whatever problems I have in regard to that offspring are not mine alone. I can count on others in predictable ways, I am not alone with the problems. . . .

Those who were supportive of the parents' decision not to permit the surgery seemed totally unaware of the possibility that they might be reinforcing aspects of our society that contribute to the sense of isolation and loneliness, aspects that work against the sense of community. (1986, p. 902)

Neither the individualistic proponents of the parents' position nor its religious opponents seemed to Sarason to give adequate weight to the complex interconnections between his triad of perspectives: those of the individual, of the collectivity, and of transcendent sources of meaning. At root he sees the human costs of our secular individualistic society as too high.

Our Berkeley colleague Robert Bellah and his collaborators, mainly from sociology, take a similarly critical view of the human costs of American secular individualism in their justly acclaimed book, *Habits of the Heart* (Bellah et al., 1985). They regret how, at least in California, the culture of psychotherapy has provided members of the affluent middle class with a language of individual costs and benefits to replace the old language of morality appropriate to problematic but committed relationships. They too lament the lack of genuine community, and of the essentially religious basis of shared meaning and value that they see as an inherent aspect of community. There is much in common among the perspectives of MacIntyre, Sarason, and Bellah.

The predicament to which they are trying to sensitize us is real. Modern Western society, and the United States especially, are uncommonly individualistic in comparison with the spectrum of contemporary and historic cultures, and this extreme individualism is at a cost. As many contributors to the classic tradition of sociological theory have noted in different ways, modern society is deficient in sense of community, deficient in moral consensus. Indeed we lack consensual first principles. But what are we to do about it?

How Can We Live without Moral Community?

Like it or not, we live in a world of pluralistic value perspectives. We cannot regain our traditional innocence, we cannot re-create community by preaching, prayer, or fiat. In ethics, our situation is the same as it is in aesthetics, where the breakdown of value consensus, the corrosion of cultural tradition, is quite parallel. Our unprecedented exposure to the arts of many times and places allows us to appreciate a wider range of artistic expression than ever before. But even though modern consumers of LPs and compact discs may prefer Bach to Bartok; even though modern orchestras can perform both to perfection, modern composers cannot validly write music like Bach's—any more than modern painters can validly paint like Leonardo, or Van Gogh, or Monet, whose works so many of us prefer to what is current. We are willy-nilly creatures of our own anomic time, and we can create only by participating in it authentically.

In this time of pluralism, those of us who are nevertheless convinced that our own assumptive world is or ought to be valid for everybody else have several options. On MacIntyre's suggestion, they might withdraw with like-minded people to cultivate their shared version of consensual community, awaiting the new St. Benedict. Given the value of diversity, it is fine that some people choose this option. Alternatively, the convinced absolutists might try to *impose* their view of the world on the others whom they cannot convince—and we have seen that others mostly cannot be convinced about these things. To an unfortunate degree, this is the strategy of the "right to lifers," who see their definitions of human life as God-given or, what amounts to the same thing, as written into Natural Law. But coercive solutions to a clash of assumptive worlds have their own heavy costs, and not only in the sphere of international conflict. Since rational persuasion mostly does not work, what remains is negotiation and mutually respectful accommodation, in light of as full a sharing as can be attained of what each party understands to be the relevant facts, including facts about one another's value perspectives. But this is just the kind of process of negotiation that MacIntyre disparaged in the Supreme Court's handling of the *Bakke* case. Compared with the alternatives, liberal democratic institutions are not all that bad! It is also a process to which empirical information of the sort that the behavioral sciences trade in can make a contribution.

From my own secular humanist perspective (chapter 5), there are simply no definitive answers to *any* ethical questions available to us except answers that we have negotiated in the past and can continue to negotiate among one another. Of course, I am using "negotiation" in a broad and informal sense. Here I am in full agreement with Norma Haan, just retired from the Institute of Human Development, and her colleagues in their new book, *On Moral Grounds* (Haan, Aerts, & Cooper, 1985). In this connection, they challenge the old conventional barrier between facts and values head on—the barrier embodied in the charge that in controversies about values, any appeal to matters of fact exhibits the "naturalistic fallacy." In effect, they embrace the naturalistic fallacy cheerfully, asserting that if we rule out revelation, unexamined tradition, and coercion, empirical evidence of one kind or another is all we have left to help us in our ethical negotiations. From this view, sensitization to the complexity of ethical issues (which ethicists can help with) and empirical facts of the sort behavioral science can provide (including facts about one another's value perspectives) can contribute to negotiated outcomes that are humanly more satisfactory. The more nearly we approximate the state of moral community, the simpler and more satisfying the negotiation, which—unlike withdrawal or coercion—at least points toward the cultivation of community.

Ethics in Health Decision: Two Instances

My discussion of the dilemmas of ethical disagreement has strayed from the area of health decisions that Andie Knutson was concerned with. To return to health, let me pick two examples from my recent reading. One is Elliot Valenstein's (1986) remarkable cautionary tale, his recent history of psychosurgery. The other is a recent discussion by Ruth Faden (1986) of the ethical implications of the powerful new methods of presymptomatic screening in fetuses and adults.

In *Great and Desperate Cures*, Valenstein (1986) tells the story of lobotomy, the grossly mutilating brain operation performed on the mentally ill around the world between 1935, when the operation was introduced by Egas Moniz, an eminent Portuguese neurologist and statesman, and 1960 when the "epidemic" was essentially ended and the procedures discredited. Between 1948 and 1952, at the crest of the wave, tens of thousands of the operations were performed; those in the United States with the enthusiastic promotion of Walter Freeman, a leading figure in the neurology and psychiatry establishment. (In 1949, Moniz received the Nobel price in medicine for his part—just when the utility of the procedure was beginning to be questioned.) Valenstein shows how the disgraceful episode arose from extreme personal ambition, organicist medical ideology, wishful thinking on the part of both the medical community and the public, and uncritical promotion without any check from carefully controlled clinical trials, and goes on to assert that the same conditions that led to the fad of psychosurgery continue to prevail in medicine today.

In our present context, however, I am most interested in his argument that we cannot turn to either scientific or ethical principles for secure guidance in regard to what risks are justifiable when patients suffer severely from conditions for which current therapies are not effective. Treatments work that we do not understand, and knowledgeable people will disagree about the theoretical justification of any innovative therapy. As for ethics,

A risk with a successful outcome is usually not questioned. Where no effective therapy exists for desperately ill patients, equally ethical and knowledgeable physicians may disagree about treatment. Some risks have to be taken, and some harm will inevitably ensue along with some benefit. (p. 295)

Firm, established procedures are needed to *limit* the harm, as it was not limited in the case of psychosurgery. Obligatory testing procedures or clinical trials that do not depend on professional self-regulation are needed, procedures such as those that have for some time been institutionalized for new drugs but are used sporadically at best in most experimental medicine.

If I read Valenstein correctly, the ethical issues involved in psychosurgery did *not* primarily involve clashes of assumptive worldviews. Rather, commonsense ethics were being applied by psychiatrist-surgeons and the public alike, and they were not good enough. Consensus conferences, had there been any, would also not have been good enough. Critically lacking were controlled data on the actual consequences of the procedures. On the psychosocial side of mental health, the case could be made that the rapid and ill-prepared deinstitutionalization of the mentally ill, for which I take some responsibility as an officer of the Joint Commission on Mental Illness and Health of the 1950s, had unexamined consequences that are socially almost as irreversible as those of psychosurgery. More than a decade ago, Donald Campbell (1969) argued for treating reforms as experiments, studying their consequences in pilot trials before putting them into general operation. In a more propitious political climate, perhaps we might get back to his good ideas on that score.

My quotations from Valenstein remind us that empirical research, including behavioral science, can bear on serious ethical issues in a much more direct, less ambiguous way than my earlier discussion may have seemed to imply. From Ruth Faden, a psychologist who is coauthor of the recent classic on informed consent (Faden & Beauchamp, 1986), I take another example that returns us to the context initiated by our concern with Andie Knutson's work.

Faden (1986) presents a complex panorama of the ethical issues posed by the human genetic techniques that are becoming available to determine susceptibility to a wide range of diseases before the symptoms appear. Down's syndrome can already be screened for in the fetus, and genetic testing for Huntington's disease was about to begin in both fetuses and adults. We were told that a genetic test for cystic fibrosis should be on the market shortly. Screening seems to be in the immediate offing for a number of other diseases in which genetic factors make for selective susceptibility rather than causing them directly. These developments raise a host of ethical problems, including the issue of whether screening is ethical before effective therapies have been made available, and how to avoid injustice—

what Faden calls "geneism"—when genetic information about disease susceptibility can be used to deny health insurance or make it unaffordable, or to screen potential employees for the financial advantage of the employer. The equivalent of clinical trials seems needed for guidance as the new technology is deployed in practice, but, as Faden notes, such trials have their own substantial moral and pragmatic difficulties.

The issues about the meaning of fetal life that Andie Knutson explored among public health professionals seem likely to be substantially reframed by the new technologies, according to Faden. Until recently, one potentially serious problem was the implicit challenge to the moral and psychological acceptability of "late" (second trimester) abortions posed by gains in early fetal viability resulting from advances in neonatal care. Selective abortions following amniocentesis usually occur at a time that is very close to what is becoming the new boundary of viability. This difficult situation seems about to be remedied by the new technology of chorionic villus sampling, which permits fetal diagnosis and selective abortion unequivocally in the first trimester. On the other side of the balance are rapid developments in the field of fetal therapy. As Faden writes, "depending on the circumstances, increasingly the same fetus could be either a 'patient' or an 'abortus' " (p. 18).

All of these unsettling developments are complicated by the unknown psychological impact of the now increasingly prevalent use of the fetal sonogram, which, as Faden says, "has the capacity to make compelling the human characteristics of the well-developed fetus, emphasizing its reality and individuality. The impact of the visual image on prospective parents and health care providers is as yet unknown" (p. 18). She cites Daniel Callahan and others as raising the possibility that the developments

in fetal visualization, fetal therapy, and the intensive care of premature neonates may be altering our communal psychological and moral views about the fetus and abortion. . . . It seems plausible that as the fetal sonogram increasingly becomes baby's first picture, and as fetuses increasingly become fully patients of fetal surgeons and the like, the fetus will move more publicly into the human social community. (p. 16)

Andie Knutson's kind of research is needed more than ever to monitor these changes, and to inform our consideration of the complex ethical issues that they raise.

Coda

We are not about to achieve the state of moral consensus, the ideal community, in which ethical solutions to novel dilemmas such as those posed by innovations in medical technology can readily be derived from first principles that are agreed upon consensually. Nor, I think, need we regard ourselves as actually on the brink of another Dark Ages, *if* we can avoid disaster and possible extinction in nuclear holocaust. In our nonconsensual, too individualistic society, negotiated ethical decisions are the best we can achieve—unless and until the new St. Benedict arrives. Until that millennium, behavioral science in the manner of Andie Knutson can contribute useful, even indispensable information to the negotiation process.

15

Hope and Despair:
Keys to the Sociopsychodynamics of Youth

The Pandora myth introduces the concept of *hope* into Western thought. According to the old story, Jupiter was angry at Prometheus for stealing fire from the gods for the benefit of humankind. To get even, he created Pandora, and every god and goddess contributed something to her perfection. She was dispatched to Epimetheus on earth, carrying with her a box that she was warned not to open. Eventually, she could no longer restrain her curiosity about what was in the box, and she lifted its cover just a little to look in. In a flash, a swarm of plagues flew out to bedevil humankind: gout, rheumatism, and colic for people's bodies; envy, spite, and revenge for their minds. Pandora slammed the lid shut as fast as she could, but only one thing was left in the box—and that was *hope*. Hope, says the myth, is what makes the rest of our human cares and troubles bearable.

The present world, and our own part of it, seems to have quite enough cares and troubles, and at times it appears that hope itself is in short supply. As a feature of the national mood, this may be rather new for us Americans, with our traditionally sanguine outlook. Even in the Depression, which pressed hard against our optimism, both Roosevelt's New Dealers and the radical intellectuals of the time could maintain hopes for the definitive solution of social problems that would be hard to muster today. Of course, the grimmer mood of the public at large, which includes the well-documented decline of confidence in most public institutions, is not so new among the guardians of high culture in the arts and letters, where anomie and despair have been a recurring leitmotif in modernist works here and abroad through most of the century.

We all need hope, not only to bear the pains and losses of the human condition but to enable us to cope with our problems and troubles in ways that make possible the outcomes that we desire. Hope and despair, that is, participate in the dynamics of self-fulfilling prophecies. The hopeful *may* realize their hopes because hope gives warrant to their actual striving; the despairing are all too likely to be confirmed in their fears by the passivity that fatalism justifies. This central theme is elaborated upon later in this chapter.

Whatever our age, whatever our location in the life course, we need hope. In the life course that has been typically human, it is the old whose situation near the end of life biases them against hope: societies that are good to the aged provide them with a variety of social and mythic supports to compensate. In contrast, young people standing at the outset of life have the world before them: we should normally expect a youthful bias toward hopefulness. When the appropriate hopefulness of children and adolescents wavers or is subjected to heavy assault, we have to be seriously concerned, since an underlying hopeful orientation is surely a prerequisite for development toward a satisfactory and satisfying adulthood.

Of course, these are familiar ideas. Pandora wasn't born yesterday, and the "basic trust" that Erikson (1959) saw as undergirding healthy development means essentially the same thing as hopefulness—in effect, "the world is a place that will do right by me." Yet there is more to be said, integrating what we have learned from recent research, about hope versus despair as a linchpin concept that helps us to formulate theories about, and cope professionally and politically with, problems of today's youth. As I have come to see it, hope versus despair is a strategic concept in understanding the causes of these problems, one that organizes into a coherent fabric ideas that come from the most divergent perspectives: cultural-historical, psychodynamic, and sociopolitical. It therefore helps us to think practically about needed and promising strategies for social policy and individual action. Old hat as the ideas may be, their implications are not widely or fully appreciated. The intent in this chapter is to illustrate and clarify this way of thinking.

Hope as a Cultural Deficit

A good starting point is the one that led to my own interest in hope as a psychological concept. During the late sixties, I was involved with colleagues at Berkeley (Smith, Block & Haan, 1973) in research on student activists—a good vantage point since the Free Speech Movement at Berkeley launched the student protest of the sixties—and also (continuing, in the 1970s at Santa Cruz) in studying the counterculture hippies, who made their initial headquarters in California. What, I have long been pondering, led to the eruption, just then, of an epidemic of lashing out at the established order (by the most destructive of the activists) or, alternatively, of dropping out of it (by the "turned on," drug-oriented hippies)?

Explanations based on the American experience in the Vietnam War or with the civil rights movement seemed inadequate since very similar movements erupted in the late sixties throughout the industrialized world. Explanations in terms of the universal oedipal conflict of generations (Feuer, 1969) were even less satisfactory since eruptions of hostility and withdrawal among the young are not constant through history. The timing still seems puzzling to me, though it is probable that the emergence into young adulthood of the relatively affluent first generation to come to consciousness after the Holocaust, after World War II, after Hiroshima, must have had something to do with it. Apart from the problem of timing, I came to feel some understanding of the underlying frame of mind that was variously expressed in lashing out, or in dropping out in search of "highs" through drugs or rock music or Eastern mysticism, or in the countercultural winds that swept over the borders of psychology in the encounter-group movement and "human-potential" centers like Esalen. (See chapter 7.)

Once, when discussing these matters with a ministerial group, it dawned on me that instead of referring to how the young people and some of their elders were responding to cultural deficits in meaning, in hope, and in human communion, as I had come to put it, I might just as well (or better) have used St. Paul's traditional Christian language and spoken of deficits in faith, hope, and love (or *caritas*)!

Deficits in *faith* (which I had been calling *meaning*): Many of us in the modern world suffer in one way or another from attrition in the supportive sense of eternal verities that has been available in the past to all bearers of intact cultural traditions. Recently, in the aftermath of war and holocaust, the secular faith in science, technology, and progress, which for many people, especially Americans, had come to replace or at least supplement religion, has also been shaken. A profusion of cults and irrational belief systems stand ready to fill the vacuum for would-be "true believers."

Deficits in *love* or *caritas*: Modern urban life with its segregated roles and bureaucratic impersonality leaves notorious deficits in occasions for true human intimacy, tenderness, and love. Like the ephemeral communes, the encounter-group movement thrived on the false profits of easy, instant love and communion. "Make love, not war" was the memorable slogan of the sixties, and a real revolution in sexual mores and practices did occur, especially among the young. But technological values (concern with "technique"), as well as recreational ones, did seem to pervade the easier sex; after the revolution, loving communion may be as elusive as ever. (Strictly speaking, *Playboy* values seem to be more prevalent among young adults; even after the revolution, adolescent social norms favor sex with affection [Chilman, 1983]).

As for deficits in *hope*: Hope is closely linked with faith, or sense of meaning, in secular as in religious matters, so the attrition of faith has made hope the more vulnerable. In the years since World War II, the widely perceived closing of frontiers of Planet Earth and the increasingly probable possibility of a nuclear Armageddon have made thoughtful people more doubtful about the goodness of the future. In the United States, the assassination of the Kennedy brothers and of Martin Luther King dramatically obliterated the national figures who earlier in the sixties seemed most to embody the hopefulness of youth. In comparison with faith and love, where the cultural losses of modern life seem to be matters of gradual erosion, hope seems more vulnerable to historical events in the short run, to immediate changes in people's situations of life.

In focusing here on hope versus despair, I do not intend to imply that it is the single key to an understanding of youth problems, in the sense in which my teacher Gordon Allport used to decry "simple and sovereign" theories of psychosocial causation generally. I *am* suggesting that since hope versus despair is the sentiment that connects present and future for people, it is central to people's behavioral morale; it is also central to their ability to make commitments to self or others or to abstract ideals or principles—and to live by those commitments. At a time, moreover, when psychologists are heavily emphasizing *cognitive* factors (we have just gotten over behaviorism, which denied them, and have seemingly been captured by the computer metaphor of information processing), concern with hope and despair commits us to dealing with beliefs and feelings together. In real people, beliefs and feelings are not separated.

Some Data

What do we really know about hope and despair among today's youth? Even if we had ideally adequate data, we know enough not to expect any simple answer. Since people are likely to be ambivalent about important matters, harboring contradictory feelings, we cannot expect to place youth cleanly on an Fahrenheit or Celsius scale that runs from deep despair to glorious hope. Also, we can be sure in advance that people's feelings of hope versus despair will fluctuate over time and across situations. What sort of data are available?

The best set that I could find in an all-too-scanty array appears to be the series of representative national surveys of high school seniors carried out annually since 1975 by the Institute of Social Research at the University of Michigan (Johnston, Bachman, & O'Malley, 1980–1983). Well-designed and carefully conducted survey research like this is no substitute for the special window on otherwise unarticulated experience that the relationship of psychotherapy can provide. But depth insights from psychotherapy are also no substitute for what can be learned from good survey interviews conducted with good national samples. Each sort of data has its distinctive contribution and its limitations.

On two items relevant to hope that were offered to the high school seniors for agreement or disagreement, there was virtually no change between 1975 and 1982. A third of the seniors said they agreed or mostly agreed with the statement, "When I think about all the terrible things that have been happening, it is hard for me to hold out much hope for the world." (Depending on your perspective, you can say either "only a third" or "fully a third," a tactic of presentation that is well known on Madison Avenue.) Slightly fewer (30 percent in 1975 and 25 percent in 1982) agreed or mostly agreed with the item, "I often wonder if there is any real purpose to my life in the light of the world situation." At the same time, exactly two-thirds (67 percent) agreed or mostly agreed with the optimistic item, "The human race has come through tough times before, and will do so again." Basic optimism or pessimism about the world seems quite stable in the responses of American youth, and the optimists remain in the great majority.

There are other ways in which the successive crops of seniors give much the same distribution of answers over the eight years. Over this period they are more hopeful for their own country than for the world, in the short run, but most hopeful for their own lives. Thus, when the students are asked, "Looking ahead to the next five years, do you think that things in this country will get better or worse?" between 33 percent and 38 percent say things will get much better or somewhat better, while 44 percent say they will get much or somewhat worse. When asked about "things in the rest of the world," the corresponding optimists include 16 percent to 23 percent, while the pessimists constitute 55 percent to 60 percent. If there is any trend, it is in the more pessimistic direction in both cases. But when the question asks, "How do you think your own life will go in the next five years—do you think it will get better or worse?" only 3 percent or 4 percent say they think it will get at all worse, while eight or nine in ten say they think it will get somewhat or much better. In the short run, at any rate, the overwhelming majority of the high school seniors say they are hopeful about their own lives, even though the prospects for the world look grim and those for their country not very good.

All the same, the mounting dangers of nuclear holocaust have made their mark on successive classes of seniors. The percentage of seniors who say that they often or sometimes worry about the chance of nuclear war has risen from 40 percent in 1975 to 64 percent in 1982. The percentage that agree or mostly agree with the item, "My guess is that this country will be caught up in a major world upheaval in the next ten years" rose from 36 percent to 45 percent, and with the extremely grim item, "Nuclear or biological annihilation will probably be the fate of all mankind within my lifetime," from 22 percent to 36 percent. The Madison Avenue phrasing seems unavoidable here: *over a third* of high school seniors rather expect to join personally in human extinction.

In spite of these increasingly gloomy expectations, the high school seniors' expressed feelings of powerlessness about the world situation seem to have increased only slightly if at all over the eight years: 47 percent versus 41 percent now agree or mostly agree that "I feel that I can do very little to change the way the world is today."

Given these figures, it is clearly impossible to assign simple barometer readings of hope versus despair to the responses given by American high school seniors over these years. The items cited focus on the world situation to a degree that can hardly be typical of their daily concerns; the high proportion of seniors expressing personal optimism in the short range is likely to be more characteristic. Nevertheless, substantial proportions of American youth agree to grim statements about human prospects in their lifetime when the issue is made salient to them. The broad division between the optimistic and pessimistic on most of the questions is in general accord with the two-thirds/one-third split frequently found between the generally satisfied and generally dissatisfied in studies of life satisfaction among adults, and with Offer's data on normal adolescents (Offer, 1969; Offer, Ostrow, & Howard, 1981).

Since writing the foregoing paragraphs, my attention has been called to a 1977 survey (Yankelovich, Skelly, & White, Inc., 1977) in which most of a national sample of parents assessed their own family lives as largely satisfactory but, like the youth described here, viewed the larger world as being heavily problematic.

Psychodynamics of Hope

Psychodynamic thinking about hope versus despair, as psychological research has been contributing to it, has dealt with two major interrelated themes. According to the first, if people cannot expect much of the future, they are likely to live mainly in the present, with a variety of consequences. The other holds that if people have learned that there is nothing at all they can do about improving their future, about avoiding bad outcomes, they will not continue to cope. Consider each briefly in turn.

If people cannot expect much of the future, it is to be expected that they will live mostly in the present and grasp such present satisfactions as they can. Present pleasures include the temptations of "careless love" with its consequences in illegitimacy. If, indeed, future prospects are disturbingly grim, the distractions of intense experience ("kicks") are very appealing. By the same token, hopelessness raises the value of chemical aids to sedation or oblivion: alcohol and drugs. The other side of the coin is that people's readiness to make commitments, to be governed by them, and to inhibit their impulses for the sake of greater long-term benefits depends upon their confident expectations of the future.

Perhaps these insights are sufficiently obvious to make empirical evidence unnecessary. In any case, psychologists have supplied relevant evidence. In a series of studies a number of years ago, for example, Mischel (1966) showed that children's readiness to wait for a larger delayed reward instead of taking a smaller immediate one depends on their confidence that the larger reward will actually be forthcoming; obvious, but that is partly what hope is about. On the complementary side of the relationship, in Zimbardo's (1970) studies of "deindividuation," when hypnosis was used to induce participants to limit their attention and concern to the immediate present, they let go with a variety of impulsive and sometimes destructive behavior.

These relationships help to make sense of the counterculture of the sixties, with its emphasis on the "here and now," its encouragement of hedonistic impulsiveness ("if it feels good, do it"), and its wariness of binding human commitments. Though the hippies are no longer with us as a social movement, we still live in the shadow of the counterculture. According to Yankelovich's (1981) surveys, mainstream youth have selectively assimilated these counterculture values to a considerable extent. Culture-critics who write for the mass media decry the so-called me generation and critics with more psychoanalytic sophistication write of the "age of sensation" (Hendin, 1975) or the "culture of narcissism" (Lasch, 1979). Present-day parents and grandparents get frustrated by the new slow schedule on which their offspring are entering the commitments of marriage, parenthood, and binding choice of career. Granted that middle-class children have an option of further extending their Eriksonian moratoriums that is unavailable to the less affluent, and that the necessity to make many explicit choices about matters that could formerly be taken for granted may be a more important factor in the delay, may not this hesitation to make risky full commitments of self also reflect the less secure hopes that the present world appears to warrant?

Many features of the orientations that have recently been characteristic of young people—and of their elders, too—can indeed be called "narcissistic" as a loose descriptive label. But if the term is to be used not just descriptively but in an explanatory sense, then an interpretation in terms of the vulnerabilities of hope needs to be considered as alternative or supplementary to one in terms of early narcissistic processes conceived in terms of one or another of the competing metapsychologies that employ the term. People who are short on hope will predictably act in ways that can be labeled "narcissistic."

The other psychodynamic theme focuses on a special aspect of hopelessness. If people have learned that there is nothing at all they can do about improving their futures, about avoiding bad outcomes, they probably won't keep on coping. The first theme hinges on whether youth expects a good future or a bad one. The second focuses rather on the element of perceived personal control: what can they do about it? Both themes are implied, I think, in the terms *hope* and *despair*, as we use them in ordinary language.

This second theme joins topics that have claimed an extraordinary amount of attention from research psychologists over the past two decades. The terms are varied, but the same underlying issues recur. White (1959) introduced the concepts of competence and effectance as requiring essential modification of both neobehavioristic and psychoanalytic theories of motivation. Rotter (1966) launched a whole stream of research, mostly independent of his own social-learning theory, when he provided an instrument to measure people's generalized expectations regarding the internal versus external locus of control of their behavioral outcomes. De Charms (1968) built on Rotter's work but reconceptualized the distinction as that between people's self-conceptions as "Origins" or "Pawns" with respect to personal causation. Weiner (Weiner & Kukla, 1970) turned the social psychologists' then-popular "attribution theory" to the analysis of how people attribute the causes of their successes and failures. Seligman (1975), having first given an account of depression in terms of learned helplessness on the basis of animal models, joined with colleagues (Abramson, Seligman, & Teasdale, 1978) in a reformulation of human learned helplessness in terms of people's coming to attribute their failures to internal, global, and stable causes. Bandura (1977), the most prominent and respected proponent of a social-learning theory in continuity with the stimulus-response behavioristic tradition, and a leader in the behavior modification movement, came increasingly to focus on the importance of self-efficacy.

As is readily apparent, these various concepts originate in different traditions of research and theory. The ideas involved are not fully sorted out as yet, and the evidence that is needed for a well-elaborated understanding of them is by no means all in. Nevertheless, some general conclusions seem clear enough, and I believe that they add considerably to our understanding of the psychodynamics of hope and despair. Following is my capsule formulation of what I think we know, drawing on research linked with the psychologists just cited.

Insofar as possible, people, like other mammals, want to be able to control the things that happen to them. Personal control and the sense of efficacy that goes with it may be said to be general human values. People will even put up with a good deal of noxious stimulation without showing stress effects if they believe they can turn the annoying or even painful input off at will. We are limited creatures in a world that is not always friendly to our enterprises, so the degree of control that we actually have, and the degree that we believe we have, varies widely among people and across situations.

Through experience, people develop enduring generalized expectations about the degree of personal control that they can exercise. These expectations involve fundamental linked conceptions about self and world: beliefs about one's self-efficacy or competence, and beliefs about the responsiveness of the world to one's efforts. The two go together, and it is only conceptually that we can tease them apart.

Here we come to the crux of the matter. People who think they are competent and that the world is adquately responsive are likely to cope actively, and their efforts therefore have a good chance of increasing their actual skill and competence—and as good a chance as social realities allow of resulting in a record of success. Conversely, people who regard themselves as incompetent and the world as unresponsive to their efforts are likely to withdraw from coping. Not investing the required effort, they are unlikely to develop new skills; as a result, they tend to fall still farther behind in competence, yielding a predictable record of failure. We are dealing, thus, with benign and vicious circles or, to put it differently, with self-fulfilling prophecies. "To him who hath shall be given; from him who hath not shall be taken away even that which he hath"—"Matthew's Law," as Robert Merton has called it.

At the extreme of the vicious circle is the state of "learned helplessness" that Seligman (1975) has shown to be implicated in depressive states. Given the training in helplessness that was a standard part of the traditional female role, and given persisting inequities in women's situations that are in fact beyond their individual control, psychologists who have been working on this line of research do not find it surprising that psychotic depression is so much a female specialty.

I have put these general conclusions dogmatically. Of course, a great many questions remain to be resolved about necessary qualifications: particularly, how truly general across life situations and spheres of competence/incompetence are these "generalized expectations"? We know, for example, that black youth from the ghetto may be heavily at risk for a thorough training in *academic* incompetence and helplessness yet still have acquired another set of competencies for life in the streets. How do these assets and deficits add up?

Some Social and Cultural Dynamics

This dual account of the psychodynamics of hope and despair in regard to self and world has obvious implications for *sociodynamics*, for the impact of discrimination and oppression, of fated membership in race and class, on problems of youth that are currently matters of widespread social concern. The causal processes linked to self-seeking impulsivity in the "here and now," given a future that is not worthwhile, on the one hand, and to the abandonment of coping because of a sense of personal inadequacy in an unresponsive, unfriendly world, on the other, provide a good start toward understanding these social problems. Drug abuse, vandalism and violent crime, teenage parenthood out of wedlock—all take their heaviest toll of youth in the ghettos of our central cities, where hope is especially untenable. Dealing with these problems, apart from the therapeutic Band-Aids that seem symbolically necessary even to the Reagan administration, is obviously a matter more for tough politics than it is for mental health professionals.

Indeed, why *should* inner-city youth be hopeful? Their job prospects, which are central to the planning of a coherent life in the American mainstream, are miserably bad. Drugs and violence provide oblivion or distraction; playing the "numbers" gives a sham of hope—and there are real jobs in running them and in drug dealing. Who is to say, in *this* setting, that virtue brings its own reward? But discouragement from trying to "make it" in the mainstream surely brings its own punishment. I sketch the situation with a broad brush, of course; we know that individuals differ, their microsituations may offer relief from the general blight, and many ghetto youth become competent and effective by the standards of the larger society in spite of the way that the cards are stacked against them. And problem behavior with essentially the same dynamics is by no means confined to youth in the ghetto.

About two decades ago, the anthropologist Oscar Lewis (1965) wrote about the "culture of poverty" only to be shot down by black ideologists and others (Leacock, 1971) who took their lead, insisting that to attend to the vicious circles of defeat that help perpetuate the ghetto is "blaming the victim." I have never been convinced by that line of criticism. Instead, I would erect a large sign over each major entry to each large urban ghetto: "The Surgeon General Has Determined That Life in the Ghetto Is Injurious to Your Physical and Mental Health.'' That would not be ''blaming the victim.'' It would recognize that actual conditions of social life are major determinants of people's hope and despair, and that despair is not only a terrible state in itself; it is conducive to other terrible consequences and damages people's ability to climb out of the wretchedness in which they find themselves.

To revert to the problems that I began with—why the disruptive student protest and why the hippies in the sixties, why the persistent reluctance of youth to enter upon future-binding commitments—it also seems to me that this analysis of hope and despair is at least suggestive about roots of historical change in what is salient in youth's prevailing mood and response. We are dealing not only with psychodynamics but also with historical dynamics! Developments in postindustrial society the world over give people in general, and youth in particular, grounds for feeling more like pawns of massive trends beyond their control, less able to shape the course of events to suit their needs. Our current sense of impasse about coping nationally with unemployment and inflation is only the most immediate instance of challenges to our national sense of competence and efficacy. Especially since our victorious conclusion of World War II as the greatest of the superpowers, our national morale has faltered in a paradoxical powerlessness in the face of problems so complex and obdurate that they seem to defy human solution. Instead of our erstwhile naive confidence in the stream of progress that sweeps us along inevitably, we now feel caught up in any number of pernicious streams that seem to have their own momentum, no matter what we try to do about them: lethal expansion of population in the impoverished parts of the world, exhaustion of resources, disruption and pollution of the environment, urban decay, *and* the nuclear arms race, a pernicious trend that threatens to trump all the others.

In this connection, consider the recent thoughtful paper by Escalona (1982), who wrote:

> Growing up in a social environment that tolerates and ignores the risk of total destruction by means of voluntary human action tends to foster those patterns of personality functioning that can lead to a sense of powerlessness and cynical resignation. . . . In short, I believe that growing up fully aware that the adult world seems unable to combat the threat [of total destruction] can render the next generation less well equipped to avert actual catastrophe than they would be if the same threat existed in a different social climate [p. 601]. . . . The adult response to ultimate danger is, to growing children, also the ultimate test of the trustworthiness of adult society. (p. 607)

From this perspective, the recent development that I myself find the most hope-inspiring is the extent to which people in Europe and the United

States have taken the initiative during the past year (I was writing in 1983), to insist on calling the arms race to a halt.

Implications for Individual and Social Action

The example of the nuclear freeze initiatives appropriately introduces a final set of considerations: What does the psychology of hope and despair suggest in regard to what we might do, as professionals and as citizens, to make more of our young people hopeful, and therefore to enable them to make commitments, to set goals, and to cope effectively toward their attainment—in sum, to live more satisfactory lives? It seems self-evident that the most urgent considerations engage us as citizens and as professional advisers to other citizens: the top priority is to move toward correcting the unjust realities, especially in the ghetto, that make hope unrealistic for so many of our youth. After a generation of social programs that have not solved the set of problems addressed in the War on Poverty, we can agree with conservative critics that the social inequities that undermine hope are indeed obdurate and can neither be wished away nor spent away. But I hope we can also agree that it is extremely damaging for the official world to give up trying to cope with them.

In the same spirit, we as citizens in the adult world can organize ourselves to confront the cluster of lethal trends that, if we simply ride them out passively, will assuredly lead us to doomsday with either a bang or a whimper. And, of course, we can invite the young to participate in the endeavor—after all, they have thinner layers of cynicism to break through, and a bigger stake in the outcome.

At the crux of our understanding of the psychology of hope and despair is the circular relationship between these basic stances in the world and how people cope with the challenges, the threats, the limitations, and the opportunities in their lives. I have been stressing one perspective on the circular relationship: how hope and sensed efficacy may lead to effective coping, while hopelessness and sensed helplessness often lead to withdrawal and defeat. But the circle runs the other way, too. If youth can be given support in coping with challenges that are suitable to their skills and abilities, the experience should feed back to strengthen their sense of efficacy and bolster their hopefulness; it should increase their subjective resources for the next round. Vicious and benign circles *are* vicious and benign in just the sense that, without intervention, they will predictably run their cumulative course. Mental health professionals are trained to intervene at the individual level. Intervention is possible and needed at the social and thus at the historical level as well. Such intervention is a matter of policy and therefore a matter for politics. We need not subside into a terminal morass of collective powerlessness.

I conclude by asking myself, for the public record, how hopeful am *I* that the course I am advocating *can* warrant and restore the hopes of youth? The answer is, I am very hopeful but I am not very optimistic. For the young, hope and optimism are probably a rather tight package. They go together, but they are not synonymous. For more seasoned participants in the adult world, especially the professional world, they may vary more independently. Hope is the conviction that a good future is possible and worth striving for. Optimism is the conviction that it is a sure thing or a strong probability. I submit that in today's world, optimism is a mistake. We should all be running scared, to bring potentially lethal problems under control. But hope is a necessity, unless our most despairing fears are to be realized. Our own hope, as mental health professionals, is essential to empower us to do what we can in behalf of the hope of youth, who in turn embody the hope of us all.

Epilogue: Social Psychology as Human Science

The writings that I have brought together in this book exemplify a social psychology conceived as value-relevant, socially involved human science. Of course, when I say "social psychology," I refer to a broad interdisciplinary area of human concern, not just to the subdiscipline of academic psychology that currently owns the label—owns it without copyright, however, since a subdiscipline of sociology with overlapping concerns and different boundaries has equally valid claims. My social psychology is value-relevant in two senses. It is much concerned with understanding the processes by which our values (our *oughts* and *shoulds*, our criteria of the preferable) are formed, transmitted, and modified in individual development in the context of history and culture—a causal analysis of human values. At the same time, it is concerned with understanding matters that are central to the protection and realization of our value commitments. That does not mean at all that I give up the *value* of objectivity in scientific inquiry. Objectivity is an ideal that is rarely attained, but I regard the attempt to approach it as a hallmark of the scientific enterprise. We cannot afford to kid ourselves or one another in the search for truth. Science involves the systematic distrust of wishful thinking.

My social psychology is socially involved not only from predilection (of course, idiosyncrasies of personal history led me to the paths that I have taken) but because I have somehow been able to keep in view the historically unique challenges that humankind now faces. On the one hand, there are opportunities for broadly increased justice, creativity, and freedom, including freedom from the previously universal tunnel vision of culture-boundedness. But on the other, for many of us our escape from culture-boundedness has entailed demoralizing attrition in the sources of human meaning. Moreover, the gap between haves and have-nots has been spreading ominously in our nation and between the nations of the world.

Most potentially disastrous, the successes of our technology and medicine have produced threats of planetary ecological collapse, with the end of human life on earth presided over by the Four Horsemen of the Apocalypse. The opportunities and the threats all hinge upon human understanding and human action. The disasters we most fear are not "acts of God" in the traditional legal sense (except maybe for a wandering asteroid every fifty million years or so); they are the predictable result of the cumulative actions of all of us, if we continue on our present course. The opportunities are within our reach, if only we seize them. So there is a serious challenge to psychology and the social sciences to contribute to our self-understanding in ways that may help us to meet the momentous challenges constructively.

I have no quarrel with basic research in social psychology or in other subdisciplines or disciplines: increased understanding is a value to be cherished in its own right, and we can never tell in advance which advances in basic understanding will turn out to be practically useful. During my professional lifetime as a psychologist, however, the subdiscipline of social psychology has been particularly subject to fads and fashions in topics and methods—a sign that social psychologists have often lacked a sense of intrinsic direction as to what to regard as scientific progress. It has always seemed to me that scientists who are convinced that they know where to look for progress should follow their inner compasses without any qualms of social conscience. In the frequent case in which map or compass seems inadequate, however, applied research that is focused on particular problems or issues has its own firmer basis for judging relevance and progress. So I am not surprised that the most interesting and productive areas of social psychology research and theory today seem to be ones tied to very practical concerns: health and gender.

Human Science as Science

Readers of chapters 8 and 9 will understand that my conception of social psychology as human science is closer to the meanings that the term *science* has had in the natural sciences than it is to the common understanding of human science in the humanistic psychology movement. In my view, the demise of positivism, which I join in celebrating, was by no means the defeat of natural science; it was, rather, the discrediting of ways in which a misunderstanding of the strategies of natural science was misapplied to studies of the affairs of people. Constructivism and other postmodern fashions have not shaken the faith of theoretical physicists, cosmologists, or molecular biologists. Natural science has never been more exciting or healthier! Contrary to constructivist views that I repeatedly encounter, science does not merely provide one myth on all fours with other myths. Its approximations of reality, which are necessarily fallible human constructions, have an aspect of discovery as well as an aspect of invention, so they have a different status from other human interpretations of reality. In spite of Kuhn, we *can* talk meaningfully about progress in science. Natural science has many enemies, among them, people who regret the disenchantment of modern life and the harms and threats of its accompanying technology, and, on university campuses, also have-nots in the humanistic disciplines who resent the disproportionate support that they see scientists receiving. But science as a unique cultural-historical invention cannot be wished away.

In the human studies, there are areas that obviously belong to the natural sciences; neuroscience with its links to experience and behavior is a clear case. There are also areas that belong to the interpretative humanities; psychobiography and psychohistory provide somewhat more debatable instances. In spite of the examples of Freud, Jung, Erikson, and Murray, psychologists have not drawn on the arts and letters for sources of insight to any substantial extent, a neglect that has been our loss. In this book I have given special emphasis to the area in which the causal/explanatory approach of natural science and the interpretative approach of the humanities intersect, which arises as a central focus for human inquiry because of the reflective, self-aware nature of human selfhood. Research and theory in this area have recently been very productive, elucidating concepts like self-efficacy, learned helplessness, hope, despair, and empowerment that intimately concern human values and are very important practically. The treatment is necessarily contextual, taking social, historical, and cultural considerations into account. But it is scientific in the traditional sense of a public and self-critical enterprise that is yielding cumulative conceptualized understanding of a domain that, in this case, merges interpretation and causal explanation.

I have recently heard colleagues give voice to anxious doubts about the future of psychology as a discipline. At a time when undergraduate enrollments in psychology are still near their peak, there is serious question whether the scientific field or graduate programs within it will preserve their historic identity. According to one scenario, the body of psychology will be carved up among an interdisciplinary cognitive science including artificial intelligence, an interdisciplinary neuroscience, and a social science of group phenomena and culture, with the practice of psychotherapy being fought over by various competing human service professions, including successors to the present products of our academically dubious free-standing schools of professional psychology. There is certainly nothing sacred about the present historically given boundaries of psychology,

which cannot claim to be a unified science and may very well be ununifia-
ble. All the same, psychologists like me, who have a sentimental attachment to the field because its history is so deeply woven into our lives,
should feel free to reject that scenario as too pessimistic. I think the human
science aspects of psychology will resist absorption into the new foci of
integration at our borders. In the sense that I have given to human science,
these include major aspects of personality and social and developmental
psychology. I do not think any of the proposed successor fields can treat
the reflexive phenomena of human selfhood adequately.

Relativism and a Critical Perspective

A second theme that recurs in this volume relates to my struggle since
early undergraduate years with the problem of relativism: how to keep our
bearings once we recognize that we learn our values and our assumptions
about ourselves and the world from our culture, and that our claims to
give them absolute or humanly universal standing therefore only convict
us of the sin of being culture-bound. Social scientists of my cohort were
sensitized by Margaret Mead and Ruth Benedict to a nonjudgmental,
culturally relative appreciation of other peoples and ways of life, but we
were also exposed to the manifest, salient evil of nazism and the Holocaust. Our reaction to Hitler was like Dr. Johnson's refutation of Bishop
Berkeley's idealism by kicking a rock: maybe we were philosophically
naive, but we could not regard the Nazis as other than evil; we were quite
unable to be nonjudgmental about Hitler's dream of a thousand-year
Reich. The direct contradiction with our reasoned relativism created
dissonance for me that I have continually struggled with.

In the context of concerns that this volume has explored, the vulnerability of our erstwhile absolute values comes under consideration in two
somewhat different ways. In the first place, when we lose faith in them as
God-given or engraved in Natural Law, we may be left adrift, literally de-
moralized. As an ingredient of anomie, the attrition of our traditional
values is part of the cultural crisis to which artists and humanists have
been particularly sensitive, and to which psychologists are belatedly
attending. There is much yearning, on the part of psychologists and other
social scientists as well as people in general, for what we imagine to have
been the old sense of community and value consensus. We are therefore,
all of us, vulnerable to false prophets who would help us become "true
believers" again. A value-relevant, socially involved social psychology
must be concerned with this sense of lack, and with ways in which people
may try to cope with it—desirable or undesirable according to our present
judgment.

But, second, the inner contradiction in our thinking about values poses a serious challenge to us as human scientists and intellectuals, which we can ill afford to ignore. Most of us have lost the faith in progress that sustained liberal commitments after the loss of supernatural foundations for our convictions. A thoroughgoing relativism not only undermines faith in progress but banishes its very meaning. If the yardsticks by which we measure progress or retrogression (our values) are themselves cultural products subject to the vicissitudes of historical change, we have no reason to believe that today's judgments about progress will be the judgments of tomorrow. Progress is in the shifting eye of the beholder.

I have come to defend and to attempt to exemplify a critical position that does not depend on attributing spurious timeless validity to my values. Taking a leaf from Marxist "critical theory" without accepting the dogmatic Marxist context, I think we have the resources in psychological and social science and in intelligent political discourse to criticize the values of our own culture; to recognize perils to be warded off and opportunities that are realistically in range if we can organize our human efforts to bring them about. That we accept the relativist criticism of all claims on behalf of values of supposedly universal timeless validity does not compel us to accept the status quo of our own society as the sole authority and to "adjust" to it. We can often come close to agreement about what is wrong (thus, about illness, for example). It is harder to agree about what is right, but some of us are convinced some of the time that we can see what is humanly preferable a step or so ahead. We can participate in a political process to identify the public interest in this longer run and to promote it.

It does not bother me that our social policies and actions will inevitably have unintended consequences, some of them unfortunate. It does not bother me that our successors, our children and grandchildren, will see matters from an emergently different value perspective. I have faith in neither Progress nor Utopia, but I have hope that intelligent human effort can cope with the problems and take advantage of the opportunities that we identify. I have neither hopes nor fears of any "end of history"—or any expectation that the interesting human adventure will come to a foreseeable end (except through our collective inattention and malfeasance).

A Socially Involved Human Science

A third underlying theme that has become more salient for me during the more than a decade over which these essays were written concerns our emerging planetary human interdependence as the prime context in which to consider the contributions needed from a socially involved human science. I write these concluding remarks in the spring of 1990, a remarkably hopeful moment in human history marked by the astonishing end of the cold war between the American and Soviet superpowers and the inspiring surge of democracy in unexpected quarters. But the challenges before us are immense. They only begin with the need to reset our national priorities so as to divert some of the astronomical resources still going for megaredundant weapons systems to aid newly democratic regimes whose hopes we have encouraged; to restore our deteriorating physical infrastructure and our floundering system of public education; to revive our badly neglected human services and restore hope among our own people; and to find ways of reducing the unjust, demoralizing, and destabilizing gap between rich and poor, the haves and have-nots at home and abroad. As we face these challenges, our individualistic cultural values seem ill-adapted to the realities that confront us. Here is a concrete example of the kind of critical perspective that I was just advocating.

Increasingly, we live in a world of interdependence. Our national weal increasingly depends on the world economy, in which each nation has limited degrees of freedom to manipulate its own economy. Autarchy is no longer possible. The frightening environmental problems that now concern us—global warming, the ozone window, acid rain, disposal of toxic wastes, the depletion of tropical rain forests and the extinction of species, the rampant overpopulation of the earth—all cut across national boundaries and require worldwide cooperation if they are to be mitigated. All involve what Garret Hardin (1968) called the "tragedy of the commons": the prototypical situation that arises when each actor in pursuing personal private interests (putting more and more sheep to graze on the common land of the village) gives rise to a cumulative result (overgrazing) that is disastrous to all. The cluster of ecological threats that humankind faces makes our current pattern of individualistic and nationalistic values as obsolete as the heroic, coup-counting way of life of the Plains Indians—an ideal that could be realized only in the brief period between the introduction of the horse by the Spaniards and the slaughter of the buffalo by the Yankees. Our individualism is obsolete, and I believe it will pass. The question is how: how soon, how painfully.

A quarter century ago, the polymath John Platt (1966) wrote a hopeful book that he entitled *The Step to Man* (we would now revise it to *The Step to the Truly Human*). After displaying the set of ecological trends that already spelled disaster unless somehow reversed, Platt observed that people will have to change their historically developed human nature if they are to survive as a species, and the change that will be required is greater than the change in people at the beginning of the Neolithic period when they began the long trek toward civilization by abandoning hunting and gathering for settled agriculture. Platt optimistically thought that because people have to change, they will change. It ain't necessarily so!— at least on a time scale to meet the problems we must anticipate.

Think, for example, of the long, painful process by which traditional medieval people were transformed into the *self*-conscious individuals of the United States and the Western world today (cf. Fromm, 1941; Trilling, 1972). True enough, in Fromm's terms, the "social character" shared by modern Europeans eventually came to support the functional requirements of modern capitalist society; people came to want to do what society needed from them. But it was no easy process. Think of the Thirty Years War, which decimated Europe; think of the human cost entailed by enclosure of the medieval common; think of the pestilent cities of the Industrial Revolution. Think of the many national wars, increasingly cruel and destructive, although people were not yet capable of the ultimate destructiveness that is now available to them. Even if the objective requirements of our new situation of mutual interdependence may produce people with motives and values to fit, in the long run of a few centuries, the process may be enormously destructive. Since we cannot put the genie of nuclear weaponry back in the bottle, and since the ominous ecological trends may pass critical points beyond which they are irreversible, we cannot even count upon lasting through a long run. If we are to survive, people must somehow take charge of their lives and see to it that benign trends replace the current vicious ones. If we can manage that, Platt was right: the opportunities for enriched human life will be unprecedented.

I see this context as providing a full agenda for a socially concerned social psychology and social science. We can and should contribute to shared understanding of causal processes—means-end relationships—that are relevant to our novel human situation. How can conditions of trust and mutual security be created to replace the Hobbesian zero-sum game that has prevailed on the international scene? How can the concern with care and relatedness that Gilligan (1977) identifies with women's perspectives be mobilized to compensate and correct for the individualism of the characteristic male preoccupation with autonomy, rights, and justice, as in Kohlberg's (1971) scheme that she criticizes? Are there transcultural universals of human nature of either a benign or of a problem-creating sort that can be leaned on or must be taken into account and counteracted as we try to learn how to become better adapted to an interdependent future? (Our knowledge in cross-cultural personality and social psychology is still primitive.) The possible agenda is unlimited. Participating in the long-term human project of self-understanding is a heady enterprise. Since our self-understanding is also in part self-constituting, both individually and collectively, we can aspire to contribute to the less individualistic reconstitution of our historically given human nature.

References

Abelson, R. P.; Aronson, E.; McGuire, W. J.; Newcomb, T. M.; Rosenberg, M. J.; & Tannenbaum, P. H., eds. (1968). *Theories of cognitive consistency: A sourcebook.* Chicago: Rand McNally.

Abramson, L. Y.; Seligman, M. E. P.; & Teasdale, J. D. (1978). Learned helplessness in humans: Critique and reformulation. *Journal of Abnormal Psychology* 87:49–74.

Adams, R. McC.; Smelser, N. J.; & Treiman, D. J., eds. (1982). *Behavioral and social science: A national resource.* Parts I and II. Washington, D.C.: National Academy Press.

Adorno, T. W.; Frenkel-Brunswik, E.; Levinson, D. J.; & Sanford, R. N. (1950). *The authoritarian personality.* New York: Harper.

Allport, G. W. (1935). Attitudes. In *A handbook of social psychology,* edited by C. Murchison. Worcester, Mass.: Clark University Press.

———. (1937). *Personality: A psychological interpretation.* New York: Holt.

———. (1943). The ego in contemporary psychology. *Psychological Review* 50:451–78.

———. (1954). *The nature of prejudice.* Cambridge, Mass.: Addison-Wesley.

———. (1961). *Pattern and growth in personality.* New York: Holt.

———. (1968). The historical background of modern social psychology. In *Handbook of social psychology,* edited by G. Lindzey & E. Aronson. Rev. ed. Vol. 1. Reading, Mass.: Addison-Wesley.

Allport, G. W.; Vernon, P. E.; & Lindzey, G. (1951). *A study of values: A scale for measuring the dominant interests in personality.* Rev. ed. Boston: Houghton-Mifflin.

Almond G. A., & Verba, S. (1963). *The civic culture: Political attitudes and democracy in five nations.* Princeton: Princeton University Press.

Altemeyer, B. (1981). *Right-wing authoritarianism.* Winnipeg: University of Manitoba Press.

255

———. (1988). *Enemies of freedom: Understanding right-wing authoritarianism.* San Francisco: Jossey-Bass.

Altman, I., & Rogoff, B. (1987). World views in psychology: Trait, interactional, organismic, and transactional perspectives. In *Handbook of Environmental Psychology,* edited by D. Stokols & I. Altman. Vol. 1. New York: Wiley.

American Psychological Association. (1973). *Ethical principles in the conduct of research with human participants.* Washington, D.C.: American Psychological Association.

Anderson, Q. (1971). *The imperial self: An essay in American literary and cultural history.* New York: Knopf.

Ansbacher, H. L., & Ansbacher, R. R., eds. (1956). *The individual psychology of Alfred Adler.* New York: Basic Books.

Arendt, H. (1958). *The human condition.* Chicago: University of Chicago Press.

Aron-Schaar, A. (1977). Maslow's other child. *Journal of Humanistic Psychology* 17 (2):9–24.

Aronson, E. (1976). *The social animal.* 2d ed. San Francisco: Freeman.

Asch, S. E. (1951). Effects of group pressure upon the modification and distortion of judgment. In *Groups, leadership, and men,* edited by H. Guetzkow. Pittsburgh: Carnegie Press.

———. (1952). *Social psychology.* Englewood Cliffs, N.J.: Prentice-Hall.

Back, K. W. (1972). *Beyond words: The story of sensitivity training and the encounter movement.* New York: Russell Sage Foundation.

Baldwin, J. M. (1897). *Social and ethical interpretations in mental development: A study in social psychology.* New York: Macmillan.

Baltes, P. B. (1979). Life-span developmental psychology: Some converging observations on history and theory. In *Life span development and behavior,* edited by P. B. Baltes & O. G. Brim, Jr. Vol. 2. New York: Academic Press.

Bandura, A. (1977). Self-efficacy: Toward a unifying theory of behavioral change. *Psychological Review* 84:191–215.

Barron, F. (1954). *Personal soundness in university graduate students.* Berkeley: University of California Press.

Bateson, G. (1972). *Steps to an ecology of mind.* New York: Chandler.

Becker, E. (1973). *The denial of death.* New York: Macmillan, Free Press.

Behavioral and Social Sciences Survey Committee. (1969). *The behavioral and social sciences: Outlook and needs.* Englewood Cliffs, N.J.: Prentice-Hall.

Bellah, R. N., & Glock, C. Y., eds. (1976). *The new religious consciousness.* Berkeley: University of California Press.

Bellah, R. N.; Madsen, R.; Sullivan, W. M.; Swidler, A.; & Tipton, S. M. (1985). *Habits of the heart: Individualism and commitment in American life.* Berkeley: University of California Press.

Benedict, R. (1934). *Patterns of culture.* Boston: Houghton-Mifflin.

Berger, P. L., & Luckmann, T. (1966). *The social construction of reality.* Garden City, N.Y.: Doubleday.

Berlin, I. (1978). Does political theory exist? In *Concepts and categories: Philosophical essays,* by I. Berlin. London: Hogarth Press.

Bernstein, R. J. (1976). *The reconstruction of political and social theory.* New York: Harcourt Brace Jovanovich.

Bersani, L. (1976). *A future for Astynax: Character and desire in literature.* Boston: Little, Brown.

Bloom, A. (1987). *The closing of the American mind.* New York: Simon & Schuster.

Bottomore, T. B., trans. and ed. (1964). *Karl Marx: Early writings.* New York: McGraw-Hill.

Boyer, P. (1985). *By the bomb's early light: American thought and culture at the dawn of the atomic age.* New York: Pantheon.

Braun, C. A. (1978). Climbing the ladder: The early-Christian psychology of St. John Climacus, hermit. Ph.D. diss., University of California at Santa Cruz.

Bridgeman, P. W. (1927). *The logic of modern physics.* New York: Macmillan.

Bronfenbrenner, U. (1961). The mirror image in Soviet-American relations: A social psychologist's report. *Journal of Social Issues* 17 (3):45–56.

Brown, J. F. (1936). *Psychology and the social order.* New York: McGraw-Hill.

Brown, N. O. (1959). *Life against death: The psychoanalytical meaning of history.* New York: Viking.

———. (1973). *Closing time.* New York: Random House.

Brunswik, E. (1956). *Perception and the representative design of psychological experiments.* Berkeley: University of California Press.

Bühler, C. (1933). *Der menschliche Lebenslauf als psychologisches Problem.* Leipzig: S. Hirzel.

Bury, J. B. (1920). *The idea of progress: An inquiry into its origin and growth.* London: Macmillan.

Buss, A. R. (1975). The emerging field of the sociology of psychological knowledge. *American Psychologist* 30:988–1002.

Butzer, W. (1977). Environment, culture, and human evolution. *American Scientist* 65:572–84.

Caldicott, H. (1980). *Nuclear madness: What can you do?* New York: Bantam.

Calkins, M. W. (1906). A reconciliation between structural and functional psychology. *Psychological Review* 13:61–81.

Campbell, A.; Converse, P. E.; Miller, W. E.; & Stokes, D. E. (1960). *The American voter.* New York: Wiley.

Campbell, D. T. (1963). Social attitudes and other acquired behavioral dispositions. In *Psychology: A study of a science,* edited by S. Koch. Vol. 6. New York: McGraw-Hill.

————. (1969). Reforms as experiments. *American Psychologist* 24:409–29.

————. (1977). Descriptive epistemology: Psychological, sociological, and evolutionary. William James Lectures. Preliminary draft. Harvard University.

Cantril, H. (1950). *The "why's" of man's experience*. New York: Macmillan.

Carlson, R. (1971). Where is the person in personality research? *Psychological Bulletin* 75:203–19.

————. (1975). Personality. In *Annual Review of Psychology* 26:393–414.

Chein, I. (1972). *The science of behavior and the image of man*. New York: Basic Books.

Chilman, C. S. (1978). *Adolescent sexuality*. Washington, D.C.: National Institute of Child Health and Human Development.

————. (1983). *Adolescent sexuality in a changing society: Social and psychological perspectives for the human services professions*. 2d ed. New York: Wiley.

Clifford, J. (1982). *Person and myth: Maurice Leenhardt in the Melanesian world*. Berkeley: University of California Press.

Cook, S. W. (1986). Research on anticipatory ideological compliance: Comment on Sargent and Harris. *Journal of Social Issues* 42 (1):69–73.

Cooley, C. H. (1902). *Human nature and the social order*. New York: Scribner's.

Coward, H. G., & Royce, J. R. (1975). Toward an epistomological basis for humanistic psychology. Fourth Center Conference on Theoretical Psychology, Center for Advanced Study in Theoretical Psychology, University of Alberta.

Cronbach, L. J. (1975). Beyond the two disciplines of scientific psychology. *American Psychologist* 30:116–27.

————. (1982). Prudent aspirations for social inquiry. In *The social sciences: Their nature and uses*, edited by W. H. Kruskal. Chicago: University of Chicago Press.

————. (1986). Social inquiry by and for earthlings. In *Metatheory in social science: Pluralisms and subjectivities*, edited by D. W. Fiske & R. A. Shweder. Chicago: University of Chicago Press.

Damon, W., & Hart, D. (1982). The development of self-understanding from infancy through adolescence. *Child Development* 53:841–64.

Davies, J. C. (1963). *Human nature in politics*. New York: Wiley.

De Charms, R. (1968). *Personal causation: The internal affective determinants of behavior*. New York: Academic Press.

Department of Health and Human Services. (1986). *Subject:* Mahlon Brewster Smith, June 26, 1957. Released document.

Deutsch, M. (1973). *The resolution of conflict: Constructive and destructive processes*. New Haven: Yale University Press.

————. (1983). The prevention of World War III: A psychological perspective. *Political Psychology* 4:3–32.

Dollard, J., & Miller, N. E. (1950). *Personality and psychotherapy: An analysis in terms of learning, thinking, and culture.* New York: Mc-Graw-Hill.

Doob, L. (1947). The behavior of attitudes. *Psychological Review* 54:135–56.

Du Bois, C. (1944). *The people of Alor: A social-psychological study of an East Indian island.* Minneapolis: University of Minnesota Press.

Edelstein, W. (1983). Cultural constraints on development and the vicissitudes of progress. In *Psychology and society: The child and other cultural inventions,* edited by F. S. Kessel & G. W. Siegel. New York: Praeger.

Elder, G. H., Jr. (1974). *Children of the great depression: Social change in life experience.* Chicago: University of Chicago Press.

Epstein, S. (1973). The self-concept revisited: Or a theory of a theory. *American Psychologist* 28:404–16.

———. (1979). The stability of behavior: I. On predicting most of the people much of the time. *Journal of Personality and Social Psychology* 37:1097–1126.

———. (1980). The stability of behavior: II. Implications for psychological research. *American Psychologist* 35:790–806.

Erikson, E. H. (1959). Identity and the life cycle. *Psychological Issues* 1 (1).

Escalona, S. K. (1982). Growing up with the threat of nuclear war: Some indirect effects on personality development. *American Journal of Orthopsychiatry* 52:600–607.

Estes, W. K.; Koch, S.; MacCorquodale, K.; Meehl, P. E.; Mueller, C. G.; Schoenfeld, W. N.; & Verplanck, W. S. (1954). *Modern learning theory: A critical analysis of five examples.* New York: Appleton-Century-Crofts.

Etheredge, L. S. (1985). *Can governments learn? American foreign policy and Central American revolutions.* New York: Pergamon.

Etzioni, A. (1967). The Kennedy experiment: Unilateral initiatives. *Western Political Quarterly* 20:361–80.

Faden, R. R. (1986). Presymptomatic screening in fetuses and adults: Moral and psychological issues. Paper presented to American Psychological Association, Washington, D.C., August 1986.

Faden, R. R., & Beauchamp, T. L., with King, H. M. P. (1986). *A history and theory of informed consent.* New York: Oxford University Press.

Fairbairn, W. R. (1954). *An object-relations theory of the personality.* New York: Basic Books.

Fenwick, S. (1976). *Getting it: The psychology of* est. New York: Lippincott.

Fernandez, J. (1974). The mission of metaphor in expressive culture. *Current Anthropology* 15:119–33.

Festinger, L. (1957). *A theory of cognitive dissonance.* Evanston, Ill.: Row, Peterson.

Feuer, L. (1969). *The conflict of generations*. New York: Basic Books.

Finison, L. J. (1986). The psychological insurgency: 1936–1956. *Journal of Social Issues* 42 (1): 21–33.

Fishbein, M. (1967). Attitudes and the prediction of behavior. In *Readings in attitude theory and measurement*, edited by M. Fishbein. New York: Wiley.

Fishbein, M., & Ajzen, I. (1975). *Belief, attitude, intention and behavior: An introduction to theory and research*. Reading, Mass.: Addison-Wesley.

Fiske, D. W., & Shweder, R. A., eds. (1986). *Metatheory in social science: Pluralisms and subjectivities*. Chicago: University of Chicago Press.

Fiske, S. T., & Taylor, S. E. (1984). *Social cognition*. Reading, Mass.: Addison-Wesley.

Fitzgerald, R., ed. (1977). *Human needs and politics*. Rushcutters Bay, N.S.W., Australia: Pergamon.

Frank, J. D. (1973). *Persuasion and healing: A comparative study of psychotherapy*. Rev. ed. Baltimore: Johns Hopkins University Press.

Frank, L. K. (1939). Projective methods for the study of personality. *Journal of Psychology* 8:389–413.

Frankel, C. (1973). The nature and sources of irrationalism. *Science* 180:927–31.

Frazer, J. G. (1951). *The Golden Bough: A study in magic and religion*. 3d ed. 13 vols. New York: Macmillan.

Frenkel-Brunswik, E. (1954). Psychoanalysis and the unity of science. *Proceedings of the American Academy of Arts and Sciences* 80:273–347.

Freud, S. (1961). *The ego and the id*. Standard ed. London: Hogarth. Originally published 1923.

Fromm, E. (1941). *Escape from freedom*. New York: Farrar & Rinehart.

———. (1947). *Man for himself: An inquiry into the psychology of ethics*. New York: Rinehart.

Gallup, G. C., Jr. (1977). Self-recognition in primates: A comparative approach to the bidirectional properties of consciousness. *American Psychologist* 32:329–38.

Gardner, D. P. (1967). *The California oath controversy*. Berkeley: University of California Press.

Geertz, C. (1973). *The interpretation of cultures: Selected essays*. New York: Basic Books.

———. (1975). On the nature of anthropological understanding. *American Scientist* 63:47–53.

Gergen, K. J. (1971). *The concept of self*. New York: Holt, Rinehart & Winston.

———. (1973). Social psychology as history. *Journal of Personality and Social Psychology* 26:309–20.

———. (1982). *Toward transformation in social knowledge*. New York: Springer-Verlag.

Gergen, K. J., & Gergen, M. M. (1983). Narratives of the self. In *Studies in social identity*, edited by T. R. Sarbin and K. E. Scheibe. New York: Praeger.

————, eds. (1984). *Historical social psychology*. Hillsdale, N.J.: Erlbaum.

Gerstein, D. R.; Luce, R. D.; Smelser, N. J.; & Sperlich, S. (1988). *The behavioral and social sciences: Achievements and opportunities*. Washington, D.C.: National Academy Press.

Gholson, G., & Barker, P. (1985). Kuhn, Lakatos, and Laudan: Applications in the history of physics and psychology. *American Psychologist* 40:755–69.

Gibson, J. J. (1950). *The perception of the visual world*. Boston: Houghton-Mifflin.

Gilligan, C. (1977). *In a different voice: Psychological theory and women's development*. Cambridge: Harvard University Press.

Giorgi, A. (1970). *Psychology as a human science*. New York: Harper & Row.

Girvetz, H. K. (1973). *Beyond right and wrong: A study in moral theory*. New York: Free Press.

Goffman, E. (1959). *The presentation of self in everyday life*. Garden City, N.Y.: Doubleday, Anchor.

————. (1974). *Frame analysis: An essay on the organization of experience*. Cambridge: Harvard University Press.

Greening, T. C. (1977). The Gestalt prayer: Final version? *Journal of Humanistic Psychology* 17 (3): 77–79.

Greenstein, F. (1975). *Personality and politics: Problems of evidence, inference, and conceptualization*. Rev. ed. New York: Norton.

Gundlach, R. H., & Riess, B. F. (1954). Criticism of Melby and Smith's "Academic freedom in a climate of insecurity" (letter to the editor). *Journal of Social Issues* 10 (1): 45–47.

Guntrip, H. (1971). *Psychoanalytic theory, therapy and the self*. New York: Basic Books.

Haan, N.; Aerts, E.; & Cooper, B. A. B. (1985). *On moral grounds: The search for practical morality*. New York: New York University Press.

Hadden, J. K., & Swann, C. E. (1981). *Prime-time preachers: The rising power of televangelism*. Reading, Mass.: Addison-Wesley.

Hall, C. C., & Lindzey, G. (1957). *Theories of personality*. New York: Wiley.

Hallowell, A. I. (1955). *Culture and experience*. Philadelphia: University of Pennsylvania Press.

Hardin, G. (1968). The tragedy of the commons. *Science* 162:1243–48.

Harlow, H. (1962). Development of affection in primates. In *Roots of Behavior*, edited by E. L. Bliss. New York: Harper.

Harnad, S. R.; Steklis, H. D.; & Lancaster, J., eds. (1976). *Origins and evolution of language and speech. Annals of the New York Academy of Sciences* 280.

Harré, R. (1984). *Personal being: A theory for individual psychology*. Cambridge: Harvard University Press.

Harré, R., & Secord, P. F. (1972). *The explanation of social behavior*. Oxford: Blackwell.

Harrell, D. E. (1976). *All things are possible: The healing and charismatic revival in modern America*. Bloomington: Indiana University Press.

Harter, S. (1983). Developmental perspectives on the self-system. In *Handbook of child psychology*, edited by P. Mussen. Rev. ed. Vol. 4, *Social and personality development*, edited by M. Hetherington. New York: Wiley.

Harvey, J. H.; Town, J. P.; & Yarkin, K. L. (1981). How fundamental is "The fundamental attribution error?" *Journal of Personality and Social Psychology* 40:346–49.

Heath, D. (1965). *Explorations of maturity*. New York: Appleton-Century-Crofts.

———. (1977). *Maturity and competence: A transcultural view*. New York: Gardner Press.

Hebb, D. O. (1974). What psychology is about. *American Psychologist* 29:71–79.

Heelas, P. L. F., & Lock, A. J., eds. (1981). *Indigenous psychologies: The anthropology of the self*. New York and London: Academic Press.

Heider, F. (1958). *The psychology of interpersonal relations*. New York: Wiley.

Heilbroner, R. (1974). *An inquiry into the human prospect*. New York: Norton.

Hellman, L. (1976). *Scoundrel time*. Boston: Little, Brown.

Hendin, H. (1975). *The age of sensation*. New York: Norton.

Holt, R. R. (1972). Freud's mechanistic and humanistic images of man. In *Psychoanalysis and Contemporary Science*, edited by R. R. Holt and E. Peterfreund, Vol. 1, 3–24. New York: International Universities Press.

Horkheimer, M. (1936). *Studien über Authorität und Familie*. In *Schriften des Instituts für Sozialforschung*, edited by M. Horkheimer. Vol. 5. Paris: Alcan.

Horney, K. (1937). *The neurotic personality of our time*. New York: Norton.

———. (1939). *New ways in psychoanalysis*. New York: Norton.

Hovland, C. I. (1959). Reconciling conflicting results derived from experimental and survey studies of attitude change. *American Psychologist* 14:8–17.

Hovland, C. I.; Janis, I. L.; & Kelley, H. H. (1953). *Communication and persuasion*, New Haven: Yale University Press.

Hull, C. L. (1943). *Principles of behavior*. New York: Appleton-Century.

Inkeles, A., & Smith, D. H. (1974). *Becoming modern*. Cambridge: Harvard University Press.

Institute for Propaganda Analysis, Inc. (October 1937–December 1941). *Propaganda analysis: A monthly letter to help the intelligent citizen detect and analyze propaganda.*

Israel, J., & Tajfel, H., eds. (1972). *The context of social psychology: A critical assessment.* New York: Academic Press.

Jacobs, M. K., & Goodman, G. (1989). Psychology and self-help groups: Predictions on a partnership. *American Psychologist* 44:536–45.

Jacobson, E. (1964). *The self and the object world.* New York: International Universities Press.

Jahoda, M. (1956a). Psychological issues in civil liberties. *American Psychologist* 11:234–40.

———. (1956b). Anti-Communism and employment policies in radio and television. In *Blacklisting,* edited by J. Cogley. Vol. 2. New York: Fund for the Republic.

———. (1958). *Current concepts of positive mental health.* New York: Basic Books.

Jahoda, M., & Cook, S. W. (1952). Security measures and freedom of thought: An exploratory study of the impact of loyalty and security programs. *Yale Law Journal* 61:295–333.

———. (1954). Ideological compliance as a social-psychological process. In *Totalitarianism,* edited by C. J. Friedrich. Cambridge: Harvard University Press.

James, W. (1890). The consciousness of self. In *Principles of psychology.* Vol. 1. New York: Holt.

———. (1985). *The varieties of religious experience.* Standard ed. Cambridge: Harvard University Press.

Janis, I. L. (1985). International crisis management in the nuclear age. In *International conflict and national policy issues, Applied Social Psychology Annual 6,* edited by S. Oskamp, 63–86. Beverly Hills, Calif.: Sage.

———. (1989). *Crucial decisions: Leadership in policymaking and crisis management.* New York: Free Press.

Jaynes, J. (1976). *The origin of consciousness in the breakdown of the bicameral mind.* Boston: Houghton-Mifflin.

Jessor, R. (1961). Issues in the phenomenological approach to personality. *Journal of Individual Psychology* 17:27–38.

Joelson, J. R. (1986). Nothing is left but Bambi or Bugs Bunny. Santa Cruz *Sentinel,* September 18.

Johnston, L. D.; Bachman, J.; & O'Malley, P. M. (1980–1983). *Monitoring the future: Questionnaire responses from the nation's high school seniors.* Annual volumes, 1975–1983. Ann Arbor: Institute for Social Research, University of Michigan.

Jones, E. E.; Kanouse, D. E.; Kelley, H. H.; Nisbett, R. E.; Valins, S.; & Weiner, B. (1972). *Attribution: Perceiving the causes of behavior.* Morristown, N.J.: General Learning Press.

Jones, R. A. (1977). *Self-fulling prophecies: Social, psychological, and physiological effects of expectancies.* Hillsdale, N.J.: Erlbaum.

Jourard, S. M. (1971). *The transparent self.* 2d ed. New York: Van Nostrand.

Jung, C. G. (1966). *Two essays on analytical psychology.* Translated by R. F. C. Hull. 2d ed. Princeton: Princeton University Press.

Kagan, J. (1981). *The second year.* Cambridge: Harvard University Press.

Kanter, R. M. (1972). *Commitment and community.* Cambridge: Harvard University Press.

————. (1976). The romance of community: Intentional communities as intensive group experiences. In *The intensive group experience,* edited by M. Rosenbaum & A. Snadowsky. New York: Free Press.

Kardiner, A. (1939). *The individual and his society.* New York: Columbia University Press.

Katz, D., & Stotland, E. (1959). A preliminary statement to a theory of attitude structure and change. In *Psychology: A study of a science,* edited by S. Koch. Vol. 3. New York: McGraw-Hill.

Kelly, G. A. (1955). *The psychology of personal constructs.* 2 vols. New York: Norton.

Kelman, H. C., ed. (1965). *International behavior: A social-psychological analysis.* New York: Holt, Rinehart & Winston.

————. (1979). An interactional approach to conflict resolution. *International Interactions* 6:99–122.

————. (1982). Creating the conditions for Israeli-Palestinian negotiations. *Journal of Conflict Resolution* 26:39–75.

Kendler, H. H. (1987). *Historical foundations of modern psychology.* Chicago: Dorsey Press.

Keniston, K. (1973). *Radicals and militants: An annotated bibliography of empirical research on campus unrest.* Lexington, Mass.: D. H. Heath, Lexington Books.

Kessen, W. (1979). The American child and other cultural inventions. *American Psychologist* 34:815–20.

Kierkegaard, S. (1944). *The concept of dread.* Princeton: Princeton University Press.

Kiesler, C., & Sibulkin, A. E. (1987). *Mental hospitalization: Myths and facts about a national crisis.* Newbury Park, Calif.: Sage.

Kilmann, P. R., & Sotile, W. M. (1976). The marathon encounter group: A review of the literature. *Psychological Bulletin* 83:827–50.

Klineberg, O. (1940). *Social psychology.* New York: Holt.

Kluckhohn, C. (1951). Values and value orientations in the theory of action. In *Toward a general theory of action,* edited by T. Parsons & E. A. Shils. Cambridge: Harvard University Press.

Kluckhohn, C.; Murray, H. A.; & Schneider, D. M., eds. (1953). *Personality in nature, society, and culture.* 2d ed. New York: Knopf.

Knutson, A. L. (1965). *The individual, society, and health behavior.* New York: Russell Sage Foundation.

————. (1967a). When does a human life begin? Viewpoints of public health professionals. *American Journal of Public Health* 57:2163–77.

————. (1967b). The definition and value of a new human life. *Social Science and Medicine* 1:7–29.

————. (1968). Body transplants and ethical values: Viewpoints of public health professionals. *Social Science and Medicine* 2:393–414.

————. (1979). Beliefs and values: Conceptualizations about a human life and the value judgments of public health professionals. Unpublished manuscript.

Knutson, J. N. (1972). *The human basis of the polity.* Chicago: Aldine-Atherton.

Koch, S., ed. (1959–1963). *Psychology: A study of a science.* Vols. 1–6. New York: McGraw-Hill.

————. (1959). Epilogue. In *Psychology: A study of a science,* edited by S. Koch. Vol. 3. New York: McGraw-Hill.

————. (1973). The image of man in encounter groups. *American Scholar* 42:636–52.

————. (1976). Language communities, search cells, and the psychological studies. In *Nebraska Symposium on Motivation 1975,* edited by J. K. Cole & W. J. Arnold. Lincoln: University of Nebraska Press.

————. (1985). The nature and limits of psychological knowledge: Lessons of a century qua "science." In *A century of psychology as science,* edited by S. Koch & D. E. Leary. New York: McGraw-Hill.

Koffka, K. (1935). *Principles of Gestalt psychology.* New York: Harcourt Brace Jovanovich.

Kohlberg, L. (1969). The cognitive-developmental approach to socialization. In *Handbook of socialization,* edited by D. Goslin. Chicago: Rand McNally.

————. (1971). From is to ought: How to commit the naturalistic fallacy and get away with it in the study of moral development. In *Cognitive development and epistemology,* edited by T. Mischel. New York: Academic Press.

Köhler, W. (1938). *The place of value in a world of facts.* New York: Liveright.

Kohut, H. (1971). *The analysis of the self.* New York: International Universities Press.

————. (1977). *The restoration of the self.* New York: International Universities Press.

Korzybski, A. (1941). *Science and sanity.* New York: International Non-Aristotelian Society.

Kövecses, Z. (1986). *Metaphors of anger, pride, and love: A lexical approach to the structure of concepts.* Amsterdam and Philadelphia: John Benjamins.

Kroeber, T. (1961). *Ishi.* Berkeley: University of California Press.

Kruskal, W. H., ed. (1982). *The social sciences: Their nature and uses.* Chicago: University of Chicago Press.

Kuhn, T. S. (1970). *The structure of scientific revolutions.* 2d ed. Chicago: University of Chicago Press. Originally published 1962.

Laing, R. D. (1959). *The divided self.* London: Tavistock.

———. (1967). *The politics of experience.* New York: Ballantine.

Lakoff, G. (1987). *Women, fire, and dangerous things: What categories reveal about the mind.* Chicago: University of Chicago Press.

Lakoff, G., & Johnson, M. (1980). *Metaphors we live by.* Chicago: University of Chicago Press.

Lakoff, G., & Kövecses, Z. (1987). The cognitive model of anger inherent in American English. In *Cultural models in language and thought,* edited by D. Holland & N. Quinn. New York: Cambridge University Press.

Langbaum, R. (1977). *The mysteries of identity: A theme in modern literature.* New York: Oxford University Press.

Langer, S. K. (1967 and 1972). *Mind: An essay on human feeling.* 2 vols. Baltimore: Johns Hopkins University Press.

Lasch, C. (1976). The narcissistic society. *New York Review of Books* 23 (15): 5–13.

———. (1979). *The culture of narcissism: American life in an age of diminishing expectations.* New York: Norton.

Lasswell, H. D. (1927). *Propaganda technique in the world war.* New York: Knopf.

Lazarus, R. S. (1983). The costs and benefits of denial. In *The denial of stress,* edited by S. Breznitz. New York: International Universities Press.

Leacock, E., ed. (1971). *The culture of poverty: A critique.* New York: Simon & Schuster.

Lee, A., & Lee, E. B., eds. (1939). *The fine art of propaganda.* New York: Harcourt Brace.

Lee, D. D. (1959/1948). Are basic needs ultimate? In *Freedom and culture,* by D. D. Lee. Englewood Cliffs, N.J.: Prentice-Hall.

Leventhal, H. (1970). Findings and theory in the study of fear communications. In *Advances in experimental social psychology,* edited by L. Berkowitz, 119–86. Vol. 5. New York: Academic Press.

Lévi-Strauss, C. (1966). *The savage mind.* Chicago: University of Chicago Press.

LeVine, R. (1973). *Culture, behavior, and personality.* Chicago: Aldine.

Levinson, D. (1978). *The seasons of a man's life.* New York: Knopf.

Levy, R. I. (1973). *Tahitians: Mind and experience in the Society Islands.* Chicago: University of Chicago Press.

Lewin, K. (1931). The conflict between Aristotelian and Galilean modes of thought in contemporary psychology. *Journal of Genetic Psychology* 5:141–77.

———. (1935). *A dynamic theory of personality: Selected papers.* New York: McGraw-Hill.

————. (1936). *Principles of topological psychology*. New York: McGraw-Hill.

————. (1951). *Field theory in social science: Selected theoretical papers*. New York: Harper.

Lewin, K.; Lippitt, R.; & White, R. K. (1939). Patterns of aggressive behavior in experimentally created social climates. *Journal of Social Psychology* 10:271–99.

Lewis, M., & Brooks-Gunn, J. (1979). *Social cognition and the acquisition of self*. New York: Plenum Press.

Lewis, O. (1965). *La Vida: A Puerto Rican family in the culture of poverty*. New York: Random House.

Lieberman, M. A.; Yalom, I. D.; & Miles, M. B. (1973). *Encounter groups: First facts*. New York: Basic Books.

Lifton, R. J. (1961). *Thought reform and the psychology of totalism: A study of "brainwashing" in China*. New York: Norton.

————. (1967). *Death in life: Survivors of Hiroshima*. New York: Random House.

————. (1976). *The life of the self: Toward a new psychology*. New York: Simon & Schuster.

Lindzey, G. (1961). *Projective techniques and cross-cultural research*. New York: Appleton-Century-Crofts.

Lindzey, G., & Aronson, E. (1968–1969). *The handbook of social psychology*. Rev. ed. 5 vols. Reading, Mass.: Addison-Wesley.

Lippmann, W. (1955). *The public philosophy*. Boston: Little, Brown.

Loevinger, J. (1966). Three principles of psychoanalytic psychology. *Journal of Abnormal Psychology* 71:432–43.

————. (1976). *Ego development: Conceptions and theories*. San Francisco: Jossey-Bass.

MacDonald, A. P. (1973). Measures of external-internal control. In *Measures of Psychological Attitudes*, edited by J. P. Robinson & P. R. Shaver. Rev. ed. Ann Arbor: Institute for Social Research, University of Michigan.

MacIntyre, A. (1980). A crisis in moral philosophy: Why is the search for the foundations of ethics so frustrating? In *Knowing and valuing: The search for common roots*, edited by H. T. Engelhardt & D. Callahan. Hastings-on-Hudson, N.Y.: Hastings Center.

————. (1981). *After virtue: A study in moral theory*. Notre Dame: University of Notre Dame Press.

Magnusson, D., & Endler, N. S., eds. (1977). *Personality at the crossroads: Current issues in interactional psychology*. Hillsdale, N.J.: Erlbaum.

Malraux, A. (1953). *The voices of silence*. Garden City, N.Y.: Doubleday.

Marcuse, H. (1955). *Eros and civilization*. Boston: Beacon Press.

————. (1964). *One-dimensional man*. Boston: Beacon Press.

Marin, P. (1975). The new narcissism. *Harper's*, October, 45–56.

Marsella, A. J.; De Vos, G.; & Hsu, F. L. K., eds. (1985). *Culture and self*. New York and London: Tavistock.

Marshak, A. (1976). Implications of the paleolithic symbolic evidence for the origin of language. *American Scientist* 64:136–45.

Maslow, A. H. (1954). *Motivation and personality*. New York: Harper.

———. (1966). *The psychology of science: A reconnaissance*. New York: Harper & Row.

———. (1968). *Toward a psychology of being*. Princeton, N.J.: Van Nostrand.

———. (1971). *The farther reaches of human nature*. New York: Viking.

May, R. (1975). Opening remarks. In Association for Humanistic Psychology. Edited transcript, AHP theory conference. San Francisco: Association for Humanistic Psychology.

———. (1977). *The meaning of anxiety*. Rev. ed. New York: Norton.

Mayr, E. (1982). *The growth of biological thought*. Cambridge: Harvard University Press.

McDougall, W. (1908). *Introduction to social psychology*. London: Methuen.

McDowell, V. H. (1978). *Re-creating: The experience of life-change and religion*. Boston: Beacon Press.

McKeachie, W. (1976). Psychology in America's bicentennial year. *American Psychologist* 31:819–24.

Mead, G. H. (1934). *Mind, self, and society*. Chicago: University of Chicago Press.

Mead, M. (1939). *From the south seas: Studies of adolescence and sex in primitive societies*. New York: Morrow.

Melby, E. O., & Smith, M. B., eds. (1953). Academic freedom in a climate of insecurity. *Journal of Social Issues* 9 (3): 2–55.

Merleau-Ponty, M. (1962). *Phenomenology of perception*. London: Routledge & Kegan Paul.

Miller, G. A. (1969). Psychology as a means of promoting human welfare. *American Psychologist* 24:1063–75.

Mischel, W. (1966). Theory and research on the antecedents of self-imposed delay of reward. In *Progress in experimental personality research*, edited by B. Maher. Vol. 3. New York: Academic Press.

———. (1968). *Personality and assessment*. New York: Wiley.

———. (1971). *Introduction to personality*. New York: Holt, Rinehart & Winston.

Morawski, J., & Goldstein, S. E. (1985). Psychology and nuclear war: A chapter in our legacy of social responsibility. *American Psychologist* 40:276–84.

Morris, C. (1956). *Varieties of human value*. Chicago: University of Chicago Press.

Mumford, L. (1967). *The myth of the machine*. Vol. 1, *Technics and human development*. New York: Harcourt Brace Jovanovich.

————. (1970). *The myth of the machine*. Vol. 2, *The pentagon of power*. New York: Harcourt Brace Jovanovich.

Murphy, G., ed. (1945). *Human nature and enduring peace*. Cambridge, Mass.: Houghton-Mifflin.

————. (1947). *Personality: A biosocial approach to origins and structure*. New York: Harper.

Murphy, G., & Likert, R. (1938). *Public opinion and the individual.* New York: Harper.

Murphy, G., & Murphy, L. B. (1931). *Experimental social psychology*. New York: Harper.

Murphy, J. M. (1976). Psychiatric labeling in cross-cultural perspective. *Science* 191:1019–28.

————. (1981). Abnormal behavior in traditional societies: Labels, explanations, and social reactions. In *Handbook of cross-cultural human development*, edited by R. H. Monroe, R. L. Monroe, & B. B. Whiting. New York: Garland.

Murray, H. A. (1981). *Endeavors in psychology: Selections from the personology of Henry A. Murray*. Edited by E. S. Shneidman. New York: Harper & Row.

Murray, H. A., & Morgan, C. D. (1945). A clinical study of sentiments. *Genetic Psychology Monographs* 32:3–311.

Murray, H. A., & others. (1938). *Explorations in personality*. New York: Oxford University Press.

Myrdal, G. (1944). *An American dilemma: The Negro problem and American democracy*. New York: Harper.

Nelson, B. (1969). Scientists increasingly protest HEW investigation of advisers. *Science* 164:1499–1504.

Newcomb, T. (1943). *Personality and social change*. New York: Dryden.

Nisbet, R. (1980). *History of the idea of progress*. New York: Basic Books.

O'Donnell, J. M. (1985). *The origins of behaviorism: American psychology, 1870–1920*. New York: New York University Press.

Offer, D. (1969). *The psychological world of the teenager*. New York: Basic Books.

Offer, D.; Ostrow, E.; & Howard, K. (1981). *The adolescent: A psychological self-portrait*. New York: Basic Books.

Onians, R. B. (1973). *The origins of European thought*. New York: Arno Press. Originally published 1951.

Ornstein, R. E. (1972). *The psychology of consciousness*. New York: Viking.

————. (1976). *The mind field*. New York: Viking-Grossman.

Ortony, A., ed. (1979). *Metaphor and thought*. New York: Cambridge University Press.

Osgood, C. E. (1962). *An alternative to war or surrender*. Urbana: University of Illinois Press.

Overton, W. F., & Reese, H. W. (1973). Models of development: Methodological implications. In *Life-span developmental psychology: Methodological issues,* edited by J. R. Nesselroade & H. W. Reese. New York: Academic Press.

Pepper, S. C. (1942). *World hypotheses.* Berkeley: University of California Press.

Perls, F. S.; Hefferline, R. E.; & Goodman, P. (1951). *Gestalt therapy.* New York: Julian.

Piaget, J. (1932). *The moral judgment of the child.* New York: Harcourt Brace.

————. (1952). *The origins of intelligence.* New York: International Universities Press.

Platt, J. (1966). *The step to man.* New York: Wiley.

Popper, K. R. (1968). *The logic of scientific discovery.* New York: Harper & Row. Originally published, 1935.

President's Research Committee on Recent Social Trends. (1933). *Recent social trends.* Vols. 1 and 2. New York: McGraw-Hill. Reprint, New Haven, Conn.: Greenwood Press, 1970.

Quine, W. V. O. (1953). *From a logical point of view.* Cambridge: Harvard University Press.

Rank, O. (1932). *Art and the artist: Creative urge and personality development.* New York: Knopf.

Reese, H. W., & Overton, W. F. (1970). Models of development and theories of development. In *Life-span developmental psychology: Research and theory,* edited by L. R. Goulet & P. B. Baltes. New York: Academic Press.

Reiff, R. (1970). Psychology and public policy. *Professional Psychology* 1:315–24.

Renshon, S. A. (1974). *Psychological needs and political behavior: A theory of personality and political efficacy.* New York: Free Press.

Rickman, H. P. (1979). *Wilhelm Dilthey: Pioneer of the human studies.* Berkeley: University of California Press.

Ricoeur, P. (1970). *Freud and philosophy: An essay on interpretation.* New Haven: Yale University Press.

Riegel, K. (1976). From traits and equilibrium toward developmental dialectics. In *Nebraska Symposium on Motivation 1975,* edited by J. K. Coe & W. J. Arnold. Lincoln: University of Nebraska Press.

Riesman, D., with Denney, R., & Glazer, N. (1950). *The lonely crowd.* New Haven: Yale University Press.

Rogers, C. (1942). *Counseling and psychotherapy.* Boston: Houghton-Mifflin.

————. (1961). *On becoming a person.* Boston: Houghton-Mifflin.

————. (1973). *Carl Rogers on encounter groups.* New York: Harper & Row, Harrow.

Rokeach, M. (1960). *The open and closed mind: Investigations into the nature of belief systems and personality systems.* New York: Basic Books.

————. (1973). *The nature of human values*. New York: Free Press.

————. (1980). Some unresolved issues in theories of beliefs, attitudes, and values. In *Nebraska Symposium on Motivation 1979*, edited by H. E. Howe, Jr., & M. M. Page. Lincoln: University of Nebraska Press.

Rosaldo, M. Z. (1984). Toward an anthropology of self and feeling. In *Culture theory: Essays on mind, self, and emotion*, edited by R. S. Levine & R. Levine. New York: Cambridge University Press.

Rosenbaum, M., & Snadowsky, A., eds. (1976). *The intensive group experience*. New York: Free Press.

Rosenberg, S.; Verba, S.; & Converse, P. (1970). *Vietnam and the silent majority: The dove's guide*. With a postscript by R. K. White. New York: Harper & Row.

Rosnow, R. L., & Georgoudi, M., eds. (1986). *Contextualism and understanding in social science: Implications for research and theory*. New York: Praeger.

Ross, L. (1977). The intuitive psychologist and his shortcomings: Distortions in the attribution process. In *Advances in experimental social psychology*, edited by L. Berkowitz. New York: Academic Press.

Roszak, T. (1968). *The making of a counter culture*. Garden City, N.Y.: Doubleday, Anchor.

Rotter, J. R. (1966). Generalized expectancies for internal versus external control of reinforcement. *Psychological Monographs* 80 (1; Whole No. 609).

Rychlak, J. F. (1977). *The psychology of rigorous humanism*. New York: Wiley.

Ryder, N. B. (1965). The cohort as a concept in the study of social change. *American Sociological Review* 30:843–61.

Ryle, G. (1949). *The concept of mind*. London: Hutchinson.

Sacks, S., ed. (1979). *On metaphor*. Chicago: University of Chicago Press.

Sampson, E. E. (1977). Psychology and the American ideal. *Journal of Personality and Social Psychology* 35:767–82.

————. (1981). Cognitive psychology as ideology. *American Psychologist* 36:730–43.

————. (1989). The challenge of social change for psychology: Globalization and psychology's theory of the person. *American Psychologist* 44:914–21.

Sandman, P. M., & Valenti, J. M. (1986). Scared stiff—or scared into action. *Bulletin of the Atomic Scientists*, January, 12–16.

Sanford, N. (1953). Individual and social change in a community under pressure: The oath controversy. *Journal of Social Issues* 9 (3): 25–42.

Sarason, S. B. (1981). *Psychology misdirected*. New York: Free Press.

————. (1986). And what is the public interest? *American Psychologist* 41:899–905.

————. (1988). *The making of an American psychologist: An autobiography*. San Francisco: Jossey-Bass.

Sarbin, T. R. (1977). Contextualism: A world view for modern psychology. In *Nebraska Symposium on Motivation 1976*, edited by J. K. Cole & A. W. Landfield. Lincoln: University of Nebraska Press.

————, ed. (1986). *Narrative psychology: The storied nature of human conduct*. New York: Praeger.

Sarbin, T. R., & Adler, N. (1970–1971). Self-reconstitution processes: A preliminary report. *Psychoanalytic Review* 57:599–616.

Sarbin, T. R., & Coe, W. C. (1972). *Hypnosis: A social psychological analysis of influence communication*. New York: Holt, Rinehart & Winston.

Sarbin, T. R., & Mancuso, J. C. (1980). *Schizophrenia: Medical diagnosis or moral verdict?* New York: Pergamon.

Sarbin, T. R., & McKechnie, G. E. (1986). Prospects for a contextualist theory of personality. In *Contextualism and understanding in social science: Implications for research and theory*, edited by R. L. Rosnow & M. Georgoudi. New York: Praeger.

Sargent, S. S., & Harris, B. (1986). Academic freedom, civil liberties, and SPSSI. *Journal of Social Issues* 42 (1):43–67.

Schafer, R. (1976). *A new language of psychoanalysis*. New Haven: Yale University Press.

Schell, J. (1982). *The fate of the earth*. Boston: Houghton-Mifflin.

Schneider, D. J. (1973). Implicit personality theory: A review. *Psychological Bulletin* 79:294–309.

Schutz, A. (1967). *The phenomenology of the social world*. Evanston: Northwestern University Press.

Schwartz, B. (1986). *The battle for human nature: Science, morality, and modern life*. New York: Norton.

Seligman, M. E. P. (1975). *Helplessness: On depression, development, and death*. San Francisco: W. H. Freeman.

Shand, A. F. (1914). *The foundations of character*. London: Macmillan.

Sherif, M. (1936). *The psychology of social norms*. New York: Harper.

Sherif, M., & Cantril, H. (1947). *The psychology of ego-involvements: Social attitudes and identifications*. New York: Wiley.

Sherif, M., & Sherif, C. (1953). *Groups in harmony and tension*. New York: Harper.

Shotter, J. (1974). What is it to be human? In *Reconstructing social psychology*, edited by N. Armstead. Harmondsworth, Eng.: Penguin Books.

————. (1981). Telling and reporting: Prospective and retrospective uses of self-ascriptions. In *The psychology of ordinary explanations of social behavior*, edited by C. Antaki. New York: Academic Press.

————. (1984). *Social accountability and selfhood*. Oxford: Blackwell.

Shweder, R. A., & Bourne, E. J. (1982). Does the concept of the person vary cross-culturally? In *Cultural conceptions of mental health and therapy*, edited by A. J. Marsella & G. M. White. Dodrecht, The Netherlands, and Boston: D. Reidel.

Shweder, R. A., & Le Vine, R., eds. *Culture theory: Essays on mind, self, and emotion*. New York: Cambridge University Press.

Sidel, V. W. (1983). Destruction before detonation: The health and social costs of the weapons race. *Health and Medicine* 1 (4): 6–15.

Skinner, B. F. (1971). *Beyond freedom and dignity*. New York: Knopf.

Smelser, N. J. (1986). The Ogburn vision fifty years later. In *Behavioral and social science: Fifty years of discovery*, edited by N. J. Smelser & D. R. Gerstein. Washington, D.C.: National Academy Press.

Smelser, N. J., & Gerstein, D. R., (1986). *Behavioral and social science: Fifty years of discovery*. Washington, D.C.: National Academy Press.

Smith, M. B. (1950). The phenomenological approach in personality theory: Some critical remarks. *Journal of Abnormal and Social Psychology* 45:516–22.

———. (1954). Comment on the "implications of separating opinions from attitudes." *Public Opinion Quarterly* 18:254–65.

———. (1955). Review of G. W. Allport, *The nature of prejudice*. *Journal of Abnormal and Social Psychology* 50:158.

———. (1959). Research strategies toward a conception of positive mental health. *American Psychologist* 14:673–81.

———. (1961). "Mental health" reconsidered: A special case of the problem of values in psychology. *American Psychologist* 16:299–306.

———. (1963). Personal values in the study of lives. In *The study of lives: Essays on personality in honor of Henry A. Murray*, edited by R. W. White. New York: Atherton.

———. (1966). Review of A. H. Maslow, *The psychology of science: A reconnaissance*. *Science* 153:284–85.

———. (1968a). Personality in politics: A conceptual map with application to the problem of political rationality. In *Political research and political theory: Essays in honor of V. O. Key, Jr.*, edited by O. Garceau. Cambridge: Harvard University Press.

———. (1968b). A map for the analysis of personality and politics. *Journal of Social Issues* 24 (3): 15–28.

———. (1969a). *Social psychology and human values*. Chicago: Aldine.

———. (1969b). Competence and socialization. In *Social psychology and human values*, by M. B. Smith. Chicago: Aldine.

———. (1969c). Morality and student protest. In *Social psychology and human values*, by M. B. Smith. Chicago: Aldine.

———. (1970). Comment on Reiff. *Professional Psychology* 1:324–26.

———. (1972). Toward humanizing social psychology. In *The psychologists*, edited by T. S. Krawiec. Vol. 1. New York: Oxford University Press.

———. (1973a). On self-actualization: A transambivalent examination of a focal theme in Maslow's psychology. *Journal of Humanistic Psychology* 13 (2): 17–33.

———. (1973b). Political attitudes. In *Handbook of Political Psychology*, edited by J. N. Knutson. San Franciso: Jossey-Bass.

————. (1974). *Humanizing social psychology.* San Francisco: Jossey-Bass.

————. (1976). Social psychology, science, and history: So *what? Personality and Social Psychology Bulletin* 2:438–44.

————. (1977). A dialectical social psychology? Comments on a symposium. *Personality and Social Psychology Bulletin* 3:719–24.

————. (1978a). Humanism and behaviorism in psychology: Theory and practice. *Journal of Humanistic Psychology* 18 (1): 27–36.

————. (1978b). Landmarks in the literature: The psychology of prejudice. *New York University Education Quarterly* 9 (2): 29–32.

————. (1978c). What it means to be human: An evolutionary and historical perspective. In *What it means to be human,* edited by R. Fitzgerald. Rushcutters Bay, N.S.W., Australia: Pergamon.

————. (1983). The shaping of American social psychology: A personal perspective from the periphery. *Personality and Social Psychology Bulletin* 9:165–80.

————. (1984). Humanistic psychology. In *Encyclopedia of Psychology,* edited by R. J. Corsini. Vol. 2. New York: Wiley.

————. (1985). Mapping humanistic psychology. *Humanistic Psychologist* 13:7–8.

————. (1989). Lässt sich eine humane Wissenschaft verwirklichen? *Report Psychologie,* July, 34–40.

————. (1990). Personology launched. Retrospective review of H. A. Murray, *Explorations in personality. Contemporary Psychology* 35:537–39.

Smith, M. B., & Anderson, J. W. (1989). Obituary: Henry A. Murray (1893–1988). *American Psychologist* 44:1153–54.

Smith, M. B.; Block, J.; & Haan, N. (1973). Activism and apathy in contemporary adolescents. In *Understanding adolescents,* edited by J. Adams. 2d ed. Boston: Allyn & Bacon.

Smith, M. B.; Bruner, J. S.; & White, R. W. (1956). *Opinions and personality.* New York: Wiley.

Smith, M. B., & Hobbs, N. (1966). The community and the community mental health center. *American Psychologist* 21:499–509.

Snell, B. (1953). *The discovery of the mind: The Greek origins of European thought.* Oxford: Blackwell.

Spence, K. W. (1948). The postulates and methods of behaviorism. *Psychological Review* 55:67–78.

Spiro, M. (1967). *Burmese supernaturalism: A study in the explanation and reduction of suffering.* Englewood Cliffs, N.J.: Prentice-Hall.

Spranger, E. (1928). *Types of men: The psychology and ethics of personality.* Halle: Max Niemeyer Verlag.

Stagner, R. (1986). Reminiscences about the founding of SPSSI. *Journal of Social Issues* 42 (1): 35–42.

Stewart, G. (1950). *The year of the oath.* Garden City, N.Y.: Doubleday.

Stone, W. F., & Schaffner, P. E. (1988). *The psychology of politics.* 2d ed. Secaucus, N.J.: Springer-Verlag.

Subcommittee to Investigate the Administration of the Internal Security Act and Other Internal Security Laws. Committee on the Judiciary. United States Senate. (1953). Stenographic transcript of hearings, March 2, 20:48–61. Released under Freedom of Information Act.

Sullivan, H. S. (1953). *The interpersonal theory of psychiatry.* New York: Norton.

Sutton, F. X. (1985). American foundations and the social sciences. *Items* (Social Science Research Council) 39 (4): 57–64.

Tart, C. T., ed. (1975). *Transpersonal psychologies.* New York: Harper & Row.

Taylor, R. B. (1989). From the president. *Population and Environmental Psychology 34 News* 15 (2): 1–3.

Tetlock, P. E. (1986). Psychological advice on foreign policy: What do we have to contribute? *American Psychologist* 41:557–67.

Thomas, W. I., & Znaniecki, F. (1918). *The Polish peasant in Europe and America.* Vol. 1. Boston: Badger.

Thurber, J. (1940). *Fables for our time and famous poems illustrated.* New York: Harper.

Thurstone, L. L. (1928). Attitudes can be measured. *American Journal of Sociology* 33:529–54.

Tolman, E. C. (1932). *Purposive behavior in animals and men.* New York: Appleton-Century.

Tomkins, C. (1976). New paradigms: Profile of Michael Murphy. *New Yorker,* January 5, 30–51.

Tomkins, S. S. (1979). Script theory: Differential amplification of affects. In *Nebraska Symposium on Motivation 1978,* edited by H. W. Howe, Jr., and R. A. Dienstbier. Lincoln: University of Nebraska Press.

———. (1987). Script theory. In *The emergence of personality,* edited by J. Aronoff, A. I. Rabin, & R. A. Zucker. New York: Springer.

Triandis, H. C. (1977). Cross-cultural social and personality psychology. *Personality and Social Psychology Bulletin* 3:143–58.

———. (1978). Some universals of social behavior. *Personality and Social Psychology Bulletin* 4:1–16.

———. (1980). Values, attitudes, and interpersonal behavior. In *Nebraska Symposium on Motivation 1979,* edited by H. E. Howe, Jr., & M. M. Page. Lincoln: University of Nebraska Press.

Trilling, L. (1972). *Sincerity and authenticity.* Cambridge: Harvard University Press.

———. (1976). Why we read Jane Austen. *Times Literary Supplement,* (London), March 5, 250–52.

Turner, V. (1969). *The ritual process.* Chicago: Aldine.

U.S. abandons attempt to deport L. I. Japanese doctoral candidate. (1986, August 21). *New York Times,* p. 1.

Vaihinger, J. (1925). *The philosophy of "As if": A system of the theoretical, practical, and religious fictions of mankind*. New York: Harcourt, Brace.

Valenstein, E. S. (1986). *Great and desperate cures: The rise and decline of psychosurgery and other radical treatments for mental illness*. New York: Basic Books.

Veroff, J. (1986). Contextual factors in the normal personality. In *Contextualism and understanding in social science: Implications for research and theory*, edited by R. L. Rosnow & M. Georgoudi. New York: Praeger.

Wachtel, P. L. (1983). *The poverty of affluence: A psychological portrait of the American way of life*. New York: Free Press.

Wallach, M. A., & Wallach, L. (1983). *Psychology's sanction for selfishness: The error of egoism in theory and therapy*. San Francisco: Freeman.

———. (1990). Rethinking goodness. Albany: New York State University Press.

Wallas, G. (1909). Human nature and politics. Boston: Houghton-Mifflin.

Warren, R. P. (1975). *Democracy and poetry*. Cambridge: Harvard University Press.

Washburn, S. L. (1959). Speculations on the interrelations of the history of tools and biological evolution. In *The evolution of man's capacity for culture*, edited by J. N. Spuhler. Detroit: Wayne State University Press.

———. (1978). Human behavior and the behavior of other animals. *American Psychologist* 33:405–18.

Weiner, B., & Kukla, A. (1970). An attributional analysis of achievement motivation. *Journal of Personality and Social Psychology* 15:1–20.

Weinstein, E., & Deutschberger, P. (1963). Some dimensions of altercasting. *Sociometry* 4:454–66.

Wertheimer, M.; Barclay, A. G.; Cook, S. W.; Kiesler, C. A.; Koch, S.; Riegel, K. F.; Rorer, L. G.; Senders, V. L.; Smith, M. B.; & Sperling, S. E. (1978). Psychology and the future. *American Psychologist* 33:631–47.

Wheelis, A. (1958). *The quest for identity*. New York: Norton.

White, A. D. (1896). *A history of the warfare of science with theology in Christendom*. 2 vols. New York: Appleton.

White, L. D., ed. (1956). The state of the social sciences. Chicago: University of Chicago Press.

White, R. K. (1970). *Nobody wanted war: Misperception in Vietnam and other wars*. Garden City, N.Y.: Doubleday, Anchor.

———. (1984). *Fearful warriors: A psychological profile of U.S.-Soviet relations*. New York: Macmillan, Free Press.

———, ed. (1986). *Psychology and the prevention of nuclear war: A book of readings*. New York: New York University Press.

White, R. W. (1959). Motivation reconsidered: The concept of competence. *Psychological Review* 66:297–333.

Whiting, J. (1966). Field guide for a study of socialization. In *Six cultures: Studies in child-rearing,* edited by J. Whiting. Vol. 1. New York: Wiley.

Why fear foreigners' free speech? (1986, November 13). Editorial. *New York Times.*

Williams, R. M. (1947). *The reduction of intergroup tensions.* SSRC Bulletin No. 57. New York: Social Science Research Council.

Wilson, E. O. (1975). *Sociobiology: The new synthesis.* Cambridge: Harvard University Press, Belknap Press.

Wirth, L., ed. (1940). *Eleven twenty-six: A decade of social science research.* Chicago: University of Chicago Press.

Wittgenstein, L. (1953). *Philosophical investigations.* Oxford: Blackwell.

Woodward, P. (1948). How do the American people feel about the atomic bomb? *Journal of Social Issues* 4 (1): 7–14.

Wylie, R. C. (1961). *The self-concept.* Lincoln: University of Nebraska Press.

———. (1974 [Vol. 1]); (1979 [Vol. 2]). *The self concept.* Rev. ed. Lincoln: University of Nebraska Press.

Yankelovich, D. (1981). *New rules: Searching for self-fulfillment in a world turned upside down.* New York: Random House.

Yankelovich, Skelly, & White, Inc. (1977). *Raising children in a changing American society.* Minneapolis: General Mills.

Zimbardo, P. G. (1970). The human choice: Individuation, reason, and order versus deindividuation, impulse, and chaos. In *Symposium on Motivation 1969,* edited by W. Arnold & D. Levine. Lincoln: University of Nebraska Press.

Index

Ryder, N.B., 169
Ryle, G., 154, 175

Sacks, S., 82
Sampson, E.E., 10, 33, 155, 185
Sandman, P.M., 220n
Sanford, N., 56, 196, 203
Sarason, S.B., 185, 226, 227
Sarbin, T.R., 44, 50, 137, 154, 156, 169, 170, 172, 174, 175
Sargent, S.S., 202
Sartre, 78
Saybrook, 1964 conference at, 99, 132
Schafer, R., 75, 176
Schaffner, P.E., xiv
Schell, J., 208
Schemas, 27
Schneider, D.J., 88
Schoenfeld, W.N., 152
Schutz, A., 45, 77, 104
Schwartz, B., 185
Science, features of 160
Scientific agenda, understanding of, 143–147
Scientific constructs, as metaphor, 45–46
Scientific psychology, Lewin's conception of, 165–166
Scientific worldview, and selfhood, 45–47
Secord, P.F., 114, 154, 163, 166
Secular humanism, xi; as a mode of collective self-representation, 110; emphasis in humanistic psychology movement, xv; underrepresented in humanistic psychology, 98–100
Secular origin myth, xv, 100–102
Self, the: archetype of, 30, 90; compared to ego, 40; compared to selfhood, xiv
Self-actualization, Maslow's theory of, 10–11, 123–125. See also Needs, Maslow's theory of
Self-conception, psychology of, 51
Self-disclosure, as a value in humanistic psychology, 134–135. See also Culture of seekership
Self-evaluation, as a social emergent, 77–79
Self-fulfilling prophecy, 51
Selfhood: archetypical aspects, 30–31; attitudes and, 50; attributional aspects of, 30–31, 51, 79, 158; in chimpanzees, 78; cognitive psychology and, 30; cross-cultural and transhistorical perspective on, xiii, xiv, 20, 23–27, 90–91; defined, xiv, 19–20, 156, 159–160; developmental perspective on, xiv, 20, 27–30; emergence in infants, 78–79; evolutionary, historical perspective on, xiv, 20–23,

41–48, 113, 115–116, 119–122; interpretive perspective on, 35, 166; interrelation of interpretive and causal points of view on, xiv, xvi, 32, 157–161, 174, 249; issues bearing on personality theory and, 30–35; metaphoric, 44–52, 73–93; modern, 33, 47, 90–91; psychology of, 33–34, 37–52; reflexive, 22, 29–30, 42–45, 104–105, 157–158; the self and, 76; symbolic, 41–52, 79; terminology of, 69–70; theory of, xiv, 19–34, 79–80, 156–160, 168–169; three perspectives on, xiv, 20–30; values and, 66–68. See also Development: dialectical; I and me; language; Marxist personality theory; Meadian theory; meaning, consensual; metaphoric conception of selfhood; modernity, selfhood in
Self-referential aspects of a person, 70
Self-regarding sentiment, 58
Self-requiredness, 6–7
Seligman, M.E.P., 51, 52, 79, 158, 209, 240, 241
Sentiments, 57–58
Sexual revolution of the mid-sixties, 133
Shakespeare, 70
Shand, A.F., 57
Sherif, C., 39, 61
Sherif, M., xi, 39, 40, 61
Shotter, J., 72n, 79, 154, 157, 163, 166, 170, 175
Shweder, R.A., 155, 159, 169
Sibulkin, A.E, 189
Sidel, V.W., 209
Sincerity, 25, 81, 89
Situation, role of the, 56, 164–165
Skinner, B.F., 7, 8, 46, 108, 139, 152, 165
Skinnerian psychology, and values, 7–8, 53
Smelser, N.J., 149, 150, 217, 223
Smith, D.H., 90
Smith, M.B., xiii, iv, xv, 4, 7, 10, 12, 16, 34n, 35, 38, 42, 48, 51, 54, 56, 59, 60, 62, 65, 67, 72n, 75, 80, 99, 111, 118, 127, 133, 141, 143, 146, 147n, 153, 156, 192, 200, 203, 206, 234
Snadowsky, A., 130
Snell, B., 43, 44, 45, 46, 48, 50, 80, 81
Social constructivism, role of evidence in, 154
Social problems: amelioration by natural science, 150; encounter group movement and, 129–130; psychology and, xiii; of youth, 233–245
Social psychology: cognitive, 154; crisis of, 38; criticisms of mainstream, xiv, 37–41; as forerunner of a humanistic sci-